A CULTURAL HISTORY OF WORK

Volume 6

A Cultural History of Work (6 vols.)

Winner of the 2020 PROSE Award for Multivolume Reference/Humanities

A Cultural History of Work
General Editors: Deborah Simonton and Anne Montenach

Volume 1
A Cultural History of Work in Antiquity
Edited by Ephraim Lytle

Volume 2
A Cultural History of Work in the Medieval Age
Edited by Valerie L. Garver

Volume 3
A Cultural History of Work in the Early Modern Age
Edited by Bert De Munck and Thomas Max Safley

Volume 4
A Cultural History of Work in the Age of Enlightenment
Edited by Deborah Simonton and Anne Montenach

Volume 5
A Cultural History of Work in the Age of Empire
Edited by Victoria E. Thompson

Volume 6
A Cultural History of Work in the Modern Age
Edited by Daniel J. Walkowitz

A CULTURAL HISTORY OF WORK

IN THE MODERN AGE

Edited by Daniel J. Walkowitz

BLOOMSBURY ACADEMIC
LONDON • NEW YORK • OXFORD • NEW DELHI • SYDNEY

BLOOMSBURY ACADEMIC
Bloomsbury Publishing Plc
50 Bedford Square, London, WC1B 3DP, UK
1385 Broadway, New York, NY 10018, USA
29 Earlsfort Terrace, Dublin 2, Ireland

BLOOMSBURY and the Diana logo are trademarks of Bloomsbury Publishing Plc

First published in Great Britain 2018
This edition published in Great Britain, 2021

Copyright © Bloomsbury Publishing, 2018

Daniel J. Walkowitz has asserted their right under the Copyright, Designs and Patents Act, 1988, to be identified as Editor of this work.

Cover image © Education Images/Getty Images

All rights reserved. No part of this publication may be reproduced or transmitted in any form or by any means, electronic or mechanical, including photocopying, recording, or any information storage or retrieval system, without prior permission in writing from the publishers.

A catalogue record for this book is available from the British Library.

A catalog record for this book is available from the Library of Congress.

ISBN:	HB:	978-1-4742-4481-7
	PB:	978-1-3502-7890-5
	Set:	978-1-4742-4503-6

Series: The Cultural Histories Series

Typeset by Integra Software Services Pvt. Ltd.
Printed and bound in Great Britain

To find out more about our authors and books visit www.bloomsbury.com and sign up for our newsletters.

CONTENTS

LIST OF FIGURES		vi
GENERAL EDITORS' PREFACE		x
CONTRIBUTORS		xii
	Introduction *Daniel J. Walkowitz*	1
1	The Economy of Work *Jennifer Klein*	17
2	Picturing Work *Cathleen Chaffee, with Michael Frisch*	39
3	Work and Workplaces *Richard A. Greenwald*	61
4	Workplace Cultures *Andrew Perchard*	77
5	Work, Skill, and Technology *Amy E. Slaton*	93
6	Work and Mobility *Nimisha Barton and Andrew Hazelton*	109
7	Work and Society *Andrew August*	127
8	The Political Culture of Work *Stephen Meyer*	141
9	Work and Leisure *Randy D. McBee*	157
NOTES		173
FURTHER READINGS		204
INDEX		210

LIST OF FIGURES

CHAPTER ONE

1.1 "Make a Wish," Bronx Slave Market, 170th Street, New York, 1938, The Crisis. Photo: Robert McNeill. Courtesy Smithsonian Institution.   19

1.2 Ben Shahn, "For All These Rights We've Just Begun to Fight," 1946. Courtesy Fogg Art Museum, Harvard University Art Museums.   23

1.3 "1919–1969 ... Benefits Then and Now," *Hercules Mixer*, employee magazine of the Hercules Chemical Corporation, a DuPont subsidiary. Courtesy Hagley Museum and Library.   26

1.4 Workers and consumers march on Illinois State Capitol, Springfield, 1992. Courtesy Wisconsin Historical Society, SEIU 880 Collection.   33

1.5 Worker at a Starbucks café, New York, c. March 2016. Courtesy © 123RF.com.   37

CHAPTER TWO

2.1 Auguste and Louis Lumière, *La Sortie de l'usine Lumière à Lyon*, 1895. Black and white film. Source: frame capture.   39

2.2 Aleksandr Rodchenko, Workers' club interior, design for the *Exposition Internationale des Arts Décoratifs et Industriels Modernes*, 1925. Alfred H. Barr, Jr. Papers, 13.I.E. The Museum of Modern Art Archives, New York. Digital Image © The Museum of Modern Art. © Estate of Alexander Rodchenko/RAO, Moscow/VAGA, New York.   42

2.3 Diego Rivera, *Detroit Industry*, north wall lower panel, 1932–3. Courtesy Detroit Institute of Arts, Gift of Edsel B. Ford. © 2017 Banco de México Diego Rivera Frida Kahlo Museums Trust, Mexico, D.F. / Artists Rights Society (ARS), New York.   43

2.4 Dorothea Lange, *Migrant Mother*, 1936. Library of Congress, Prints & Photographs Division, FSA/OWI Collection, LC-USF34-009058-C.   44

2.5 Milton Rogovin, Untitled, 1976. (Doris McKinney, 1976). Courtesy Center for Creative Photography.   50

2.6 Milton Rogovin, Untitled, 1976. (Doris McKinney, 1976). Courtesy Center for Creative Photography.   51

2.7	Milton Rogovin, Untitled, 1987. (Doris McKinney, 1976). Courtesy Center for Creative Photography.	52
2.8	"Handshake Ritual" with workers of New York City Department of Sanitation. Mierle Laderman Ukeles, *Touch Sanitation Performance: Fresh Kills Landfill*, 1977–80. Courtesy the artist and Ronald Feldman Fine Arts, New York.	55
2.9	Fred Lonidier, detail from *The Health and Safety Game*, 1976. Courtesy the artist; Essex Street, New York; Michael Benevento, Los Angeles; and Silberkuppe, Berlin.	56
2.10	Installation view of Harun Farocki's *Workers Leaving the Factory in Eleven Decades*, 2006. Courtesy Harun Farocki, GbR in *Overtime: The Art of Work*, Albright-Knox Art Gallery, Buffalo, New York, March 8–May 18, 2015. © Image courtesy Albright-Knox Art Gallery Digital Assets Collection and Archives, Buffalo, New York. Photo: Tom Loonan.	58

CHAPTER THREE

3.1	Garment workers in the N.M. dress shop in New York, 1943. Photo: Marjory Collins. Courtesy Library of Congress.	63
3.2	Bangladeshi garment workers, during a protest march in Dhaka on July 28, 2010. AFP Photo/Munir uz Zaman. Courtesy Getty Images.	64
3.3	Container cargo freight ship working crane bridge. Courtesy Getty Images.	66
3.4	The Levee, New Orleans, Louisianna, c. 1900. Courtesy Library of Congress.	69
3.5	Young man doing a freelance job from his home office in Berlin, Germany. By lechatnoir. Courtesy Getty Images.	70

CHAPTER FOUR

4.1	"Here in Youngstown": Bruce Springsteen visiting the abandoned Jenny blast furnace, 1996. Photo: Dale Maharidge. Courtesy Dale Maharidge.	78
4.2	Growing up in the shadow of the winding wheel: gala day float, Loanhead, Midlothian, Scotland, 1920s. Courtesy National Mining Museum, Scotland.	83
4.3	"Anticipatory socialization" in the coalfields: Cubs visiting Lady Victoria Colliery, Newtongrange, Midlothian, Scotland, 1970s. Courtesy National Mining Museum, Scotland.	84
4.4	Protesting closures: steelworkers protesting the closure of Usinor Longwy Steel Works, Lorraine, France, January 30, 1979. Courtesy Getty Images.	91

4.5 Miners embrace each other after their last shift at Kellingley Colliery, England, December 18, 2015. Courtesy Getty Images. 91

CHAPTER FIVE

5.1 Charlie Chaplin as the American factory worker driven to madness in Chaplin's film *Modern Times*, 1936. Courtesy Getty Images. 94

5.2 Computer terminals at the headquarters of the Washington Suburban Sanitary Commission, Laurel, Maryland, c. 1980–2006. Photo: Carol M. Highsmith. Library of Congress. Public domain. 95

5.3 Pouring concrete in construction of Umatilla ordnance depot, Hermiston, Oregon, 1941. Photo: Lee Russell, Library of Congress. Public domain. 99

5.4 Women working on Second World War aircraft assembly, c. 1950s. Photo: George Marks. Courtesy Getty Images. 101

5.5 Container facility at Harbour, Oakland, California, c. 1980–2006. Photo: Carol M. Highsmith, Library of Congress. Public domain. 102

CHAPTER SIX

6.1 A nineteenth-century map of the world depicts the spread of European dominion across the globe. Courtesy Falkensteininfoto, Alamy. 111

6.2 Mexican migrants wait to cross the border at Nuevo Laredo, Tamaulipas-Laredo, Texas, c. 1948. Courtesy Andrew Hazelton (private collection). Photographer unknown. 118

6.3 Supporter holds a sign as Republican presidential candidate Donald Trump speaks at a rally February 19, 2016, in Myrtle Beach, South Carolina. Courtesy Aaron P. Bernstein. Getty Images. 123

6.4 Approximately thirty Syrian war refugee family members arrive at a Red Cross Centre on April 4, 2014 in Malaga. Courtesy Jorge Guerrero/AFP/Getty Images. 124

6.5 June 24, 2016: French far-right leader Marine Le Pen holds a press conference at the National Front political party headquarters during the 2016 controversy surrounding "Brexit." Photo: Vincent Isore/IP3/Getty Images. 126

CHAPTER SEVEN

7.1 Worker assembling a bomber in Nashville, Tennessee, 1943. Photo: Alfred T. Palmer, US Office of War Information. Public domain. 129

7.2 Striking machinists from the Ford facility in Dagenham, 1968. Courtesy Getty Images. 131

LIST OF FIGURES ix

7.3 Minister of Health Aneurin Bevan at a hospital near Manchester
on the first day of the National Health Service, July 1948. University
of Liverpool, Faculty of Health and Life Sciences. Creative Commons. 135

7.4 Hunger marchers in Washington, DC, claim rights to employment and
relief, December 1931. Courtesy Getty Images. 139

CHAPTER EIGHT

8.1 Ford Assembly line, 1923. Photographer unknown, Library of Congress.
Public domain. 143

8.2 On strike, these Flint sit-downers occupy themselves with an activity
that normally could not be done under the strict production regime of
auto work: reading newspapers. Photo: Sheldon Dick, Library of
Congress. Public domain. 147

8.3 Two women and a man have lunch in the Ford Willow Run plant.
Photo: Anne Rosener, Library of Congress. Public domain. 149

8.4 Post-war British assembly line for small automobile in unidentified
factory, 1945. Photographer unknown. Imperial War Museum.
Public domain. 150

8.5 Robots have greatly reduced the proportion of human production
workers in modern automobile plants. Photo: Monty Rakuen. Courtesy
Getty Images. 152

CHAPTER NINE

9.1 Poolroom constructed in 1940 near the Shasta Dam in Shasta
County, California. Photo: Russell Lee, Library of Congress. Public
domain. 159

9.2 The Rialto Theater in Casper, Wyoming, 2015. Photo: Carol
H. Highsmith, Library of Congress. Public domain. 160

9.3 A bowling alley in Barnsley, England, located at the Monk Bretton
Miners Social Centre, 1965. Photo: National Coal Board. Courtesy
UK National Archives. 163

9.4 Motorcyclist Jack Troop competing in a hill-climbing competition in the
United States, mid-1950s. Photographer unknown. Courtesy Don Troop. 164

9.5 An abandoned drive-in theatre in Chester, West Virginia. Photo:
Carol H. Highsmith. Library of Congress. Public domain. 168

GENERAL EDITORS' PREFACE

Issues around work and the workplace seem to be having a renaissance and are no longer embedded solely in the discourses around Marxism and labor movements. Similarly, new and fresh research has been taking place around guilds, skill, control and gender issues. *A Cultural History of Work* takes an approach that focuses on culture in order to explore the subtleties of the character and dynamics of work and the people and relationships involved in working and the workplace in a theoretically holistic way to bring together disparate historical traditions and historiographical approaches. The aim and scope of *A Cultural History of Work* is to offer a comprehensive survey of the social and cultural construction of work across six historical periods. This approach that focuses on the *cultural* history of work provides an opportunity to explore the dynamics of work and the people and relationships involved in working and the workplace, helping to rethink boundaries and the issues of work. This is not an "economic" history of work, but a cultural one. Of course, we talk about economics, but the fundamental concept is to explain the ways in which work was situated in and influenced cultural dynamics of the western world. It is a key contribution to the process of rethinking boundaries and issues of work.

A Cultural History of Work draws on "the western world." Contributors approached their essays with a great deal of freedom, drawing on their specific expertise in national and regional histories, but throughout the thirty-six essays that make up the series, they have tried to embrace the "West." The series does not intend to "cover" all of western culture, or even all of Europe and North America. Authors instead have aimed at *representing* the broad trends and nuances of the culture of work from antiquity to the present. Thus *A Cultural History of Work* concentrates on the central themes in western work, with some sensitivity to areas we know less about.

This is a work of scholarly reference designed to provide scholars and students with a detailed, nuanced overview. Each contribution has been written as an original essay presenting an *overview* of a theme in a period, but each also includes a wide range of case material and has a particular thrust or point of view (or points of view) informing the organization of the piece. The series is structured into six time periods—though historians will always quibble about what these periods mean and will blur the edges. That is part of the process of understanding the past. And time does not have the same meaning across regions, much less countries or continents. Each volume covers a long period of time and a broad geography that can and will introduce a range of variables. Each volume uses the same chapter titles so that readers can read on a theme across volumes, or read through a period exploring the range of themes and nuances that each volume presents. There are also overlaps within volumes and across them that enrich the discussion.

The editorial decision to study work rather than labor is suggestive of a broader, more encompassing field of study that lends itself more readily to different periods. For example, in particular it is more appropriate to use *work* for periods such as antiquity and the Middle Ages because labor looks in one sense as an eighteenth- or nineteenth-century concept. English is rather unusual in having two words whose meanings overlap considerably, but are not identical. For example, there is only one word in French, *travail*, like *Arbeit* in German, *arbejde* in Danish/Swedish/Norwegian, *lavoro* in Italian. Some other languages tend to have one primary word also e.g *trabajo* in Spanish, though there are other usable words. From a definitional point of view we can argue that *labor* means the use of mental or physical capacities/faculties, so it implies suffering and difficulty, whereas *work* has to do with the simple act or fact of doing something/the activity/the action in progress. From the point of view of the political economy, *labor* seems to refer to the Marxist discourse; *work* is more pragmatic and less laden with cultural overtones. So, work describes the parameters of this project while *labor* is one aspect of it, which is more important in the nineteenth and twentieth centuries, and to a lesser extent in the eighteenth. Thus we argue *work* seems more neutral and general and therefore more applicable across six centuries.

Moving from the world of antiquity and into the twenty-first century, the culture of work has shifted considerably as technologies, organization and locations have changed. Workplace relations have also undergone transformations from small-scale and familial settings to large-scale and potentially less personal environments. And yet, the world of work remains complex with great variations between national cultures, political and economic approaches to managing the fields of work, and especially in the ways that people have negotiated their own spaces and places within them. Work retains many meanings from the simple need to survive to senses of deep satisfaction for the character of the job and the creativity one can achieve. It may be valued for the income, or wealth it can generate; conversely some choose to work less and on their own terms. Part-time, job-sharing, self-employment, and the IT revolution have offered different routes for some people. Workers can, however, remain tied to an employer and though nominally slavery does not exist in the West, there are those, like sweated immigrant workshops, and live-in domestic workers who may feel that little has changed. *The Cultural History of Work* traces and explores many of these routes and their implications for people and their cultural experience of work.

CONTRIBUTORS

Andrew August is Professor of History in the Abington College of Penn State University, Pennsylvania. His work focuses on modern British social, cultural and gender history. He is the author of *How Separate a Sphere? Gender, Work and Poverty in Late-Victorian London* (1999) and *The British Working Class, 1832–1940* (2007).

Nimisha Barton is Associate Director of the Freshman Scholars Institute and Programs for Access and Inclusion at Princeton University, New Jersey. In this role, she designs, innovates and administers programming for first-generation and low-income students at Princeton University. She received a dual BA in History and Religious Studies from UC Berkeley and her Ph.D. in History from Princeton. She is presently at work on her book manuscript, *Reproductive Citizens: Gender, Immigration and the State in France, 1900–1945*.

Cathleen Chaffee, Ph.D., is Chief Curator at the Albright-Knox Art Gallery in Buffalo, New York. Previously, she has worked at the Yale University Art Gallery, New Haven, Connecticut, the Museum of Modern Art, New York, and the Cleveland Museum of Art. In 2015 Chaffee curated "Overtime: The Art of Work," an exhibition that included artists from Honoré Daumier to Josh Kline and considered the different reasons modern and contemporary artists have depicted work, workers, and working conditions.

Michael Frisch is Professor of History & American Studies, Emeritus, University at Buffalo, State University of New York. He is an American social and urban historian with extensive oral and public history experience. He is the author of *A Shared Authority: Essays on the Craft and Meaning of Oral and Public History* (1990) and (with photographer Milton Rogovin) the prizewinning *Portraits in Steel*, (1993). His recent work with media indexing technology has been developed through The Randforce Associates, LLC, in the University at Buffalo's Technology Incubator.

Richard A. Greenwald is Professor of History and Dean of the College of Arts and Sciences at Fairfield University, Connecticut. Author of *The Triangle Fire, the Protocols of Peace and Industrial Democracy in Progressive Era New York* (2005), coeditor of *Sweatshop USA: The American Sweatshop in Historical and Global Perspective* (2003), and editor of *Exploring America's Past: Essays in Social and Cultural History* (1996), his most recent book is a coedited collection (with Dan Katz), *Labor Rising: The Past and Future of American Workers* (2012).

Andrew Hazelton is an Assistant Professor of History at Texas A&M International University. He completed his Ph.D. in History at Georgetown University. His research interests encompass labor, migration from Mexico, Mexican-Americans, borderlands, and agricultural history in the twentieth century. His current project is a book manuscript titled *Blue Sky Sweatshops: The Bracero Program, Mexican Immigration, and Organized Labor, 1942–1964*. He lives in Laredo, Texas, with his wife, son, and the faithful family dog.

Jennifer Klein is Professor of History at Yale University. She is author of *For All These Rights: Business, Labor, and the Shaping of America's Public-Private Welfare State* (2003). She is coauthor (with Eileen Boris) of *Caring for America: Home Health Workers in the Shadow of the Welfare State* (2012). She is the 2014 winner of the Hans Sigrist Prize awarded by the University of Bern and the Hans Sigrist Foundation in Switzerland, for her work on gender and economic precarity. She serves on the Editorial Board of International *Labor and Working-Class History*.

Randy D. McBee is Professor of History at Texas Tech University where he teaches a wide range of courses on US social history, gender, and the working class. He is the author of *Dance Hall Days: Intimacy and Leisure among Working-Class Immigrants in the United States* (2000) and *Born to be Wild: The Rise of the American Motorcyclist* (2015).

Stephen Meyer is a retired Emeritus Professor from the University of Wisconsin–Milwaukee. He is the author of *The Five Dollar Day*, "*Stalin Over Wisconsin,*' and *Manhood on the Line* (1981), and coeditor (with Nelson Lichtenstein), of *Manhood On the Line* (2016).

Andrew Perchard is Senior Lecturer in the Division of Management, Work and Organisation, Stirling Management School, University of Stirling, UK. He is the author of *Aluminiumville: Government, Global Business and the Scottish Highlands* (2012), and editor (with Steven High and Lachlan MacKinnon) of *The Deindustrialized World: Confronting Ruination in Post-Industrial Places* (2017) and (with Mats Ingulstad and Espen Storli) of *Tin and Global Capitalism, 1850–2000: A History of the "Devil's Metal"* (2014).

Amy E. Slaton is Professor of History at Drexel University in Philadelphia. She holds a Ph.D. from the University of Pennsylvania. She has written on ideologies of race, gender, sexuality and disability in technological work and education and on the role of technical standards in the control of American labor.

Daniel J. Walkowitz is a social and cultural historian who in nearly a dozen books, many articles, and four films for public television, has worked to bring America's past to both academic and broad public audiences. Professor Emeritus of History and of Social and Cultural Analysis at New York University, his more recent work includes *Working with Class: Social Workers and the Politics of the Middle-Class Identity* (1999), *City Folk: English Country Dance and the Politics of the Folk in Modern America* (2010), and (with Donna Haverty-Stacke) *Rethinking U.S. Labor History* (2010), and *The Remembered and Forgotten Jewish World: Jewish Heritage in Europe and the United States* (2018).

Introduction

DANIEL J. WALKOWITZ

Changes in production and consumption fundamentally transformed the culture of work in the industrial world during the century after the First World War. Prior to 1920, rural migrants and immigrants moving to the industrializing metropoles across Europe and North America served as the backbone of the factory labor in garments, steel, and a host of nineteenth-century industries. Manufacture extended to the countryside, too, where mammoth textile mills, characterized by worrisome reformers as "Satan's strongholds," and large-scale coal mines, similarly dotted the landscape. Struggling to compete and maximize profits, the proliferating mills and factories strategized. Some economized by lengthening hours, lowering wages, deploying "labor-saving" technologies, or speeding up production. Some also pursued economies of scale, buying out competitors to create monopolies or oligopolies (horizontal integration of industry) and acquiring industries such as banking and railroads to save on costs (vertical integration).[1] Little of this changed in the aftermath of the First World War, but in the search to find and create new markets and rationalize work, management also engaged new strategies of advertising and scientific management. They also deployed new workforces in labor increasingly tied to consumption rather than production.

The Marxist sociologist C. Wright Mills traced the basic components of this shift in his landmark 1951 book *White Collar: The American Middle Classes*. The title, an abbreviation of the white-collar *worker*, prefigured scholarly confusions about class identity and worker subjectivity in the latter half of the century. The book's major focus was a new substantial and critical component of the working class: white collar middle-class workers. Looking at work in America, but noting shifts that also characterized work across the western industrial landscape over the course of the twentieth century, Mills described the rise of a new middle class. According to Mills, the "old middle class" of free professionals and farmers had given way in the twentieth century to a "new middle class" of white-collar workers in service, clerical, professional, and managerial work engaged in the generation, selling, and distribution of commodities. As significant, the new labor sector also reflected a major change in the nature of the work in modern industrial societies from "blue-collar" production to white-collar (and pink-collar) jobs distributing, marketing, and consuming products. While Mills's focus was the United States, his account described a process in which the United States played a leading role in reshaping the culture of work in industrial cities elsewhere. Manufacturing continued in mid-twentieth-century industrial centers much as it had a half-century earlier, but over the course of the twentieth century, industrialists steadily moved mass-production industries, such as coal, steel, and auto and clothing manufacture to cheaper labor markets in less developed and poor parts of Asia and Central America. Older industrial cities became sites for postindustrial labor in finance, transportation, communication, and financial services.

Monopoly capital, or more precisely oligopoly—the rule of a small number of giant firms—encouraged the rise of Mills's new middle class while it also reshaped labor in the old middle class. As family farms fell victim to industrialized agricultural combines, and doctors and lawyers increasingly moved into factory-like firms or large medical groups, over the course of the twentieth century the old middle class of independent farmers and free professionals declined in both number and status. By the end of the twentieth century, the modern, industrial urban workforce came to resemble what the industrial world had long dismissed as "third world" urbanites where a large poorly paid (and often "nonwhite") service sector ministered to a small number of privileged (and typically "white") elites. Rather than the older professions, the elite sector in the new millennium focused on work in finance, real estate, accounting, advertising, fashion and media, and production technologies.[2]

These changes affected both the culture of the workplace and the home, as the gendered family economy of the modern worker struggled with the vagaries of a changing gendered labor market and the inequalities that accompanied them. Men and women often concentrated in labor sectors with different work regimes: for example, male blue-collar workers concentrated in mass-production industries, and female employees in white- and pink-collar workplaces. Wherever they worked, however, society discriminated against women workers: men (and many women) expected working wives to do the "double day" and return from the job to do housework and childcare; the paternalist state generally privileged male workers as "breadwinners" and required means tests for female-oriented benefits such as family assistance; and for women, who received less pay than men for comparable work, a glass ceiling also limited occupational advancement.

Gender also shaped the postindustrial culture of work and worklessness. As manufacturing and industrial jobs disappeared in the last half of the twentieth century, many workers turned to "middle-class" service work and increasingly identified themselves, at least at home, with a consumerist middle-class identity. Consumer goods—especially a private home and car, but also the full panoply of "labor-saving" machines, "modern" conveniences, and clothes in "la mode"—became the base for a hybrid, ambiguous nonclass identity, that of the "middle-class worker." The shift mirrored the decline of older male-dominated industrial unions that had sustained the male-breadwinner ideology, and the privatization of daily life and institutions in late twentieth-century neoliberal economies.[3]

Indebtedness, once the scourge of the worker that led to debtors' prison, characterized and made possible the new middle-class consumer lifestyle. Advertising advanced in the 1920s to drive production further. It was facilitated by the expansion of an advertising industry that encouraged consumers to buy autos, cloths, vacations, and second homes "on credit." Debt, rather than being a path to prison, was a mark of status—to be "credit worthy." But credit was a double-edged sword. With a new status to buy came fragility. Homes typically were not owned but held on a mortgage, and payments came due regardless of changing personal or familial circumstances. And the next debt or credit payment was only as secure as the job. Thus, by the end of the twentieth century, deindustrialization, capital flight, and increasing corporate reliance on foreign back-office labor undermined security. Gender trouble further strained the culture of work as many male industrial workers who lost their jobs to deindustrialization also felt their manliness threatened by the family's increased dependence on the earnings of wives and daughters who filled new lower-paid clerical and service jobs. These new jobs too often also came without medical or retirement benefits or the benefit of a union to advocate for the workers. With deepening social and economic inequalities, job insecurity, and strained social relations at home, workers and their families increasingly grew angry, anxious, and fearful. In this context, it remained unclear how or if their identity as middle-class workers would reverse a politics of *resentement* that focused hostility on immigrant labor rather than on their bosses as the source of their troubles.

This introductory chapter focuses on two distinct illustrative cases: white-collar social workers and blue-collar miners. The two cases highlight the uneven development and timing of changes in the modern culture of work over the course of the long twentieth century. The chapters in this volume, while typically also drawing on case studies, detail the segmented character of labor and worker culture across the industrial world.

THE INTERWAR YEARS

World historic events framed the culture of work in the years between the two world wars. First, the Russian Revolution in 1917 and the subsequent rise of a communist "workers' state" inspired many workers, whom socialist and communist labor leaders further mobilized, to fight for improved living and working conditions. Second, in reaction to growing socialist and communist labor movements, fearful corporate leaders and their allies in government advanced patriotic nationalism (Americanization, English, German and French nationalism, etc.). Further, they mounted anticommunist purges against trade unions, restricted immigration, or sought to replace urban labor with more contract labor from rural areas or with foreign migrants. Third, economic depression, whose signs first appeared in agricultural areas of Europe in the early 1920s, became the Great Depression of the 1930s. While the Depression brought great hardship to both rural and industrial workers, protests and organizations by workers led to the large-scale expansion of social welfare. Meanwhile, a vibrant trade-union movement expanded into mass-production industries and organized previously unorganized workers in the new clerical and professional sectors. Fourth, the rise of fascist regimes in Germany, Italy, Spain, and Japan led to the militarization of economies in these countries. As other nations in Europe and North America came to appreciate the imperial aims of the axis powers, they militarized their economies as well. War production ultimately brought the Depression to a close, and the enlistment of men gave opportunities to many traditionally discriminated against in the labor market, notably women and racial "others." But the war, of course, also had serious deleterious effects on workers. Nazis forced millions of Jews, gypsies, radicals, and homosexuals to "migrate" to extermination camps masquerading as "labor camps." Allies did not exterminate enemy aliens, but did ride herd on immigrant aliens: the United States, for example, restricted and isolated Italians and Germans and, in the case of Japanese-Americans, interned them for the duration of the war; the British interned Italian and German immigrants, including some German Jews. Calls to patriotism by state policymakers required industrial workers subordinate any labor complaints and pledge not to strike.

THE CASE OF SOCIAL WORKERS

Social work as it emerged in the early part of the twentieth century, exemplified the rise of the welfare state in the industrial world, the growing role of the service sector, and the new gendered relations of work and the family economy. Welfare state bureaucracies expanded dramatically in the last two decades of the nineteenth century in Great Britain, France, Germany, and the United States. As noted by historians Seth Koven and Sonya

Michel, this development "leads to the expansion of care-taking professions dominated by women: social work, nursing, health visitors—both as volunteers and professionals."[4] Female volunteers dominated the sector. Characterized as "Lady Bountifuls" in the US case, they were typically wealthy women engaged in charity work. A similar development occurred in Britain, where in 1890, an estimated half a million women engaged in public social welfare work, but only twenty thousand were employed in salaried positions.[5]

In the early twentieth century, the entry of rural migrants to overcrowded cities and increased radical labor agitation increased the call from both urban reformers and industrialists for more social-service workers. The two groups, which often overlapped, variously sought to adjust, help, and discipline workers. As a result, new service work institutions and would-be professionals emerged in the form of social workers and visiting nurses. In 1884, Toynbee Hall pioneered a settlement house movement in London's East End and inspired settlements throughout the industrial world. Schools for training social workers, professional associations through which they could advance their standing, and agencies in both the public and the private sector arose to offer their services. One well-known early example was the Ford Motor Company's deployment of social workers in the years just prior to the First World War. Building on Frederick Winslow Taylor's pioneering work in scientific management, Ford's program was his radical social experimentation in human engineering. Having developed the assembly line to maximize production, Ford's challenge was to reduce absenteeism and high turnovers by creating an industrious worker willing—and preferably even happy—to work at the routine. Ford's solution was to employ a new category of service worker, the industrial social worker, to oversee worker habits and attitudes in a new division of his company, the Sociological Department. Many of these service workers were men, but the new occupation, immediately recognizable as a "caring profession," would soon be marked as a female occupation. The social worker's job was to "care" for workers by making them more productive. In this sense, service work was an expansion of work into new arenas, both making service a form of twentieth-century commodity production and making workers more productive.[6]

Across the industrial landscape, managers in the 1920s celebrated and deployed welfare capitalist programs rooted in the experiments in human engineering. Creating business unions, companies sponsored sports program and education classes to teach ethnic workers how to be good Englishmen (sic) or Americans. Manager efforts to discipline workers extended to the workplace, too. New developments in scientific management modelled on lessons at the Hawthorne Electric Company in Chicago in the 1920s encouraged better ergonomics and lighting—but not better pay or shorter hours—to increase production. In the next decades, lessons of the Hawthorne Experiments led to the development of both business schools and employee-counselling programs. American companies pioneered these developments, but managers in industrial sites across Europe adopted them in the next decades. With its scientific management roots, both management studies and the counselling programs evolved with assumptions that workers need to adjust to industrial conditions, not that adjustments had to be made to the work process. To administer the adjustment, these programs employed another kind of social worker—the clinical social worker. As one union newsletter would describe them, counsellors became "cow sociologists" who believed "contented workers would give more milk."[7]

In the 1920s, some workers advanced alternatives to welfare capitalism and newly imposed taylorized work routines. Socialists and communists played important leadership roles in actions that some historians have depicted as heroic and others as quixotic. Often ending in defeat, for some these actions represented the end to an era of worker radicalism; to others, they demonstrated potential in collective action that workers would build on a decade later. For example, militant socialists and communists in the British Trades' Union Congress led 1.7 million workers in a general strike in May 1926 to force the government to pressure mine companies to withdraw wage reductions. The strike brought transport and heavy industry to a halt for nine days, only ending when the government brought in the army to crush strikers on the dockyards. In the same year, a textile strike in Passaic, New Jersey, galvanized the support and attention of American workers to the possibilities of unionization. Although they ultimately lost their struggles, under the leadership of the Communist Party, seventeen thousand textile workers gamely fought for sixteen months a 10 percent wage reduction.[8]

Communist and socialist trade unionists had more success in some places but not others during the Depression years of the 1930s, as governments—with the profound exception of fascist Germany and, later, Italy and Spain—began to support worker claims for better wages. However, the new welfare states of the industrial world differed in the benefits they provided and in the ways they met or encouraged industrial worker demands, especially during the hard times of the 1930s Depression. Fascist Germany, which had the strongest state and provided the most comprehensive program of benefits for women and children, had the most ineffective worker movement. By way of contrast, the United States, which had the weakest state, had the most powerful reform movement for worker entitlements. The French case resembled the German one while the British more closely approximated the American case. As Susan Pedersen notes, in France, paternalist employers and social Catholics united to support a family-centered social policy in order to forestall trade unionism; by way of contrast, in Britain, gender politics of a strong male trade-union movement committed to a breadwinner ideology weakened state interest in a strong family allowance program.[9]

In each particular context, often under the leadership of socialists and communists, workers struggled to build their own institutions and survive hard times. In Britain and the United States, the creation of worker educational institutions was one strategy and occurred well before the Depression: Ruskin College, first established in 1899 to educate British workers, served as a model for worker education in the UK and other countries. US labor colleges such as Brookwood Labor College (1921–37) and Bryn Mawr Summer School for Women Workers in Industry (1921–38) followed.[10] Workers during the Depression, most notably in the United States, recorded major successes in the industrial arena as well, establishing and sustaining worker institutions and gaining policy victories.

The case of New York social workers illustrates the historically contingent nature of work cultures. The history of radical social worker unionization and professionalization places the subjectivity of a feminizing professional labor sector in relief. It also highlights how both left-wing organizers and state anticommunism shaped the culture of work in a mid-century city with a particular radical cadre.

Prior to 1930, as the idea of the "caring professions" suggests, a professional ethos shaped the efforts of these new service workers. A male-dominated job until the early 1920s, by 1930 four out of every five people working in or preparing for a career in social work or teaching was female. These women constituted a very different social group from their charity predecessors. No longer daughters of native-born elites, a majority were now immigrants, daughters or granddaughters of male immigrants who had themselves been skilled workmen or clericals.[11] To win status and job security these women turned to professional and trade-union associations. In both fora, they had to overcome opposition from some men (and women) who regarded paid labor and the demands of professional "objectivity" to be "unwomanly." They also had to overcome the managerial logic of scientific management. One woman, a Miss Levy, a Milwaukee social worker, did so.

Writing in 1923, Levy turned the language of scientific management on its head, making it stand for workers' rights rather than for managed routine: "why don't the social workers of the United States and Canada organize themselves so that will have a standard salary, a standard vacation and standard rights?"[12] Levy urged workers to join the American Association of Social Workers, the professional organization, which most, in any case, did. However, in the Depression, as social workers faced deteriorating work conditions with rapidly rising workloads, they also turned to trade unions.

The material conditions of the Depression era required workers to rethink what they had to do to improve their lot and reimagine their identities in doing so. For social workers, this meant imagining themselves to be both white-collar professionals and trade unionists. This also meant they came to see themselves as both middle class and proletarians. New conditions and new leaders facilitated investment in new institutions.

To begin with, private charities that employed most social workers could not keep up with demands for help. Recognizing state commitments to self-help and reluctance to take a role in relief, US ethnic groups had historically developed institutions to aid their own communities. To do so, they relied on contributions from wealthy benefactors who gave only as they wished or felt they could. With the onset of the Depression, the local state, first New York State, and then the federal government, stepped in with new programs, relief agencies, and funding. The result was the expansion of a new cadre of social workers in a vastly expanded public sector that found their work increasingly focused on overseeing relief aid.

The Depression presented a different challenge for the smaller number of private agency staff that continued to work in ethnic- and religious-based institutions consolidated in Catholic Charities, Federation of Jewish Philanthropies, and Federation of Protestant Welfare Agencies. Faced with limited resources for both relief and their own wages, they acted to distinguish themselves from their public-sector counterparts who they saw as engaged in lower status and more proletarian work. With social service in the public sector increasingly focused on administering relief, private staff case workers moved to focus on clinical casework. Claiming expertise rooted in psychoanalysis they distinguished their work as therapy rather than relief. As we shall see below, the wartime use of psychiatry in military recruitment evaluations and postwar trauma would lead to a fuller blossoming of this division in the 1950s. But while the roots of the division of the occupation lay in the 1930s, social work conditions in the Depression solidified their unity.

The same Depression conditions that unified social workers mobilized many other industrial workers in US industries who the labor movement had hitherto ignored. Historians have detailed, for instance, the growth of unionization among the unorganized and less skilled in US mass-production industries such as textiles and auto. They have also documented the central role of radical communist and socialist leadership in these unions. And, with the important exception of Germany where the Nazis imprisoned and executed communist leaders, unionization took place across the industrial economies in which these radical parties thrived, such as France, Italy, Spain, and the United States.

While less well known, trade-union organization and struggle extended to service workers, from department store clerks to professionals in teaching, nursing, and social work. In all these cases, women played a major part, and not simply as "auxiliaries."[13]

In all cases, aid discriminated against women. Men were thought to be breadwinners, so wives lost jobs if their husbands worked in the same shop. Aid traditionally administered to women, as in Aid to Families and Dependent Children, was means tested; aid typically provided to men, such as Social Security and Disability Insurance, generally had no income test.

Social work and state welfare policy also privileged white immigrants, discriminating against those seen as nonwhite "others." State and private welfare, for instance, rarely aided farmers. Moreover, welfare did not cover domestic service jobs, part-time labor, or marginal jobs "off the books," occupations filled by African Americans. Ironically, as social workers were relatively poorly paid working women, they both suffered from these distinctions and implemented them.

Sometimes social workers recognized these paradoxes and aligned with the usually female and poor (and in the 1960s, often African American) public welfare recipients/clients who fought for basic income, food, and housing. Supported by welfare workers and radical organizers, women in poor communities where one in three was out of work, led rent strikes. Mobilized by tenant activists from the local communist-led Unemployment Council, a "Great Rent Strike War" erupted in 1932 to fight evictions and demand rent reductions in privately owned East Bronx high-rise apartments. As the historian Mark Naison notes,

> By an accident of geography and sociology, this neighbourhood contained one of the largest concentrations of Communists in New York City. On the corner of Bronx Park East and Allerton Avenue stood the "Coops"—two buildings populated entirely by Communists who had moved to the neighbourhood as part of a cooperative housing experiment and had remained when the buildings reverted to private ownership [were] filled with people for whom "activism was a way of life."[14]

With the support of the courts, evictions continued, but so too did the strikes. Over the next two years rent strikes took place in the East Village section of Manhattan as well as in several Brooklyn neighborhoods, each of them communist communities. In all these actions, neighborhood women and many of the female social workers played major roles. And while the strikes failed to stop most evictions, the organizers did succeed in their major objective: to mobilize the unemployed.[15]

Social workers also organized themselves. Approximately 3,300 private agency social workers in America, the largest number of them in New York, joined the Social Service Employees Union (SSEU) of the United Office and Professional Workers of America (UOPWA); another 8,500 workers in the public sector joined the State, Country and Municipal Workers of America (SCMWA), an industrial union of clerical and professional workers that became the United Public Workers (UPW) in 1946. With dedicated communist leadership, these unions demonstrated the possibilities for solidarity across white- and blue-collar lines within the working class. Although fleeting, such moments were nonetheless examples of what was and might be possible. For instance, New York social workers in both Jewish agencies and the Department of Welfare walked picket lines during the mid-1930s. They did so again in the 1960s, when they fought agency wage reductions and high caseloads while also demanding better services and more benefits for clients.[16] New York social workers, led by a radical rank-and-file movement, developed a panoply of advanced social and cultural institutions, from journals to sports activities and social gatherings. Their culture of work raised money, built solidarity and generally solidified their families behind their cause. To be sure, radical social worker unions were especially evident in New York, but social workers elsewhere in the United States organized to meet urban challenges that accompanied the influx of migrants and immigrants to Depression-era cities. Outside New York, their efforts drew upon less militant professional associations. But New York social worker militancy and organization reflected heightened worker self-consciousness about work and leisure in the 1930s. As historian Lizabeth Cohen observes in her classic cultural history of working-class Chicago, *Making a New Deal,* workers came together as ethnics, African Americans, women and men in the workplace, the union hall, and neighborhoods. They did so as both workers and consumers, forging a collective political identity, political culture, and social democratic ethos in defense of rights and entitlements.[17]

POSTWAR CHALLENGES

For social work, the end of the Second World War brought some profound challenges and opportunities that epitomized a changing culture of work both within this sector and elsewhere. In the nineteenth century, male psychiatrists (or "alienists") had been low-status functionaries who treated low-status insane-asylum patients. Conscious of the precedent of shell shock and postwar trauma during and after the First World War, governments turned to psychiatrists to evaluate Second World War recruits' emotional stability. As front-line troops on the home front, psychiatrists (and the female cadre of psychiatric social workers) emerged from the war with enhanced status, new ambitions, and new possibilities for therapy as a valued commodity of the postwar consumer society.

For many social workers, then, the new "problem" of postwar traumatic stress and readjustment was an opportunity. Clinical social work, often in private practice and with paying customers, became a preferred niche. Meanwhile, public-sector social workers, increasingly augmented by clerical staffs, administered heavy caseloads with impoverished clientele for low pay. That is to say, social work, as with the more general division between blue-, white-, and pink-collar work, became increasingly fractured along distinct cultural and social lines. Clients receiving public assistance were an under- or unemployed fraction of the working class, and were often women with children. Mid-1950s plays and films such as *West Side Story* and *Blackboard Jungle*, depicted the racial divisions that also marked working-class culture. Set in a poor urban New York City high school, *Blackboard Jungle* was a breakout debut for Sidney Poitier as a leader among troubled black youth. The jungle metaphor reflected the racialized concerns of the day: when an angry student traumatizes the white teacher's pregnant wife, urban youth culture is seen to threaten the white family. The soundtrack for the film, "Rock Around the Clock," also heralded the onset of a new urban youth culture embedded in marginalized communities and set them against a white-collar sector of service professionals who identified with a new suburban middle class. This conflict led to the film being banned in some cities for fear that its uninhibited, wild music might incite "respectable" audiences to inappropriate sexual behavior.[18]

West Side Story and *Blackboard Jungle* imaginatively refigured the convergence of opportunity, white flight, and racism that shaped the segmentation of work, labor, and working-class cultures in mid-century New York, social and geographic divisions that would persist and deepen in the next half-century across the industrial world. Immigrant labor and the poorest within the working class would constitute the racial "other" everywhere. However, postwar European countries also confronted major devastation that required them to rebuild factories, institutions, and houses. Labor reorganized after the war to win deferred wartime wage increases, but Cold War anticommunism complicated its efforts, most especially in the United States where McCarthyism was particularly virulent. Following a strike wave in 1946, for instance, US business interests lobbied state and federal government to pass a series of laws that hamstrung labor. The passage of the Taft–Hartley Act over President Truman's veto in 1947 seriously restricted the power of labor unions, outlawing secondary boycotts, limiting union shops, and allowing the government to impose injunctions on strikes. Equally important was the act's requirement that union leaders sign an affidavit that they were not communists. This, in turn, led the Congress of Industrial Organization (CIO) in the United States to purge radical leaders and replace their unions with centrist "bread-and-butter" organizations less committed to the wider social issues of discrimination that affected both skilled and unskilled workers at home, in the neighborhood, and at the workplace.

Both social workers and their working-class clients felt the effects of postwar anti-communism. Conservative local and state politicians, who believed many of those on welfare received undeserved benefits, oversaw the public welfare bureaucracy. Boards of governors for the private agencies consisted almost exclusively of male, white businessmen-philanthropists, who faced resistance from radical unions in the department stores and garment factories they owned. As staunch Cold War anti-communists, both these authorities proceeded to eviscerate radical social worker unions in both the public and the private sectors. This led to the decline of an active pro-client faction in social-worker ranks, with dire implications for clients, who were increasingly African Americans and Puerto Ricans. Insisting many women welfare clients had "men hiding under their beds" and made illegitimate claims, a new cadre of conservative welfare administrators in the 1950s instituted a new "business regime." In the names of efficiency and justice, they oversaw rollbacks in welfare rolls and benefits. In the 1960s, these rollbacks would come under attack by revitalized left-wing unions, and a poor peoples' movement led by African American women would reverse these assaults on worker entitlements. But the 1950s cutbacks illustrate the uneven development of the new consumer society.[19]

The racialization of welfare and its cutbacks also reflected the geographic dispersion and segmented history of working-class communities.[20] "White flight" led white-collar families, including families of social workers, into the suburbs where they would participate in the new consumer society; the situation of urban "communities of colour" was considerably more constrained. Many workers may have willingly exchanged postwar economic opportunity for loss of militant leadership. But not everyone did. While European workers continued to endure rationing, the American economy boomed: wartime US production converted into postwar production of consumer goods production, and the state made substantial investments in a robust Federal Housing program, an Interstate Highway system, and the vast expansion of public education. However, even in the United States, economic realities of "the Affluent Society" did not extend to all workers. The white-industrial and white-collar working class benefited but not African American and Latino urban workers. Agitation from and on behalf of these people by radical social workers and others in the 1960s led to programs for "equal opportunity," but such policies belied a new reality. Opportunity meant little if jobs were unavailable. Ironically, the resurgence and winning of equal opportunity masked early signs of deindustrialization, which as the historian Judith Stein found, began in the 1950s.[21]

DEINDUSTRIALIZATION AND THE CASE OF MINING

A second case of work culture, that of mining, also exemplifies changing job opportunities and frustrations in Europe and the United States in the last half of the twentieth and early twenty-first centuries. The coal industry in the three largest coal-producing nations—the United States, Great Britain, and Germany—suffered similar declines. However, mining in a fourth nation—Ukraine—illustrates how the impact of deindustrialization in the modern age was historically contingent. In parts of the industrial world such as Ukraine the culture of work for miners continued to have one foot planted in the premodern era.

Mining was one of the most dangerous industrial occupations: in the poignant words of one miner, when the men went down the shaft, they "said goodbye to life."[22] As late as 1989, the life expectancy of Ukrainian miners was only about forty-eight years. Life expectancy gradually improved in other industrial nations over the course of the century but remained considerably below average. And disproportionate numbers of those who did not die on the job experienced serious injuries.

Mining communities everywhere drew on a unique culture of solidarity to resist assaults on their living and working conditions by coal companies and to actively protest mine closures. Mining companies often tended to be absentee-owned and controlled; miners possessed solidarity nurtured by their work culture and by life in isolated rural communities. Close working relationships and reliance on one another below ground further instilled solidarity. So, when faced with deteriorating work conditions or loss of work, miners historically responded with unusual militancy. And, as the historian Herrick Chapman has observed, in countries with strong social democratic movements such as Germany, France, and Great Britain, miners gained new housing, job restructuring, and health benefits to ease some of the worse effects of job loss.[23] Moreover, militant strikes led by militant unions addressed twentieth-century wage reductions and pit closures. In the United States, for example, the Western Federation of Miners, and later the United Mine Workers, organized major strike campaigns that regularly punctuated the history of Midwest and southern mountain coalfields. In the UK, before it suffered a devastating loss to a determined anti-union Thatcher government in a 1984–5 strike, the National Union of Mineworkers won wage increases after two bitter strikes in 1972 and 1974.

The history of American mining illustrates the impact of deindustrialization on work in the modern age and the culture of work miners mobilized to meet its challenges. Mining was a leading sector of the rural US economy at the end of the nineteenth century, employing almost half a million workers in 1900 and nearly three-quarters of a million in 1920. Between 1950 and 1960, an era considered the heyday of the "American century," the number declined precipitously from 488,206 to 188,451. Intensified work regimes and automation, not industry decline, accounted for some of the loss: per capita production doubled while the labor force shrank. After 1980, the industry suffered a second major loss, declining to 83,462 in 1995. By April 2016, US coal miners numbered only 56,600. Dramatic fourfold gains in per capita production since 1980 demonstrated that the shift was the result of the intensification of work and automation, more than deindustrialization.[24]

The decline of mining in the UK and Germany mirrored the US experience. Britain's National Coal Board (NCB) counted 700,000 employees in 1950; its number declined by a comparatively modest 10 percent in the next decade. Pit closures followed, as coal seams were exhausted, as power stations increasingly relied on cheaper imported coal and gas, and as a result of privatization of the nationalized coal industry under Thatcher. The closure of the Kellingley mine in West Yorkshire, in mid-December 2015, brought the era of deep coal mining in Great Britain to an end. So, too, ended the glory era in the history of the once powerful miners' union. The National Union of Miners, over half a million strong earlier in the twentieth century, was left with just 100 members; in the end, the pits' 450 miners received severance packages equal to only twelve weeks' pay.[25]

The Ruhr and Saar coalfields made Germany the third leading coal producing nation. Mine production resumed after the war, but the decline of mining soon afterwards followed the US pattern. Between 1960 and 1980 the number of mines dropped from 146 to 39, although the industry still employed more than half a million people. In 2000, only twelve mines remained open and provided jobs to well under fifty thousand people.[26]

The era of mining deindustrialization represented job decline, a loss of labor vitality, in all three countries. Mine jobs, which had been almost exclusively the province of men, disappeared, but their absence was visible in profound ways; in reconstituted social relations for women, men, and children in the family, and in new attitudes within distraught working-class communities who felt society and government ignored their plight, the disappearance of mining jobs threatened the survival of long-standing working-class bonds of solidarity.

The impact of job loss on mining communities and the drama of protracted and bitter miners' strikes across the mid-twentieth century also resonated within popular culture in film and video. From John Ford's 1941 poignant depiction of Welsh mining community in the 1930s, *How Green Was My Valley*, to Barbara Kopple's 1976 documentary, *Harlan County, USA*, films captured and publicized the contested history of exploitative mining conditions for national and international audiences. Others, such as John Sayles's powerful 1987 account of West Virginia miners' struggles in the 1920s, *Matewan* and the 1993 French film by Claude Berri based on the Émile Zola novel, *Germinal*, appeared after the fate of mining communities had largely been determined. While prolabor productions did nothing to support contemporary miners, they coexisted alongside romantic representations of deindustrialized regions in the British Midlands and the North. *Brassed Off* (1996) gave audiences a chuckle while seeing how the closures affected a miners' band; *The Full Monty* (1997) exposed audiences to male striptease as a survival strategy for six unemployed miners; while a miner's son in *Billy Elliot* turns to ballet to soar above the sorry history of the 1984–5 strike. Finally, in another comedy-drama drawn from that same strike, *Pride* (2014), London gay activists and Welsh miners unite in a south Wales mining community.

Such films won large audiences, particularly among urban liberal audiences comprised of many of the white-collar service, managerial, and professional classes who constituted the more affluent sector of the hybrid social class of middle-class workers. For blue-collar workers like miners such representations might lighten a day, but did nothing for their social plight. The example of Pittsburgh's miners is a case in point.

Pittsburgh, located in west Pennsylvania's Allegheny County, was the quintessential smokestack city at the center of one of American's premier coal- and steel-producing regions. The Pittsburgh coal seam, the best and most extensive coal bed in the eastern United States, extended south eleven thousand miles from Allegheny's Mon Valley into western Maryland and West Virginia and employed hundreds of thousands of coal miners. The coal, in turn, fuelled steel mills such as Andrew Carnegie's famous Homestead Works. Acquired by Carnegie in 1883 from the Pittsburgh-Bessemer Steel Company, Homestead become a byword around the world for its brutal use of private Pinkerton police against striking workers in an 1892 strike. In the next century, Homestead and a host of sister steel mills would dominate the Pittsburgh economy and labor market.

As elsewhere, signs of deindustrialization first scarred Pittsburgh in the 1950s, just after the city reached its peak population growth. From a high of almost 700,000, the city lost about 10 percent of its population over the decade. During a 116-day steel strike in 1959 local construction companies chose to import steel. The use of cheaper foreign product escalated in the next years, leading to the closure of twenty-nine Pittsburgh steel mills in the next forty years. A mass layoff of 153,000 steel workers followed a 1981–2 recession. And in 1991, Homestead was demolished. In a cruel irony of the new consumer culture, a few years later an upscale Waterfront Shopping Mall, at which unemployed miners and steelworkers would be hard-pressed to shop, replaced it.

The closure of the mines and mills transformed Pittsburgh, leaving a sharply segmented workforce in its wake. With the shift from heavy industry to service, medicine, higher education, tourism, banking, and high-tech industry, nearly one in five people moved out of the city during the 1970s, many into the adjoining suburbs. Many of those who remained were affluent, unemployed, or too old to leave. The city cleaned up its air and water, but in the interim lost almost 40 percent of its 1950 population: by 1980, Pittsburgh's population had fallen to 369,878. Remade as a white-collar and corporate city, it gained the praise of Rand McNally editors who announced in 1985 that Pittsburgh had become the "most liveable" city in the nation: it was now "a smoke-free city of tall office buildings set in a stunning natural setting."[27]

The "most liveable" moniker belied another reality for blue-collar workers who had lost their jobs. Unemployment in the Pittsburgh metropolitan area in 1983 reached 18.2 percent; in the surrounding region, where coal mines had closed, the number soared to well over 20 percent.[28] Allegheny County had the dubious distinction of having the oldest population in America after Dade County, the retiree center in Florida. As with the mining villages of Britain, the loss of work and an increasing dependence on the wages of wives and children created a crisis of masculinity among men who had been raised to be "breadwinners." For instance, Pittsburgh's two major employers in the 2010s were the University of Pittsburgh Medical Center (twenty-six thousand employees) and West Penn Allegheny Health System (thirteen thousand employees). But while male steelworkers and miners lost jobs, work in the large number of service jobs in these expanding white-collar industries often went to women. Pay rates in these jobs on average constituted only two-thirds of what a miner or steelworker had earned. Most private-sector work was nonunion labor without benefits. Thus, the century ended with an increasingly discouraged and aging blue-collar labor force troubled by class and gender anxieties. White-collar professionals and workers in the burgeoning high-tech and financial industries could partake of the amenities of the consumer economy and the status conferred by a consumer identity. By way of contrast, the blue-collar working class, embittered and angry by the lack of security and opportunity for themselves and their children, soured on "politics as usual," retreated into nationalism, and looked for a strong leader who could fight foreign imported workers and their products.[29]

The story of Pittsburgh's workers was not unique, but it vibrated in the eastern Ukrainian city of Donetsk, its sister city. The history of miners in Donetsk also reframes the US, British, and German stories. Highlighting the historically contingent nature of the changes in work culture in the industrial world, coal miners there continued to work at the end of the twentieth century, albeit with a marked decline in status and in conditions that had barely modernized.

Donetsk was the capital of the Donbass region and home to the Soviet Union's oldest and largest coalfields. As late as 1989 its 121 mines employed approximately 120,000 miners. The work was difficult and dangerous, but coal fuelled the Soviet state and thus the work gave them considerable social power. As such, miners were a privileged, high-status occupation in the Soviet Union. The high status of miners turned the conventional labor values of capitalist states on their head: miners received two to three times the wages of teachers, doctors, engineers, or other industrial workers. While they knew their job was dangerous, they took pride in their work and their role in the state. Generations of young men followed their fathers into the mines and young girls dreamed of marrying a miner. But by 1989, as living conditions in the Soviet Union declined, Donetsk miners also suffered a loss of status.[30] An exchange with some young girls interviewed following the 1989 strike lightheartedly intimated the miners' lessened value in the marriage market:

GIRL 1: Marry miners?
GIRL 2: They make more money [laughter].
GIRL 1: [Seriously] Yes, it's true.
INTERVIEWER: You personally would you do it?
GIRL 3: We, personally, are going to America [laughter].[31]

The Donetsk miners' experience, however, differed in important ways from European miners elsewhere. First, rather than experiencing the onset of deindustrialization, after being left flooded by the Nazis, the mines were entirely rebuilt in the postwar years. By 1990, while mines mechanized elsewhere, Donetsk mining technologies remained little changed from the pick and shovel work common in mines elsewhere half a century earlier. Accidents and mine explosions were frequent, and the average miner did not live to see his fiftieth birthday. In contrast to the experience of miners in the United States and Great Britain, however, neither automation nor deindustrialization drove Donetsk miners to strike in 1989. Rather, mining continued as a backward industry but it no longer sustained miners' privileged position. When Donetsk miners went out on strike, they demanded a restructuring of society and of their mine management (as well as basic provisions such as soap in the mine showers). Their action in 1989 was one of the first real strikes in the Soviet Union's history. It helped to bring about the resignation of Mikhail Gorbachev and played a critical role in the downfall of the Soviet Union. But in mobilizing to restructure the mine management, miners encountered some painful contradictions: the mines were in horrific condition and safety conditions were abominable, but the mine seams were largely exhausted. What little coal was left was also miles deep. In 1989, it could take an hour to get to the face of the seam, and what a miner extracted there was of poor quality with high sulfur content. In the face of growing environmental concerns with pollution from burning coal, the state offered little hope to Donetsk miners. Most mines needed to be closed, but Donetsk miners, as elsewhere, found few employment alternatives.

Some miners, like Valery Samofalov, a strike leader, dreamt of becoming an "entrepreneur" living a "normal life." Based on Hollywood film and TV images for information, he and his workmates blindly imagined "normal" to be the life of Pittsburgh-area miners, little knowing they had been made redundant. The bankrupt and corrupt Ukrainian government in Kiev offered them few alternatives. Increasingly nationalist, it showed little sympathy or understanding of a region where half the population viewed itself as Russian-speaking Russian-ethnics. Since 2014, when they were caught up in civil war as the capital of a separatist campaign, Donetsk miners scoured old mine shafts for nuggets of coal they could sell on the black market. These miners' desperation resembled the plight of miners elsewhere. In Donetsk, mining became the survival strategy of working-class scavengers in a scavenger economy.

CODA

The contrasting experiences and attitudes of blue-collar workers highlights the segmentation of the working classes and their work culture in the modern age. Unemployment rates and real wages improved modestly for blue-collar workers in the years following the Great Recession of 2008, although income inequality in the industrial nations dramatically increased. Meanwhile, government authorities held out little hope that environmentally unfriendly work in industries such as coal would return. Barraged by advertising for consumer goods that seemed beyond their reach and jobs they saw outsourced to cheap labor elsewhere, embittered blue-collar sectors turned to nationalist, nativist policies and politicians for help. In the UK, older industrial areas led the vote for Brexit, the withdrawal of the country from the European Union, which they associated with immigrant labor and global trade. Industrial workers in the United States supported the election of Donald Trump on a similar platform, while distressed workers supported the comparable election of far-right regimes in Poland and Hungary.

The category of the white-collar worker was not unitary, however: there were significant economic, political, gendered, and racialized cultural divisions. In the United States, African Americans and Latino/as, often first and second-generation immigrants, filled the ranks of the more lowly paid service worker engaged in intimate labor; elsewhere, immigrant and migrant occupied a similar niche. In contrast, predominantly white professional-managerial-technical workers remained well educated and better paid. However, the new workplaces they encountered bore a resemblance to corporate culture that had transformed work at Ford Motor Company and the Hawthorne Works a century earlier at the beginning of our story. In the twenty-first-century workplace, for instance, Google took care of employees' everyday needs, such as dry cleaning and commuting, offering play stations at the workplace, and flexible hours and workplaces. Compass, a high-end New York-based 2014 start-up company with hundreds of realtors in cavernous open-design rooms glued to monitors, further typified the opportunities and challenges of the new workplace culture. Compass described itself as a tech company, but the workplace looked like a factory. Its large advertising and IT staff supported the realtors, who could retreat to play ping-pong, go to a yoga class, or relax with a cappuccino. They worked to their own schedule, but without a contract or salary—or benefits. Rather, they lived on their sales' commissions, 30 percent of which went to Compass.[32]

Thus, the twenty-first-century professional-technical sector, which labored in a tech-driven "agile-type" work culture that echoed the assembly line of a century ago, experienced both new opportunities and new challenges. Technology-driven, the new workplace imagined itself as a tech company where "agile work," a new management concept, represented "the new organizational pattern." But as one perspicacious labor journalist notes, "standard corporate organization charts looked something like assembly-line factories, with strictly defined jobs moving up narrow silos of production." "We don't talk about work/life balance anymore," said one chief executive. "It's work/life mix" where workers organize their own schedule. But what do "flexible hours ... really mean?" According to the journalist, it means "that they [workers] are expected to work all the time. And they are expected to react faster to bosses' demands with more varied skills."[33]

Over the course of the century, most workers gained a higher standard of living, but gender and racial inequities persisted. In recent decades, inequality reached dramatically high levels not seen in a century. Economists estimated that 1 percent of the world's population owned as much as the other 99 percent, while a super-rich group of sixty-two people owned as much as half the world.[34] Automation led the shift away from manufacturing jobs into service and technical work that carried their own challenges. The differences between the cases of distressed blue-collar miners and professional-technical workers, ranging from social workers to IT staff in "new economy" industries, illustrate how segmentation, though less extreme, continued to characterize the work and culture of new sectors of workers. Blue- and white-collar workers encountered many of the same challenges—to sustain a family living wage, and to find and hold on to a good job. However, facing these challenges, each group drew up a different culture of work with distinct skill sets, income, and educational resources. In the twenty-first century, while economic reasons to unite remained, the divisions between these cultures increasingly pitted sectors of the class against one another.

CHAPTER ONE

The Economy of Work

JENNIFER KLEIN

INTRODUCTION

Viewing the period from the 1920s through the early twenty-first century, we see not only the moments or conditions when workers gained greater leverage over the wage bargain (or lost it), but also the profound effects of state regulation, economic policy, and labor policy on the demand for and conditions of labor. Prior to the 1930s, individual firms had unrivalled prerogative over labor markets in their region and industry. As a result of New Deal and Second World War labor policies in the United States, the idiom of contract—based on an utter imbalance of power—shifted to a set of collective working-class rights and economic citizenship that held business power in check. Through economic policy, labor standards, and unionism, the state and organized labor challenged firms' domination of the economics of labor, generated redistribution of wealth more broadly, and compressed the gaps in social stratification. Yet because of labor markets segmented by race and gender, contract would have a very different meaning for women and people of color.

In the 1960s and 1970s, a new generational labor movement in the public sector and service sector changed the terms of this labor: its compensation, cultural worth, and political leverage. Within two and a half decades, women composed 45 percent of unionized workers, the percentage of Latinos in the unionized workforce more than doubled, and one in eight union workers was an immigrant.[1] But labor law remained rooted in the structures of employment of the mid-twentieth century, making it difficult for workers to maintain rights and security as the economics of labor continued to change. By the end of the twentieth century, business had conquered both the legal and the socio-political institutions and culture that had enabled workers to gain some self-determination over working conditions, job markets, and aggregate employment. Companies used politics, technology, and outsourcing to build new forms of insecurity into jobs and labor markets, resurrecting employment "at-will" and disposable labor.

THE PRE-NEW DEAL ERA

The popular image of the 1920s showcases the burgeoning pleasures of mass consumption with a widening array of goods available. For much of the working class, however, wage work was so undependable as a source of steady income, their lives remained conditioned more by scarcity. Consequently, social workers, settlement house reformers and US Women's Bureau researches found the working-class economy relied on "wage earning outside the home, wage-earning inside the home, and cash replacement activities," including taking in boarders, bartering care support, trading second-hand clothing, extending and receiving loans, and "putting out" children to work in others' homes. Forms of reciprocity patched the holes left by the labor markets such workers faced.[2]

While some new manufacturing firms sought to create stability through vertical integration, variegated internal labor markets, scientific management, and personnel management, they were still subject to the ups and downs of the business cycle. Employers shifted the burden of downturns to workers in the form of slack work (short hours) and short weeks. Among the new mass of semi-skilled and unskilled factory operatives, slack work was as much part of the labor-market experience as long hours. Adding up the impacts of technological change, irregular work, strikebreaking and punitive responses to labor militancy, and seasonal production, "insecurity and instability of employment would remain a part of men's occupational experience."[3]

Prior to the New Deal, then, wage work was no ticket to independence. Neither industrial employment nor wages in and of themselves conferred freedom or independence. Despite the idiom of contract that seemed to infuse individual employment and the functioning of markets for wage labor, the experience of work was discontinuous, contingent, and precarious. Legal, structural, and political barriers rendered wage work insecure. Rooted in centuries-old "master and servant" law, a worker was legally "free" to enter into an employment contract, yet the employer could also dismiss the worker "at will" for any reason or no reason. "Management's absolute right to discharge at-will employees for any reason whatsoever was repeatedly reaffirmed by the courts ... as sacrosanct." If a worker quit, wages could not be demanded as a right.[4] Management could reinforce its prerogatives through access to force—state militias or private company guards.

In the wake of the First World War, European leaders and reformers perceived Americans as having a uniquely high standard of living, especially defined by high wages and mass-produced goods. Charged with the function of improving standards of living and reforming the conditions of labor internationally, the newly created International Labour Organization (ILO) set out to systematically measure and assess the American working-class standard of living. Yet once the investigation began, it became clear that nobody had an exact idea of the standards of living of average workers in industrial cities such as Detroit. ILO investigators found that the high wage was a "flexible concept" and goods were often bought on credit.[5]

Anti-vagrancy statutes shaped labor markets for the poor and African Americans. In both the post-Civil War South and the urban North, anti-vagrancy laws made it a crime not to have a job. In northern cities, new uniformed police forces conducted dragnet sweeps, herded unemployed people or those cobbling together a living on the street into night court, charged them with vagrancy, and upon release directed them into the labor market or, possibly, military service. Women who were paupers and ended up in the alms-house were sent to work—either in textile mills or in domestic service.

Adrift from patriarchal homes, an individual woman's precariousness threatened others and threatened the social order. Charity reformers and leaders of public and private welfare organizations, asylums, and orphanages therefore channelled girls and women into domestic work. The social, legal construction of the home as private enabled the persistence of interminable hours, on-call overnight, few days off, arbitrary surveillance, vulnerability to sexual assault, lack of food and extreme hunger, and nonpayment of wages. Middle-class employers insisted that domestic labor simply could not be shoehorned into the frame of an eight-hour day.[6] This assumption would have a lasting legacy throughout the twentieth century.

For many workers, the insecurity of selling one's labor power was repeated daily, through the shape-up Each morning, men of all sorts would gather, bunched together on docks, construction sites, warehouses, and fields ready for harvest, hoping the foreman would choose them for that day's work. They stood outside in any kind of weather, their time expropriated and exploited, as they waited, yet were not paid. Whether it was men gathering on the Embarcadero in San Francisco for waterfront work or African American women in the Bronx waiting to be hired for a day's domestic labor, workers and labor organizers referred to the shape-up as a "slave market."[7]

Once inside the factory gates or the shipyard, workers faced the petty tyranny of foremen. Personal discretion—and indiscretions—of front-line supervisors, favoritism, and arbitrary discipline defined life on the job. The drive system was a corollary to at-will employment: using fear and coercion foremen compelled high output, driving out those who could not keep up or chafed under the system. High quit rates and high discharge rates were different sides of the same coin.[8]

Seasonal labor churned the workforce of common laborers not only in agriculture. Railroads, mining, urban construction of subways and skyscrapers, canning, and garment manufacturing had seasonal peaks and layoffs. In garments, small manufacturers produced on a "rush-order basis," setting up a perpetual war of cost cutting, price-cutting competition and, thus, swift surges and contractions of employment, season after season.[9] Hull House labor reformer Florence Kelley observed, manufacturers "constantly aim to concentrate work of the year into the shortest possible season."[10] Even Ford Motors,

FIGURE 1.1 "Make a Wish," Bronx slave market, 170th Street, New York, 1938, The Crisis. Photo: Robert McNeill. Courtesy Smithsonian Institution.

which through the $5 day, personnel management, and welfare capitalism had sought to create more long-term employment, shut down production in 1927 in order to retool for the production of a new Model A auto, throwing 100,000 employees out of work.[11]

Large corporate employers attempted to combine the imperatives of productive stabilization, worker loyalty, employee welfare, and managerial prerogative through welfare capitalism. Welfare capitalism encompassed social welfare benefits and health, safety, or leisure programs established and directed by the employer. They ran the gamut from cafeterias, athletic clubs, leisure activities, and Americanization classes to more pecuniary forms such as profit sharing, savings and loans, life insurance, sick pay or accident compensation. American corporate leaders saw workplace social welfare as an alternative to unionism and a private, managerial response to pressure from the state and workers, especially when workers sought to use the state to improve working conditions and guarantee economic security.[12]

In the 1920s, prominent welfare capitalists believed that individual employers could use private, firm-based mechanisms to mitigate unemployment. In Rochester, New York, General Electric (GE) and Eastman Kodak gathered fourteen local companies to join in a regional unemployment prevention program. Each company would make contributions to a reserve fund based on its particular layoff history—or experience rating. Allegedly, that would provide incentive for firms to plan better, spread work, and prevent layoffs. No state involvement was necessary, Kodak and GE executives confidently assured everyone.[13]

For progressive reformers and labor advocates Louis Brandeis, John R. Commons, Florence Kelley, and newly emerging union leaders in consumer goods industries, though, business voluntarism did not address what linked intermittent employment, unemployment, and low wages: the imbalance of power within the world of work. Until workers had participation as "citizens" in industry to shape the conditions of labor and collective organization equal to that of the corporation, they could not achieve regular employment, a reasonable income, safe working conditions, and health and leisure.

Labor leaders such as Sidney Hillman and John L. Lewis, aligned with Progressive reformers, pushed forward an alternative means of technocratic management of particular industries' erratic ups and downs and spasmodic employment. This 1920s "new unionism" promoted mechanisms of social cooperation and compromise in the workplace that would promote greater efficiency and well-being, not through the pure coercion of floor bosses, or the "adjustments" of Taylorism, but through workers' participation and rule-making, dispute resolution, and contractual obligation. Within this *aspirational* vision of industrial democracy, joint responsibility would balance the imperatives of managerial efficiency, adaptation to new technology, and workers' control and democratic consent.[14] Industrial democracy, though, was an elastic concept. It could entail more radical workers' control or merely substitute new bureaucratic institutions "at the expense of more direct, less predictable forms of shop floor power."[15]

THE NEW DEAL ERA

For most of the working class, the Great Depression represented a change in degree of employment and income insecurity, more than a sharp break. After the stock market crash and the Great Depression sunk in, business turned back instead to the old practices. Large corporations cut hours and workforces and spread the work. Textile plants used the stretch out: forcing fewer workers to tend more machines more intensively. By 1932, at the nadir of the Great Depression, even the unemployment fund instigated by the

Eastman Kodak Company in Rochester as part of its welfare capitalist program could not keep up with need and, within a year, half of the participating companies had dropped out. Regional, voluntarist micro-regulation could not weather the storm of severe economic crisis and mass unemployment.[16]

"The depression was simultaneously a set of distinctive national phenomena and an interconnected global event," writes historian Mary Nolan. Attempting to preserve jobs for whites, the United States deported over one million Mexicans and Mexican Americans. France similarly expelled Algerians, Spaniards, Poles, and Italians. Many of the new governments in industrialized nations improvised with reform but also drew on earlier social policies and forms of economic reorganization.[17] "In the face of unprecedented unemployment, two dozen states on both sides of the Atlantic, including the United States, Germany, Britain, Switzerland, Sweden, and Bulgaria, established labour services"—although they tended to focus on men, prioritizing male unemployment as both politically threatening and destabilizing to family and gender roles.[18]

In the American South, Nazi Germany, and the Soviet Union, the state used coerced labor and political prisoners. Labor's right to organize and bargain collectively was smashed in fascist Italy and Germany. French West Africa also used forced labor, especially on sisal and peanut plantations, despite the fact that in 1937 France had signed the ILO Convention Against Forced Labour.[19]

The New Deal drew on the experiments of the progressive era and the 1920s but also opened an era in which both some politicians and labor began to address unemployment as a question of industrial democracy and economic citizenship. From 1935 on the New Deal changed the economics of labor fundamentally. Through more permanent legislation, the New Deal created a "standardized work" week and security in sync with a particular structure of industrial mass production. The large-scale public corporation represented the apotheosis of American capitalism at that point. The goal of New Dealers was not to take them down in size or disaggregate them. Rather it was to recast corporations as social institutions that must be subject to democratic refashioning and accountability. It was not size per se that posed a problem but the unfettered concentration of self-serving, authoritarian power.[20] Employment would no longer be simply the private prerogative of corporations. Unemployment could not be isolated from the unequal workings of labor markets as a whole. With Keynesian countercyclical fiscal policy, the federal government would stimulate the economy when it lagged or slow down growth when inflation threatened. The booms and busts that had been a routine feature of American economic life would instead be turned into steady growth and more widely shared benefits. In addition, through unemployment insurance linked to experience rating (a component of the 1935 Social Security Act) employers were held responsible for regular employment. Economic modernization was not to be achieved at the expense of the working class or middle class.

Understanding the New Deal political economy also requires locating where and how New Deal forms of security intersected with democracy in the workplace. Essential to the New Deal order were the various elements that restructured the world of work. To begin with, the New Deal tossed out the fictive notion of "freedom of contract": that an individual worker could somehow equally negotiate with a corporate employer over the terms of work. The feudalistic control of the foremen's regime, argues Nelson Lichtenstein, ended.[21] Workers could organize and take collective action legally, while collective bargaining between unions and management was now seen as rectifying the imbalance of power, extending freedom of association, and facilitating the free flow of commerce and economic growth rather than impeding them.

A new union movement emerged, grabbing hold of the possibilities for industrial democracy: the Congress of Industrial Organizations (CIO). The craft-based unionism of the American Federation of Labor (AFL) represented a rather shrinking share of the overall labor force, given its focus on skilled, white, native-born or northern European male workers. The American economy, however, was now dominated by mass production industries with semi-skilled and unskilled operatives, many of which were immigrants and the children of immigrants. The AFL was not prepared to organize them. But as the Depression and the New Deal generated new levels of worker resistance, new organizers stepped in to create industrial unionism in basic manufacturing. Industrial unionism would organize all workers regardless of skill, tradition, or place in the shop. Allied with organizers from the ranks of the socialist and communist left, industrial unionism swept through basic industry and through sheer force, creativity, and dynamism—and the crucial support of the state—won its foothold. Between 1933 and 1937, five million workers joined unions.

Congress passed Senator Robert Wagner's National Labor Relations Act (NLRA) in 1935, but most employers had little intention of accepting it and looked to their long-time allies, the courts, to rule it unconstitutional. With the 1937 *NLRB v. Jones Laughlin* decision, the US Supreme Court subordinated the doctrine of "at-will" employment that had governed employment relations, instead allowing Congress's power to regulate interstate commerce to restructure the economics of labor. Recognizing a new authority of Congress over labor relations, the ruling was intended to support Congress's broader economic policy: industrial peace augmented by sustained purchasing power and employers' duty to bargain. A cohort of liberal businessmen in mass consumer goods industries, industrial unionists, labor-minded social scientists, and proto-Keynesian economists reoriented labor politics and public policy around mass consumption and the mass market. Federal public policy would promote unionism, tying it to economic growth.[22]

The 1938 Fair Labor Standards Act (FLSA) finally achieved workers' almost century-long struggle for the eight-hour workday—accompanied by a legally mandated minimum wage. Workers would be paid time and a half for every hour they worked beyond the newly constituted forty-hour workweek. Yet one had to be designated as meeting the legal definition of "employee" in order to be within the "boundaries of workplace democracy."[23]

The legal definition of employee was firmly rooted in a Fordist model of production. Industrial relations law was molded onto the factory hierarchy. Although original drafters and proponents of the NLRA believed foremen or supervisors could unionize, by the late 1940s front-line supervisors were expected to hold the line against worker power on behalf of upper management.[24] Thus, on the one hand, for those who labored in mass production industries, the Wagner Act "liberated millions of workers from the arbitrary rule of management." On the other hand, workers who made decisions, strategized about the organization of work, and held some form of authority, or who did not fit neatly into an industrial hierarchy, did not win such rights to freedom of association at work. Management and labor would continue to spar over this—through the National Labor Relations Board (NLRB) and the courts—during the 1950s and 1960s, with the NLRB and the courts increasingly leaning toward classifying knowledge workers, technicians, and semi-professionals outside the boundaries of employees with rights.[25] The designation of employee also eluded those at the bottom rungs of the occupational hierarchy doing labor not recognized as work in places not acknowledged as workplaces—e.g. home-based care jobs.

Nonetheless, the new relationship between the state and labor altered the relationship between wage work and security significantly. The Fair Labor Standards Act and Wagner

Act extended control over the undulating experience of too much work and not enough work. Social Security—through its unemployment compensation and old-age pensions—replaced wages when one no longer had work. Its passage, along with minimum wage law, mortgage protection, and regulatory laws finally brought American workers benefits many European workers had had for decades from more generous welfare states. These policies reflected a new recognition within American political culture that everyone in an industrial society at some point faced the risks of lost income owing to unemployment, old age, and child-rearing on one's own. Protection could be extended to all by sharing that risk—pooling it together while income was coming in—across the entire society. Security entailed an element of public power.

The New Deal did not simply create a welfare state; it reoriented economic relationships around a widespread political ideology of security. Before and during the Second World War, community groups and physicians were engaged in local experimentation—in building citizen-based or citizen-responsive medical care institutions at the local or even regional level. Yet participants in this budding health security movement hoped to use the power of the federal government to bolster these efforts, and they often worked closely with advisors within the new Social Security Board and US Public Health Service. They saw health security as a two-tiered project: federal subsidy for an insurance mechanism nationally, and group medical centers or risk-pooling plans at the community level. These types of programs continued to germinate as America shifted its focus to war.

FIGURE 1.2 Ben Shahn, "For All These Rights We've Just Begun to Fight." Courtesy Harvard University Art Museums.

POSTWAR REMAKING OF INDUSTRIAL LABOR MARKETS

Second World War mobilization policies continued the social tasks begun in the Depression and set the stage for a postwar social Keynesianism. In exchange for labor's unimpeded participation in continuous war production, the federal government settled labor disputes through a National War Labor Board and facilitated union growth with a "maintenance of membership" policy that required every worker in a unionized workplace to join up and pay dues. With millions of workers pouring into industrial manufacturing, national union membership soon jumped to fifteen million in 1945, about 30 percent of non-farm employment. Through seniority, union work rules, grievance procedures, restraints on speed-ups, and other work standards, industrial unions fundamentally transformed the formerly "capricious autocracy" of the industrial shop floor. At their height, unions compelled managers to share governance of the American workplace.[26] Collective bargaining and the steward system established routinized means of dispute resolution. Labor advocates and lawyers' overriding faith in contractual procedures led them to see contractualism as a rational system of industrial jurisprudence that would eliminate labor-management strife.[27]

The industrial unionism of the CIO instituted seniority. Albeit a flawed principle in some ways, seniority offered a form of job security, displacing some of the most insecure aspects of wage work: the day-labor shape-up, arbitrary layoffs, and employment at will. By eliminating deference and favoritism, seniority enabled long-time workers to feel there was respect for their tenure and amassed knowledge and experience; it served as a workplace analogue to security as established through the New Deal welfare state.[28] As mass-industrial unionism swept through basic manufacturing from the late 1930s through the late 1940s, jobs would not simply be assets held by corporations. Unions had determination over jobs as well and they used the jurisprudence of industrial democracy—contracts, grievance procedures, and shop steward representation—to exercise it. On the downside, seniority could also become forms of white male privilege, blocking the access of African Americans and women to better paying, more secure jobs.

In the late 1940s, organized labor and its New Deal allies saw the movement for greater purchasing power and security as a battle on two fronts: the economic and the political. Facing corporate employers, labor demanded not only higher wages, protections against inflation, and job security but also social welfare benefits: paid vacation, sick leave, health insurance, and pensions. The NLRB, eventually sustained by the Supreme Court, endorsed this bargaining strategy, thus forcing management to accept a widening sphere for collective bargaining. The strategy proved most successful in oligopolistic sectors of the economy (auto, steel, tire and rubber, airplane manufacturing) where the market power of the corporations and the bargaining clout of the unions made it possible to take wages out of competition. This generated "pattern bargaining": when one of the leading corporations signed a new contract, the other top companies in the sector agreed to almost all of its main provisions. Consequently, the presence of a strong, dynamic union movement helped drive wages up in primary labor markets across the economy. As inflation ebbed and women entered the workforce in a proportion that exceeded even that at the height of the Second World War, median family incomes rose in dramatic fashion, doubling in just over a generation. As Jack Metzgar recalled about his father, a unionized steelworker at US Steel Corporation in the 1950s, "no regular guy in the history of the world had seen the material conditions of his life improve more dramatically."[29]

After unions began to focus on getting Social Security demands included in a labor-management contract, as a demand extracted from management, the labor movement gradually shifted away from the independent health projects initiated prior to the war. The trade unions' emphasis on Social Security benefits obtained through collective bargaining, in the long run, refocused health security, and to some extent old-age security, on to the employer and what they were willing to provide. Indeed, American corporations organized to make sure they did not face the national-level labor-management bargaining taking shape in the Netherlands, Sweden, and Norway, nor even the industry-level bargaining of Germany or Great Britain.

Insurance companies provided an alternative strategy: group insurance policies that management—the sole legal policyholder—could dominate, firm by firm, even plant by plant. Insurers expanded the range of group hospital insurance policies employers purchased by offering to "tailor" policies to meet the particular needs of each employer. The purchaser of a group plan could pick and choose exactly which services it did and did not want included and the amount of an employee's contribution.[30] Consequently, American business firms and commercial insurance companies became partners in creating and expanding private alternatives to public social insurance and community-controlled social welfare institutions. "The American working man must look to management," Ford Motors' vice president John Bugas told the American Management Association.[31]

From the late 1940s on, insurance companies and corporate employers constructed a new ideology around risk and health security. Instead of community rating used by the health cooperatives and earlier models to share risk evenly, insurance companies used medical underwriting and experience rating. With medical underwriting, insurance plans divided people up and separated them according to their health profile. Insurers made the notion of risk an individualized one: "each insured will pay in accordance with the quality of his risk." Individuals or groups who were perceived to have higher risk for medical problems were charged more money and received less coverage. Or insurers might avoid them all together.[32] Experience rating allowed firms with better conditions (or at least fewer workers seeking high-cost medical care) to pay less; industries deemed poor risks or firms with older or sicker workers paid more, fragmenting the social pooling of risk, isolating labor markets. Many occupations were left completely uncovered. Finally, because group insurance covered employees only during the term of their employment, in the long run it generated cultural assumptions that health security was an achievement of individuals solely through their persistent hard work. It shrouded both the collective struggle that won these benefits and the role of politics and public power. In the late 1950s, the US Congress put the final stamp of ratification on the private, employment-based insurance system: unilateral control by employers, little regulatory oversight, and tax subsidy through tax deductions of employer contributions to pension plans and trusts. Welfare capitalism once again proved an effective strategy—a way of checking the expansion of the state and the unions.[33]

So, throughout the 1950s and 1960s, workers in unionized sectors won an ever-widening range of social benefits—medical insurance, surgical insurance, pensions, supplementary unemployment benefits, support for kids' college, retiree benefits—but at the cost of weakened union power. In addition, at this point a broader gap opened between those in union and nonunion jobs. Structurally, the private, employment-based welfare benefits meant that millions of Americans had no direct claim to health insurance as citizen-workers. Nationally, private health insurance coverage peaked at 69 percent of the population and then receded after the mid-1970s. The regional and sectoral disparities of

FIGURE 1.3 "1919–1969 ... Benefits Then and Now," *Hercules Mixer*, employee magazine of the Hercules Chemical Corporation, a DuPont subsidiary. Courtesy Hagley Museum and Library.

welfare capitalism's labor markets persisted. Health insurance coverage and benefits lagged, for example, in the Southeast, Central Plains south of Texas, Oklahoma, Louisiana, and Southwest. Black, Hispanic, and female workers were always far less covered at work than white men. Benefits negotiated with employers also left out all those who were not employed. Family members, especially women, had no direct claim to health care if they were not wage earners, and family medical benefits were less in both unionized and nonunionized sectors.[34]

The development of European welfare states also hinged on the politics of industrial relations. Not only did industry-wide or national-level bargaining expand the range of issues at the table in Britain, Germany, Belgium, Austria, the Netherlands, and the Nordic countries of Sweden, Norway, and Denmark. It gave labor a role in retraining and redeployment of workers to new industries and locales. Such bargaining could also be tied to national industrial policies and wage or incomes policies. In Belgium and the Netherlands, union leadership eventually became fully integrated into the process of social and economic policymaking.[35]

It was thus in the latter part of the 1950s that the divergence from Europe, with respect to the welfare state, widened. For it was finally in the late 1950s and 1960s that the comprehensive, universalist European and Canadian welfare states really took shape. Governments boosted the social wage—"the share of the nation's resources that is distributed according to social rather than strict market criteria"—through rent control, housing, health care, family allowances, and pensions.[36] In Sweden, after several years of bargaining, both the employers' and labor confederations turned to the welfare state and the landmark "active labor market policy" in 1956. Sweden enacted comprehensive health insurance, which included free hospitalization, medical benefits, and guaranteed sick pay, and a new pension system guaranteeing all workers a standard of living in retirement that matched that of their last working years.[37] They succeeded in making a full claim for security upon private employers, drawing business into politicized bargaining with labor and the state over workers' compensation and families' standard of living.[38] This is precisely what American employers were determined to avoid.

PRECARITY AND THE CASE OF HEALTH-CARE WORKERS

Other types of labor remained outside this new regime. For example, the spaces and sectors of labor heavily dominated by women were placed outside the New Deal laws' coverage and protections—laws won with the support of activist women! In some cases, it was because certain categories of work did not fall under the rubric of interstate commerce, the constitutional bedrock used for the new legislation; nurses, hospital workers, teachers, nonprofit workers of various sorts, and sales clerks and purchasers remained outside the law. In other cases, the law did not recognize the very workplace itself—the home—as a truly constituted waged workplace open to state regulation. New Dealers explicitly excluded agricultural and domestic workers in a deal with Southern legislators, who sought to maintain their control over black labor. Thus, labor market discrimination, as well as gender and racial divisions in labor, were reproduced in the welfare state.

By contrast, domestic workers in some nations made surprising use of courts, legal reform, economic cooperatives, newspapers, reform organizations, and trade unions. In twentieth-century Argentina, domestic workers found they could successfully use courts, owing to the passage of a 1956 domestic labor protection law that also established the Tribunal of Domestic Work. Domestic servants in Brazil lodged demands for compensation and other entitlements in the courts.[39]

At the same time, a different regulatory regime applied to US women's labor. So-called "protective" labor legislation had been established during the progressive era to protect women's "health and morals": maximum hours, prohibitions on night work, and regulations against working in certain areas or during pregnancy. Reformers and labor advocates who originally pressed for these laws also believed they would act as an opening wedge for broader labor regulations for all workers. When that took a slightly different track during the New Deal (through the Fair Labor Standards Act), women increasingly encountered these earlier "protective" proscriptions as impediments to better paying jobs. A generation later, labor-union women and feminists found themselves working to overturn these through the Women's Bureau of the Department of Labor or the new President's Commission on the Status of Women in the 1960s. They wrestled with how to revise "out-dated laws ... without sacrificing basic protections" of federal labor standards and new rights such as equal pay, childcare, and fair employment practices prohibiting sex discrimination that would bolster women's employment and security.[40] After 1964, they would turn to using Title VII of the Civil Rights Act and the Equal Employment Opportunity Commission it created.

The dramatically improved standards of work and life under the unionized collective bargaining regime also, to an extent, relied on the precarious, low-paid labor of others. A decade after bargaining for health insurance took off the number of workers covered by negotiated health insurance plans reached twelve million, up from one million prior to 1946.[41] Hospitals, whether public or "private," quickly became the beneficiaries of the health-care policies that emerged from the New Deal and Fair Deal. Fuelled by public spending and private insurance, Americans encountered a generationally new health-care sector—services they could access without being indigent wards of the state. In the two decades after the Second World War, admissions to hospitals rose by 64 percent, to twenty-three million admissions or discharges in 1964 alone, and outpatient visits increased by 247 percent. As a result, employment in health services rose by 704 percent. Medical employment ranked third among major sectors and industries in the nation. The proportion of this work being done by physicians, however, dropped by more than half, while the number of subsidiary, semi-skilled, paraprofessional, and unskilled workers mushroomed.[42]

Numbering 1.5 million in the 1960s, these positions included technicians (x-ray, medical records, occupational and physical therapy, medical and dental) and assistants (licensed practical nurses (LPNs), nurse's aides, and psychiatric aides.) In the late 1960s, four out of five such workers were women, they had education ranging from elementary school completion to a year or two of college, and they were either in their late teens/early twenties or over forty years of age (that is, they returned to the workforce after their children had entered school or grown up). From 1950 to 1965, the percentage of aides, orderlies, and attendants grew by 70 percent, practical nurses by 50 percent, and homemaker/home health aides by 360 percent. Within nursing as a whole, the roles of LPNs, nurses' aides, and home aides grew most significantly. Hospitals drew in the surplus of low-wage labor in their immediate surrounding area. The workforce also reflected the growing shift of women into paid employment and hospitals' ability to absorb large numbers of untrained workers. Not only were most of them female, but the racial profile differed from that of other sectors as well, having more than twice the percentages of nonwhite females relative to all other industries. Women of color were concentrated in the positions of attendants, aides, and LPNs.[43] Despite this growth, top administrators, professionals, and planners tended to overlook or dismiss the role of supporting personnel.[44] With the passage of Medicare and Medicaid, as well as anti-poverty policies of the 1960s, the types of health-care institutions proliferated and began to form deep interconnected networks of service provision, reaching from hospital all the way into home.

The spread of health insurance coverage—in both private and public forms—rested on the low-wage labor of hundreds of thousands of women and people of color. Even as the medical/health sector became a major growth industry after the Second World War, inside its walls, the ideology and assumptions of "charity" still undergirded the structuring of work. New Deal reformers and labor-liberals of the 1940s repeatedly emphasized that the social insurance and even the "fringe benefits" of the 1950s were the very opposite of the charity principle.[45] Rejecting the charity principle, these were the "earned" benefits of citizen workers. But the workplaces of hospitals, nursing homes, and home care continued to operate under these assumptions. Moreover, hospital by laws and regulations of a 24-hour institution presented a quandry for those seeking conformity to the new labor standards regime.

Left out of New Deal labor laws, the America Nurses Association initiated a major postwar push to improve labor standards for registered nurses, whose wages and working conditions lagged behind other professionalizing occupations. The 1947 Taft-Hartley Act ensured their exclusion from NLRA coverage. It took until 1961 for amendments to FLSA to cover hospitals, nursing homes, and residential-care facilities.

For the nonprofessional staff within the hospitals, labor conditions resembled those of involuntary servitude. Not covered by the nation's basic wage and hour law, FLSA, hospital staff in New York, for example, often made less than the minimum wage per hour and were forced to turn to public assistance, as even hospital administrators acknowledged. Wages were deducted to pay for uniforms, reminiscent of sweatshop practices from the turn of the century. Staff routinely faced twelve-hour shifts; laundry workers had been made to work as many as thirteen hours in a shift. For hospital dietary workers, custodians, laundry staff, orderlies, there was no five-day workweek. Instead, they endured erratic and arbitrary schedules, ofter working ten to twelve days without a day off. Arbitrary treatment was the norm. Lunch breaks served as tools of managerial favoritism, with supervisors adding or subtracting time based on personal favoritism. Supervisors could fire workers on the spot. No form of resolving grievances existed; workers quit or were fired. When it came time to "retire," the Department of Social Services would conduct a welfare investigation, home visit, assessment of assets and needs, and determine a small "pension" for the worker.[46] In a sense, they were as much charity cases as the medically indigent patients. Compounding the exemption from FLSA, in 1947 Congress added an amendment to the Taft-Hartley Act, in response to intensive lobbying from the American Hospital Association, exempting nonprofit hospitals from union elections.[47]

Spurred by Blue Cross, Hill-Burton Act hospital construction funds, and then Medicaid, the case of Duke University Medical Center's dramatic growth between the 1960s and the 1970s illustrates what has been described as increasingly commodified, assembly-like care. Duke built new facilities for teaching, patient care, and research between 1948 and 1960. In the 1960s, it received an influx of money from the National Institutes for Health. Yet for the black workforce, "this new-style industrial efficiency" was combined with "old-style paternalistic racism."[48] Up north, in cities such as New York, the workforce consisted of African American southern migrants and Puerto Ricans, those entering the local labor market at the bottom rungs. In New York City, blacks and Puerto Ricans made up 80 percent of the hospital service and maintenance workforce.[49] On the West Coast, hospitals employed Latin Americans, Filipinas, and other Asians.

RACE AND THE POSTWAR ECONOMY OF LABOR

Beginning in the Second World War and extending for four decades, the economics of labor was also shaped by contract labor. Carrying the taint of slavery, foreign contract labor had been formally outlawed in 1885. Yet it was reinvented in the mid-twentieth century through "guestworker" programs. Agribusiness strategically and politically drummed up claims of "labor shortage" to push government to meet employers' demands for cheap, contingent, and pliable foreign workers. Behind growers' rising claims that local workers were not available lay a story of social struggle. Agricultural labor generally had been excluded from New Deal programs and laws. Nonetheless, farm hands had begun to gain sufficient leverage to push wages up and press employers into negotiations, especially where they had the added security and decency of federal migrant labor camps.[50]

Bowing to pressure from growers, New Deal liberals in the 1940s instituted a guestworker program through which the US government recruited workers, gave them visas or work contracts to enter the United States, and promised pay and conditions superior to those of their home country and even to those of American farmworkers.⁵¹ The two main programs were the Bracero Program, which brought in Mexican nationals to work the fields of the Southwest and West, and the H2 visa guestworker program, which recruited farm laborers from the Caribbean to employment along the East Coast and in Michigan. Implemented initially to meet wartime needs, both programs were allowed to continue long after the war ended, but as they did, the state increasingly backed away from supervising conditions and deferred to employers. Between 1948 and 1964, the United States imported an average of 200,000 braceros a year, ultimately totalling 4.6 million workers. In 1951, Congress ended the nineteenth-century ban against contract labor.⁵²

Officials revised the original Migrant Labor Agreement in 1954 to allow employers to recontract at the border. Growers used this ability not only to hire braceros but also increasingly to hire illegal labor, at lower wages, which of course perpetually reshaped the labor market and undercut the wages and conditions of both braceros and domestic workers.⁵³ From that point on, growers were less likely to abide by the agreement terms and labor conditions slipped over the course of the 1950s. Workers encountered problems with housing, illegal deductions, rotten food, low wages, and mistreatment. The Department of Labor gave local growers carte blanche in setting "prevailing" wage rates, without conducting independent investigations of the labor market. In places such as the San Joaquin Valley in California, wages for tomato picking dropped 40 percent in a decade. Rather than managing and modernizing agricultural labor markets, it created a vast workforce that remained outside federal labor standards and workers' rights and the program led to a steep decline of agricultural wages.⁵⁴

The H2 visa guestworker program brought workers from the Bahamas, Jamaica, Barbados, and the West Indies, again recruited with promises of decent labor standards. Jamaicans—proud citizens of the British Empire not used to American-style Jim Crow— soon became the predominant group of "H2 workers" and they especially went to work in the Florida sugar industry.⁵⁵ In practice, the system allowed a resurgence of employment "at-will" in an era when it was supposed to have been displaced by new terms of employment. Guestworkers were tied to a particular employer they could not legally quit, they could not settle in the United States, and employers could and did deport workers en masse directly.⁵⁶ (Among Western European nations that used guestworkers, private employers did not have the power to deport and guestworkers over time gained the rights and benefits of other workers.) The regime of contract in the United States therefore had a very different meaning in these labor markets and for these workers than for workers in unionized manufacturing and transportation.⁵⁷ Guestworker programs represented not just a means of recruiting foreign labor but also policing it. Florida sugar growers, such as the US Sugar Corporation, used explicit threats of injury, arrest, and death and displays of violence to corral workers and force them to stay. Nor were these practices some vestige of an antiquated system. As the Florida sugar industry expanded in the 1960s, the guestworker program burgeoned and took root even more firmly. Consequently, disfranchised migrant labor played a major role in shaping the modern political economy of the Southeast and Southwest.⁵⁸

PUBLIC SECTOR WORK

Caribbeans, African Americans, and women who worked in the public sector had also stood outside the New Deal system of labor rights, but that began to change in the 1960s with the surge of a new union movement. From the early 1960s to the mid-1970s, unionism would take hold in sanitation departments, hospitals, nursing homes, social welfare agencies, schools, police departments, fire departments, and numerous other state and local government agencies. Prior to that moment, workers' organizations in the public sector lacked legal rights. There was no right to bargain, arbitrate disputes, or strike, rights that private-sector industrial workers had won decades earlier. Government workers could be fired simply for joining a union, again something that had been rendered illegal for other workers since the early 1930s.[59] As Local 1199, Union of Hospital and Health Care Employees, began to organize among housekeeping, dietary (cooks, dishwashers, and aides), orderlies, and maintenance workers, their initial demands centered on winning some of the basic features of employment middle-class Americans and manufacturing workers had come to take for granted: eight-hour day, a standard workweek, paid sick days and holidays, grievance procedures, standard rates of pay, legally enforceable overtime pay, and insurance. For hospital, nursing home, community-care center, and home workers, 1199 aimed to peel back the veil of "charity" that cast workers as those who were supposed to selflessly serve. Self-sacrifice and denial were considered essential to care provided in other contexts—individual homes, nursing homes—seen as "caregiving," rather than care work.

Unions such as American Federation of State, County and Municipal Employees, Service Employees International Union (SEIU), American Federation of Teachers and Social Service Employees Union fought to bring public-sector labor standards into alignment with those of the private sector; their struggle was also aligned with civil rights. The jobs of school custodians, cafeteria workers, hospital orderlies, or teachers had been stigmatized, associated with dirt, refuse, bodies, welfare, and dependence. The new unionism sought human dignity by redefining the status of low-wage work that had been racialized and feminized. Notably, public workers also made the case for high-quality services, dependable benefits, and fair procedures.

By the mid-1970s, following a decade of significant militancy, over four million public workers belonged to unions. While they made gains on the state level, what they could not win was a national public-sector equivalent of the Wagner Act. Consequently, even as public-sector unionism became almost 40 percent of labor's total membership, it remained geographically confined; large sections of the country especially the South and Southwest, never joined the ranks of public unionism. According to Joseph McCartin, ultimately "one-half of all union members lived in only six states by 2000."[60]

THE HOME CARE WORKER CASE

Home care workers illustrate the plight and successes of workers in this sector. Perennially excluded from New Deal labor provisions, home-based workers honed a successful organizing strategy, changing the economics of labor for this growing sector of the economy. One of the fastest growing occupations of the late twentieth century, home health care long existed in a clouded netherworld between public and private, employment and family care. Alternatively called personal attendants, home aides, or home care workers, they were America's front-line caregivers, who perform intimate daily tasks—such as bathing bodies, brushing teeth, putting on clothes, cooking meals—that enabled the elderly or people with disabilities to live decent lives at home. Although home attendants labored in domestic spaces and sometimes were the direct employees of home-health franchises and nonprofit social welfare agencies, government monies and regulations determined pay, standards, and overall conditions of employment. They labored in a labor market sustained by public institutions: the welfare office, public hospital, state department of rehabilitative services, and various agencies for the aged. Those with significant disabilities qualified for Supplemental Security Income, Medicaid, and various targeted programs, can use such resources for home care. The occupation and labor market has been fundamentally shaped and maintained by the state since its expansion in the New Deal public works programs. Government dramatically increased this labor market through the War on Poverty in the 1960s and workfare programs in the 1970s and 1980s. That the United States relied primarily on means-tested social services available only to the poorest people fundamentally shaped the entire labor market for care, whether "public" or "private," no matter how much some policymakers assumed that middle-class people can just go out and hire someone to look after their loved ones.[61]

The contemporary political economy of home-based long-term care reflected the historical convergence of two labor market transformations: the privatization of public caretakers, who worked for public welfare agencies and clearly provided service to indigent elders; and the burgeoning domestic temp employment agencies. These jobs—numbering well over two million—are also increasingly important because they cannot be offshored. Work site as had been the case with manufacturing a century earlier, waves of new immigrants continually replenish these jobs. Women's labors—once considered outside of the market or at the periphery of economic life—became the strategic sites for worker struggle and the direction and character of the American labor movement.[62]

Home care workers have turned the public welfare state itself into a terrain of social struggle. Structurally, unions seeking to organize home care workers had to deal with the reality that the jobs were so dispersed; while there were tens of thousands of workers, there was no common work site. Most workers never saw each other, and many had little sense that there were many others out there doing the same kind of work. Further, the work is different. Essential to the job is emotional labor, affection, and building trust. They had to enter into alliances with the receivers of care (who have labelled themselves "consumers"). Moreover, state funding and provision of the service were organized differently state by state, or even within states, depending on whether clients were disabled or elderly. Given this structure of home care, it was never enough just to win collective bargaining rights with individual vendor agencies. To make economic gains, the union had to go to government. Between the 1990s and 2012, unions successfully used community organizing, political activism, strategic alliances with consumers and some home care agencies, and structural innovations such as county-level public authorities and state home care commissions to compel states to recognize them as public employees (or to represent the state as coemployer), negotiate, and change the economics of this labor. By 2010, four hundred thousand home care workers had unionized and engaged in collective bargaining with the state in Illinois, California, Oregon, New York, Washington, Maryland, New Jersey, Massachusetts, and Missouri. The spread of unionization not only resulted in higher wages, coverage under state worker compensation programs (for job-related injuries), safety training, grievance procedures, and health benefits for the workers (in Illinois, wages rose from $7 an hour in 2003 to $13 in 2014), but also, where the union had real clout, in more hours of service for the clients and due process rights, such as hearings if they faced termination of benefits.[63] The state came to recognize collective bargaining offered an effective means to rationalize the labor market, stabilize home care service, and attract and maintain good providers.

FIGURE 1.4 Workers and consumers march on Illinois State Capitol, Springfield, 1992. Courtesy Wisconsin Historical Society, SEIU 880 Collection.

THE "POSTINDUSTRIAL" ECONOMY OF WORK

The explosion of public sector organizing has been accompanied by the steady evisceration of unions in the private sector beginning in the 1970s. Part of this lay in the structural shift from manufacturing jobs to service jobs. Manufacturing firms had already spent two decades shifting production to lower-wage areas within the US South, where states such as Mississippi eagerly lured northern firms with promises of a union-free and lax regulatory environment. From the late 1970s on, firms sought yet another spatial fix, moving production out of the country all together. But there was an increasingly successful political assault on unionism as well. A new conservative political movement inspired by Friedrich Hayek and Milton Friedman set out to liberate the free market from the shackles of the welfare state, regulation, and labor unions. In the 1970s, conservatives successfully chipped away at the New Deal. Employers hired anti-labor management "consulting" firms to disestablish unions. Indeed, within two decades, the union avoidance industry became a multimillion-dollar sector of its own, unique among advanced industrialized nations.[64] In Britain, legislation in the early 1980s "rescinded trade unions' particular immunities under the law," restricted strikes, and relaxed oversight of police in dealing with picket lines and labor disputes.[65] Most often associated with Reaganism and Thatcherism, but in fact supported by both Republican and Democratic presidents (and Labour and Tory prime ministers), a new free-market ideology instituted deregulation and the privatization of much public-sector work. Chile was also ground zero for implementation of so-called "neoliberal policies." In the shift, unionism increasingly lost its hold economically and culturally. Unionism was no longer seen as key to what had been the central formula of Keynesian policymaking: full employment, high wages, mass purchasing power, and economic growth.

Business gained hegemony over American labor law. Its anti-union tactics and public relations often derailed union certification elections or resulted in losing elections. The number of union elections held dropped by 72 percent. Where the union won, employers delayed signing contracts for as long as possible. The NLRB itself became a tool management could use to subvert unions, as business-friendly presidents appointed business-oriented members to the NLRB board. Courts, with a new generation of conservative appointees, began to step into labor-management relations again, increasingly restricting the subjects of bargaining, the ability to strike, and the range of workers covered by the NLRA, stripping from them that necessary and coveted designation of "employee." Companies or municipalities could hire permanent replacement workers for striking employees. These tactics affected workers not only in manufacturing labor markets but throughout the growing labor markets of health care—especially nursing.[66]

"THE FISSURED WORKPLACE"

As service workers found ways to organize, American business developed a new mode of operation to utterly fragment the employer–employee relation upon which "industrial democracy" was premised: the temp industry. In the 1950s and 1960s, temp agencies (Kelly Girl Service, Manpower Inc.) recruited white women to meet corporate employers' need for additional employees at peak seasons. To assuage concerns about threats to "breadwinning full-time jobs," agencies cast temp work as women's work—merely secondary or auxiliary jobs, filled by those simply earning "pin money." The temp agency acted as legal employer of temps and yet attenuated the employment relationship. Workers signed up with one or several agencies and were sent out to jobs at a variety of businesses. Hiring through temp agencies, businesses avoided the costs of recruiting, interviewing, screening, and training, as well as health benefits, pensions, workers' compensation, and unemployment taxes; plus, they could dismiss them with little threat of legal action (and then call them back if needed). In fact, starting in the 1970s, temp agencies also marketed a strategy—"transfer of personnel" or "payrolling"—in which companies could hand workers back to the temp agency and then when needed, they would get rotated into the same workplace as before. Companies could outsource entire departments to a temp agency—billing, mail, marketing, technical support. With these practices, a company got the benefits of a permanent workforce without any of the costs. The temp agencies now also recruited male workers and sold temp work for what previously had been characterized as "male breadwinning jobs." By the late twentieth century these had become common and legitimate practices, culturally as well as economically acceptable.[67]

Not only did temp workers not receive the private or public social welfare benefits of welfare capitalism or the welfare state, temp agencies themselves aggressively worked to eviscerate the income support that linked employment and the welfare state. Evading workers' compensation and unemployment claims became a particular agency expertise. Temp agencies disputed such claims persistently and with success, using the courts to subvert statutory benefits. Being able to appear in court posed enormous and costly barriers for precarious workers. Further, the industry lobbied to influence labor law—such as laws that denied temps' claims for unemployment insurance.[68] The erosion of industrial democracy reinstituted labor market conditions of a century ago; instead of business shouldering the accountability of unemployment, individuals should take responsibility for the failings of industry.

Temp agencies then went on to create the "perma-temp" or semi-permanent employee. Rather than the original practice of filling in for a few days or weeks, these workers would be there for several months, as the temp agencies marketed it, "to help your business grow more profitably ... by shrinking pay roll." Progress and modernity was "slim and trim," lean and mean. At first these practices helped create the two-tiered workforces that spread in the 1980s—one group of workers receiving decent wages and benefits, another that wouldn't. Eventually entire job categories were permanently subcontracted out.[69]

As the temp industry changed cultural expectations about jobs and work, it grew exponentially. In the 1980s, it tripled, expanding across all sectors of the economy, including pink-, white-, and blue-collar work. General Electric, Hewlett Packard, Motorola, IBM, Lockheed, Xerox, Westinghouse used the temp model in their corporate restructuring. At Apple Computer, temps accounted for as much as 30 percent of the workforce in the mid-1980s. Bank of America created its own pool of temps. The industry grew by penetrating deeper into firms, providing managers as well as workers, pushing into new occupational sectors, and taking on high-end professional and technical labor markets (information technology, engineering, finance, telecommunications, scientific research). And it made inroads into unionized sectors and civil service; the use of temps further weakened the bargaining position of unions. In the early 1990s, Manpower became one of the largest employers in the United States. Between 1990 and 2000, the number of people employed as temps on a daily basis rose from less than a million workers a day to three million. Industry sales quadrupled from $15.6 billion in 1990 to $64.3 billion in 1999, accounting for 10 percent of the nation's employment growth. It also moved into low-wage day labor with agencies such as Labor Ready, Labor Connection, Labor Finders, and Able Body Labor, based in inner-city and immigrant neighborhoods and providing construction, landscaping, road, and industrial work.[70] A Swiss company, Adecco—having merged several times to become the largest temp agency in the world—has a global reach, competing in the United States on these terms. The shape-up and employment at will were back.

The structural result is what David Weil calls "the fissured workplace." Facing pressure from capital markets to become lean and mean, employers off-loaded different components of the company's work to subcontractors, shedding many of the responsibilities and services formerly done in-house. For example, a hotel chain such as Marriott contracted out cleaning services, laundering, food preparation, and service, although the procedures, pace, and quality standards must conform to those set by Marriott. In fact, "more than 80 percent of hotel staff are employed by hotel franchises and supervised by separate management companies that bear no relation to the brand name of the property where they work."[71] Thus it appeared that no one is really in charge of labor conditions. For the supplier or franchisee at the bottom of the labor supply chain, the labor costs were the only variable. So, they had to slice and dice labor time to gain the extra profit margin. The burden of precarious work was put on the subcontractor but the parent company had complete control. The parent company thus used high turnover to its advantage, churning those at the bottom.[72]

Precarious labor, of course, was nothing new. It has been the norm under capitalism everywhere, with work occurring under unstable conditions and without regulation. Once again, though, "precarious labour is on the rise globally." The questions then raised are: what new technologies and political arrangements facilitate and structure precarity? Informal, precarious employment in retail and services is also common throughout the global south. There is "continuous casualization in the ... retail industry" from South Africa to Mexico.[73] Sari embroidery firms left Indian cities for the southern Bengali countryside in the early twenty-first century, moving casualized labor into homes and makeshift shack workshops. South Asians and Southeast Asians migrate to the Middle East and Europe to work in services, domestic work, and construction labor on short-term, seasonal, or temporary "contracts," lacking legal status and therefore any forms of labor protection. Linking social, ethnic identities to particular jobs, racial management is still in use.[74]

(Mis)classifying employees as independent contractors saved employers at least 30 percent of their total labor costs. Subcontractors paid low wages and minimal or no health care; workers also experienced workplace "pay or workplace conditions that violate one or more workplace laws." In fissured industries, these violations included off-the-clock work, unpaid overtime, and failure to pay minimum wage.[75] Certainly there were some workers who were truly independent contractors, but in the majority of cases, it was an opportunistic misclassification imposed up and down the occupational ladder, from clerical services to warehouse logistics and trucking, nurses, home health aides, dental hygienists, editors, paralegals, accountants, and college professors. As a result, in the final decades of the twentieth century, widening circles of American workers became excluded from the legal classification and protection of "employee," with almost a third of the American workforce no longer covered by the FLSA.

Hard-nosed practices shaded into regulatory cheating and illicit practices. Various means of nonpayment of wages have spread through the economy, as the federal government abdicated its mandate to regulate the labor market. According to the US Department of Labor, by the late 1990s, "only 35 per cent of apparel plants in New York City were in compliance with minimum wage and overtime laws; in Chicago, only 42 per cent of restaurants were in compliance; in Los Angeles, only 43 per cent of grocery stores were in compliance; and nationally, only 43 per cent of residential care establishments were in compliance."[76] Among day laborers about half of them reported never receiving their pay at least once in the previous two months.[77] In total, the Wage and Hour Division of the US Department of Labor uncovered nearly $1 billion in illegally unpaid wages since 2010; and the victimized workers were disproportionately immigrants.[78]

Within the new economics of labor, workers in the US economy find themselves facing the paradox of overwork and not enough work. With pared-down workforces, mandatory overtime became a common practice. "In 2005, over a quarter (26 percent) of American workers were subject to regular mandatory overtime that added, on average, almost ten hours a month to their work schedules." Nurses at major hospitals had to do two shifts of overtime on top of their regular one. Whether working in a factory, call center, or warehouse, bathroom breaks were not allowed.[79] Rotating schedules in retail and food service challenged any possibility of the standard workweek. Retail workers were expected to be on call, but if the computer program said sales were slow at a particular time, they were sent home without pay. Workers were not guaranteed work hours and the length of the shift varied. Control over the schedule became a source of power for management; as one worker put it, the hours are "flexible" but "they are flexible for the boss, not for you."[80] When historian Bryant Simon asked Starbucks workers what they disliked about the job, they yelled, "SLEEP!" In short, "this job messes with your sleep." If they ask for a day off in advance or for more than a week's notice of one's weekly schedule, management responded by cutting the person's hours! Indeed, the "chronic crisis of the clock" makes it difficult to maintain just about any aspect of life beyond subsistence: education, childcare, medical care, rent, time off.[81] So much for bread and roses in the new economics of labor.

FIGURE 1.5 Worker at a Starbucks café, New York, c. March 2016. Courtesy ©123RF.com.

The logical extreme of this instability was reached with the technological revolution of the so-called "sharing economy": the app-based income-earning activities of Uber, TaskRabbit, Fiverr, and Instacart. Through these task service brokers people used their own cars and tools to provide one-time and quick services directly to individuals. There was no workplace, no boss, and often only a race to the bottom bidding for work. There were unending hours of work but not enough work. The precarity of temp and low-paid part-time work had already driven many to use these apps. They now tried to cobble together a living in the app economy working as much as seven days a week, hustling to assemble a living from one-off gigs. The consumer could change his or her mind instantly. If the company changes its model, a "provider" has little recourse. It's a survival game.[82]

CONCLUSION

The new economics of labor did not serve workers or families in the New Millennium well. Between 2000 and 2015, the share of income generated by corporate profits going to wages declined to the lowest level since the Great Depression, amounting to $535 billion less for workers. Indeed, wage growth was stagnant for almost three decades for middle- and working-class Americans. More people found themselves in the labor markets of low-wage work. About one in four American workers were in low-wage jobs (those paying less than two-thirds of the median wage), a share that was growing—and easily the highest rate among our democratic and developed peers. In thirty-one states (as of 2011), more than a quarter of the workforce worked at a wage insufficient to pull a full-time worker above the poverty level.[83] Precarious labor moved from the margins to the center of the economy. The racial and gender gap in wages, incomes, and wealth persisted. Minimum wage workers were no longer teenagers. Their average age in 2015 was thirty-five; more than a third were over forty and only 12 percent were below the age of twenty. More than 55 percent were women.

Reversing the decline of the labor movement could challenge these trends. Prosperity historically has been most evenly distributed in periods when workers had high levels of bargaining power.[84] As Jake Rosenfeld has found in examining private and public workforces, organized labor "was *the* core equalizing institution" of postwar America: "counterbalance[ing] corporate interests at the bargaining table, while acting as a powerful normative voice for the welfare of non-elites."[85] Workers' organizations, at their most ambitious, also gave people the space and the tools to articulate a just economic vision and build political power to get them there.

CHAPTER TWO

Picturing Work

CATHLEEN CHAFFEE, WITH MICHAEL FRISCH

INTRODUCTION

December 28, 1895. On the cusp of a new century, inventors Louis and Auguste Lumière (French, 1862–1954 and 1864–1948) debuted a forty-six-second film *La Sortie de l'usine Lumière à Lyon* (Workers Leaving the Lumière Factory in Lyon; see Figure 2.1). It was the first of ten short films the brothers screened that day for a paying audience at the Grand Café on the Boulevard des Capucines in Paris. It has been considered the very first motion picture presented as entertainment to the public.

The film's narrative is scant: a man opens a large factory gate at 25 Rue St. Victor, Montplaisir on the outskirts of Lyon, France, and a steady stream of around one

FIGURE 2.1 Auguste and Louis Lumière, *La Sortie de l'usine Lumière à Lyon*, 1895. Black and white film. Source: frame capture.

hundred people emerge until eventually the gate is closed. In an appropriately modernist representation, these workers had helped fabricate, in the Lumière brothers' own photographic plate factory, the very materials this new technology would in many ways supersede. On first viewing, the film appears purely documentary in nature: the filmmaker, with his newly invented Cinematographe camera at the ready, waits for shift's end and then captures workers at the pivotal moment when they shake off the obligations of labor and quite literally step into leisure time and the pleasures and responsibilities of family life. However, multiple existing outtakes confirm that the film was staged for the camera. The Lumière factory workers, hired for one job, had been asked or required to become actors. The sheer number of workers represented in this foundational film also demonstrated the apparent success and productivity of the inventors themselves. This nearly original "documentary" film was a carefully staged advertisement and a form of showmanship, demonstrating the brothers' accomplishment among the many other inventors who presided in these experimental years over the birth of cinema.

This film is one of the most formative visual representations of work in the twentieth century because its representation of workers also heralded the invention of an entirely new medium that would come to define the century itself. But it lacks in almost every way a representation of work. It does not valorize or celebrate the workers it depicts, either as individuals or as a powerful collective as was characteristic of social realist visual art twenty or thirty years later. Nor does it show their experience *as* workers, in the way Charlie Chaplin's *Modern Times* tackles this forty years later. Nor does it examine or represent working conditions, as in documentary photography by artists such as Louis Hine (1874–1940) in the 1920s and 1930s, and again by conceptual artists picturing work in the 1960s and 1970s. Instead *Workers Leaving the Lumière Factory in Lyon* focuses on a group of workers at a break or at the close of day, moments when they apparently cease being workers. It documents and helps naturalize an approach to the worker's identity that is both liberating and powerfully divisive. On the one hand, such a view affirms that workers are not simply the jobs that they do. On the other hand, the common reduction of labor's depiction to the moment when labor *ceases* creates a disembodied picture of the worker, whose "other" nonwork life is somehow magically separated by those gates from the physical, emotional, and political realities of the job.

This chapter traces broad shifts in the representation of workers throughout the century that followed the Lumière brothers' semi-fictional portrait. From the 1920s onward, artists in some parts of the world would valorize and allegorize the worker and his or her productivity as the critical engine of revolutions. Elsewhere the medium of photography would provide artists a more immediate, activist role in documenting dangerous labor, advocating for better working conditions, and protesting workers' inability to earn a living wage. Between these two extremes, a great deal of art since the 1920s was dedicated to depicting workers both as "types," their jobs representing a culture in microcosm—as German photographer August Sander (1876–1964) would so famously undertake with his multivolume study *People of the Twentieth Century* (1924)—and as poignantly specific individuals—as Kata Kálmán (Hungarian, 1909–1978) would do for exploited industrial and agricultural workers in Hungary and Milton Rogovin (American, 1909–2011) would do for workers in the American Rust Belt. Later, a case study of the work of Milton Rogovin, which depicted workers in many parts of the world, will highlight the themes of the chapter.

This chapter begins with a return to the nineteenth-century's realist tradition that manifested itself, among many other ways, in a documentary photography tradition established in the 1920s and 1930s that remerged in new forms in the 1960s and 1970s before being transformed again with the emergence of video art in the latter decades of the twentieth century. Although it was marked by dramatic improvements in working conditions, at least in the West, and periods of great prosperity reflected in art, in retrospect the twentieth century saw an overall erosion of workers' collective power. Much of the best art from this century witnessed and even registered protest against that loss, while many more recent artists focused less on depicting workers than on developing ways to picture the flow of capital itself.

Notwithstanding the onset of the First World War, the early decades of the twentieth century were marked by extraordinary experimentation. Artists as different as Pablo Picasso (Spanish, 1881–1973), Marcel Duchamp (French, 1887–1968), and Hannah Höch (German, 1889–1978) rejected purely representational art in favor of new, often abstract, forms. For the first few decades of the new century, realist painting was derided as the stuff of academics; the most radical and politically engaged art was, if not purely abstract, dedicated to using the language of abstraction to change the way people saw the world around them. Artists playing a central role in communicating postrevolutionary ideals often focused on work and workers in Russia (1917) and Mexico (1920). Along with Futurist artists in Italy and Russia, Dadaist artists making protest art and performance in Germany and Switzerland, and De Stijl art and design in the Netherlands, Russian constructivists such as Vladimir Tatlin (Ukrainian, 1885–1956), El Lissitzky (1890–1941), Kazimir Malevich (Russian, 1878–1935), and Lyubov Popova (1889–1924) were part of a powerful and international avant-garde dedicated to abstraction's apparently universal power. After the revolution, these Russian artists sought to marry avant-garde principles with post-revolution demands that art serve a new Russian people and specifically the Russian workers who had helped make the revolution possible. They largely set aside painting and sculpture and turned to designing architectural monuments to the revolution and its leaders (such as Vladimir Tatlin's 1919 *Monument to the Third International*, a proposal for the headquarters of the Comintern in St. Petersburg), interior designs for workers' clubs, which were to set the stage for a newly communal social life (such as Aleksandr Rodchenko's 1925 workers' club design for the *Exposition Internationale des Arts Décoratifs et Industriels Modernes* in Paris, see Figure 2.2), sets and costumes for plays (such as Lyubov Popova's designs for *The Magnanimous Cuckold*, 1921), advertisements for state-sponsored goods, and workers' overalls.[1]

But realism and representational art soon returned with a vengeance. In Russia, the constructivist artists' experiments at using elements of avant-garde art to more universally communicate with newly empowered workers were silenced with the formal implementation of Stalin's doctrine of Socialist Realism in 1934. It called for art that was "Proletarian," relevant to and understandable by common workers; "Typical," representative of everyday life; "Partisan," designed to support and further the state; and "Realistic," naturalistic and figurative in style. With this shift towards a highly proscribed and propagandistic revolutionary Romanticism, most Russian art became overwhelmingly dedicated to a realist style and the depiction of happy and prosperous factory or farm workers, bathed in sunlight. Abstraction, even in the attempted service of modern workers, was brutally censored, as was any form of critique. The return of realism was not limited to Russia's socialist realism; indeed, it took the form of social realism and regionalism in the United States during the Great Depression and in Mexico after the revolution. It dominated a great deal of international art until the Second World War and remained the lingua franca of political art until at least the 1960s. After the vibrant, defiantly new

FIGURE 2.2 Aleksandr Rodchenko, Workers' club interior, design for the *Exposition Internationale des Arts Décoratifs et Industriels Modernes*, 1925. Alfred H. Barr, Jr. Papers, 13.I.E. The Museum of Modern Art Archives, New York. Digital Image © The Museum of Modern Art. © Estate of Alexander Rodchenko/RAO, Moscow/VAGA, New York.

and unfamiliar representations that characterized avant-garde art in the early years of the twentieth century, the widespread return to realism and figuration represented a large step backward for many artists and critics. Interpretations of figurative art are, to this day, tainted by real or perceived associations with Russia's political propaganda and the pervasive influence that propaganda had on the realist aesthetic program of other authoritarian and fascist regimes throughout much of the twentieth century.

During the same period, the leaders of the postrevolutionary Mexican government from 1923 to 1939 also called on artists to promote its ideals, specifically a renewed emphasis on Mexico's rich indigenous and rural identity alongside its Spanish history. Rather than the easel painting and large-scale state monuments promoted by the Russian government, Mexican officials turned to artists including David Alfaro Siqueiros (Mexican, 1896–1974), José Clemente Orozco (Mexican, 1883–1949), and Diego Rivera (Mexican, 1886–1957) who referenced Mexico's long pre-Hispanic history of mural painting to devise a program of mural commissions that would communicate socialist ideals to a then largely illiterate populace. These so-called "Mexican muralists" designed monumental wall paintings to educate the populace, illustrate the history of the country's indigenous peoples, and, crucially, to promote the heroic image of the worker and revolutionary. Mexico's transition from a rural to an industrial nation was seen as important to the success of the postrevolutionary government. And the artists' own Marxist politics led them to feature themes of class struggle. Muralists such as Rivera and Siqueiros painted images of factory workers with an idealizing heroism that had previously been reserved for religious subject matter. Perhaps Rivera's most famous mural in Mexico is *La historia de México—de la conquista al futuro* (The History of Mexico—from the Conquest to the Future, 1929–35), in the Palacio Nacional, Mexico City. The monumental three-walled mural celebrates the indigenous peoples so central to Mexico's history, specifically the Aztecs. It represents the country's history of seemingly constant warfare and struggle, with a particularly pointed depiction of the brutality of Spanish and French conquistadors against native Indian Mexican peasants and farmers. And it proposes a brightly optimistic view of the changes industrialization and education would bring to the workers of Mexico's future. Rivera's best-known extant mural cycle outside of Mexico is the *Detroit Industry Murals* (1932–3), dedicated to the workers of Detroit and based largely on his study of Ford's River Rouge plant (Figure 2.3).

The Mexican Muralists inspired many of the social realist painters in the United States in the 1930s, even if their own political statements were comparatively restrained. Their movement was prompted and even necessitated by the country's plunge into the Great Depression (1929–39), when economic collapse, a lack of work, and a fear of starvation were near-universal constants. As part of the Federal Art Project (1935–43) of the Works Progress Administration (WPA), the US government employed as many as five thousand artists in a work-relief program to make posters, decorate public spaces with murals and sculpture, document folklore and culture, and photograph the plight of farmers. The artists of this period made commonplace workers and farmers their main subjects. Some, like Ben Shahn (American, 1898–1969), were openly political and critical of social injustice, xenophobia, and the mistreatment of immigrants. The Farm Security Administration (FSA) employed photographers as part of its own publicity department to help illustrate for the public and for Congress the problems of farm workers that it was trying to solve, and many of the best-known images of workers during the Great Depression were taken as part of this program, including those by Dorothea Lange (American, 1895–1965), Walker Evans (American, 1903–75) and Margaret Bourke-White (American, 1904–71). Lange's 1936 portrait of Florence Owens Thompson, catalogued by the Library of Congress as "Destitute pea pickers in California," came to be known as *Migrant Mother*, one of the most iconic images of the Great Depression (Figure 2.4).

FIGURE 2.3 Diego Rivera, *Detroit Industry*, north wall lower panel, 1932–3. Courtesy Detroit Institute of Arts, Gift of Edsel B. Ford. © 2017 Banco de México Diego Rivera Frida Kahlo Museums Trust, Mexico, D.F. / Artists Rights Society (ARS), New York.

FIGURE 2.4 Dorothea Lange, *Migrant Mother*, 1936. Library of Congress, Prints & Photographs Division, FSA/OWI Collection, LC-USF34-009058-C.

This documentary photograph capturing fear and hopelessness was also a full-throated protest against the economic status quo. Lange described making the image:

> I saw and approached the hungry and desperate mother, as if drawn by a magnet. I do not remember how I explained my presence or my camera to her, but I do remember she asked me no questions. She told me her age, that she was thirty-two. She said that they had been living on frozen vegetables from the surrounding fields, and birds that the children killed. She had just sold the tires from her car to buy food. There she sat in that lean-to tent with her children huddled around her, and seemed to know that my pictures might help her, and so she helped me. There was a sort of equality about it.[2]

American Regionalist painters such as Thomas Hart Benton (1889–1975) and Grant Wood (1892–1942) also made workers and farmers the subjects of their paintings, but with an approach more likely to romanticize the life of the American worker than to criticize its hardships.

Alongside the development of politically conscious documentary photography in the United States, a loose-knit and significantly more activist association of publications and photographers emerged in Germany and the Soviet Union. In March 1926, the German Communist magazine *AIZ* (*Arbeiter Illustrierte Zeitung* or Worker's Pictorial Newspaper) first called for contributions by amateur photographers. The magazine went on to establish a network of worker/photographer groups across Germany and the Soviet Union. Both Germany's *Der Arbeiter Fotograf* (The Worker-Photographer, the publication of the German Association of Worker-Photographers) and *Sovetskoe foto* (Soviet Photo, the publication of the Union of Russian Proletarian Photographers) were also founded in 1926. This marked the birth of what came to be known as the "worker-photography movement" (WPM) of the 1920s and 1930s, a coalition advocating self-representation. Its ideas eventually spread to most of Europe and the United States before being widely silenced by the rise of fascism and the Second World War.[3] Many of the photographers published by these magazines were initially untrained worker-photographers, but the professionals of the movement shared with them sensitivity to abjection and even ugliness, and deliberate rejection of aesthetic photographic tropes.[4] Edwin Hoernle, a regular contributor to *Der Arbeiter Fotograf* captured some of the movement's ethos, declaring the necessity to "proclaim proletarian reality in all its disgusting ugliness, with its indictment of society and its demand for revenge ... We must present things as they are, in a hard, merciless light."[5] Perhaps the most famous example of the widespread influence of the WPM came with the 1931 photo-essay "24 Hours in the Life of a Family Working in Moscow," by Maks Al'pert (1899–1980), Arkady Shaikhet (1858–1959), and Semen Tules published in *AIZ*.[6] The labor of the workers in the Filippov family was valorized in the photo-essay, but it also showed members of the family as complete people, engaged in all manner of educational, domestic, and leisure activities outside of the workplace. They were portrayed as a "typical" Soviet family in conditions that were inspiring, given widespread unemployment in Germany at the time, if perhaps impossibly good. The treatment of the Filippov family influenced numerous companion pieces, including a photo-essay that illustrated relatively poor conditions for workers in a comparable German family at the same time. Without the Filippov portrait, it is difficult to imagine the photo-essay format that became so prevalent in popular photography magazines such as *Life*. Less well appreciated, but no less influential, was the empowerment of the thousands of members of more than one hundred local worker photographer clubs that developed as part of the movement before Hitler's appointment as chancellor silenced the presses in Germany and led many of the photographers and publishers into jail or exile.

The all-encompassing struggle of the Second World War broadly halted creation of the masterpieces of social realism and documentary photography that we associate with the interwar years. Yet the immediate postwar years were a time of incredible artistic creativity in the United States. Many of the great artists who led the emergence of American abstraction in the 1950s had, as young artists, found employment making figurative, social realist work in the WPA—among them Jackson Pollock, Willem de Kooning, Lee Krasner, Mark Rothko, Arshile Gorky, and Philip Guston. They were able to pursue artistic careers as abstract artists after the war, some with the support of the GI Bill. The industrial ramp-up during the war had transformed the US economy, and the postwar era was a time of incredible prosperity when the struggle and strife experienced by workers in the 1930s seemed to belong to another life. These were, in many ways, the best years in the history of the United States to be a white male worker.

Many social realist painters and sculptors were left out in the cold, perhaps by this very prosperity, but certainly by the widespread shift in art towards abstraction during the postwar years. Numerous photographers who had worked for the FSA successfully transitioned to creating documentary photography for mass-market magazines such as *Life* and *Time*. Many of their works were included in *Family of Man*, a wildly popular photography exhibition organized by Edward Steichen at the Museum of Modern Art in 1955.[7] The representation of workers in *Family of Man* substituted a kind of universal spirit for the specificity and critique associated with interwar documentary photography, both the highly political worker-photography movement in Europe and the Soviet Union and the activist FSA photographers of the United States. Using more than five hundred photographs taken around the world, the organizers endeavored to illustrate the commonality of global human experience. As Fred Turner described it, "Visitors gazed at photographs of children dancing, families gathering, and men and women of myriad nations working, walking, marrying, fighting … Together, the installation and the images left few places where visitors could turn and not encounter a picture of another person doing something they were likely to recognize."[8] Although the exhibition was almost universally embraced when it opened and went on to travel for an audience of millions around the world in a US State Department-sponsored tour, it has also been the subject of pointed criticism. Susan Sontag for one, accused the exhibition of "sentimental humanism." She continued: "Steichen's choice of photographs assumes a human condition or a human nature shared by everybody. By purporting to show that individuals are born, work, laugh, and die everywhere in the same way, *The Family of Man* denies the determining weight of history—of genuine and historically embedded differences, injustices, and conflicts."[9] Although there is much to criticize in the exhibition, it was in itself emblematic of a certain depoliticization in the representation of workers, which characterized the 1950s more generally and can be associated with McCarthyism and anticommunism. Nonetheless, the exhibit and its critics would in time lead to a reemergence of the political documentary tradition. One such artist, the photographer Milton Rogovin, in a career that spanned the century, both exemplifies this transition and highlights the larger themes of work pictured in the modern age.

Case study: Milton Rogovin
Michael Frisch

The work of the long-lived American documentary photographer Milton Rogovin (1909–2011), whose practice was defined by a focus on work, workers, and their families, communities, and cultural settings, highlights this chapter's focus on how work has been pictured across much of the twentieth century.

Rogovin achieved international eminence as a photographer dedicated to working people and the poor. "The Rich have their own photographers," he liked to say.[10] An optometrist by profession and a life-long activist, Rogovin became a target of McCarthyist persecution of communists and leftists in the 1950s. He was stigmatized and pilloried in his adopted hometown of Buffalo, New York, in ways that destroyed his optometric practice and stilled his voice politically. What he lost because of his politics pushed him into beginning, already in his late forties, what became a lifetime's worth of serious documentary photography. He remained active as a photographer well into his nineties, and was still participating in social justice and antiwar demonstrations as he passed his 100th birthday.[11]

Rogovin's orientation as a photographer was broader and deeper than political identifications as such, although it was always defined by his commitment to the representation of workers and ordinary people. Throughout the years of his ascendant renown, when asked about his worldview, Rogovin's favorite response was to recite, in its entirety, Bertolt Brecht's long poem, *A Worker Reads History* which begins:

Who built the seven gates of Thebes?
The books are filled with names of kings.
Was it the kings who hauled the craggy blocks of stone?
And Babylon, so many times destroyed,
Who built the city up each time? In which of Lima's houses,
That city glittering with gold, lived those who built it?[12]

To this central axis of political and social-ethical commitment, shared with so much social documentary photography, film, painting, and theater in the second half of the twentieth century, Rogovin brought two additional defining axes—portraiture and serial photography—that complemented and complicated his social-documentary aesthetic. The result is a body of work especially resonant with this chapter's inquiry into how art and aesthetic practice—not just politics or social orientation—shaped the picturing of work and its contexts in twentieth-century culture.

Portraiture is the second defining axis of Rogovin's work: his subjects are almost exclusively pictured looking directly at the camera. As in all portraiture, this evokes social and personal context brought into sharp focus through the artist's direct engagement. The portrait subject's being and social presence are conveyed through the literally embodied revelations of face and figure, and the implicit self-representational choices of stance, gesture, expression, and gaze. To these Rogovin brings his own choices of angle, lighting, focus, and distance. The result is, by definition, a dialogic cocreation of photographer and subject.

Much of the distinctive power of Rogovin's portraiture flows from his career-long use of a Rolleiflex camera held at waist level.[13] Images are mostly shot from slightly below. Rogovin, as he shoots, is looking down into his viewfinder, not directly at the subject. The respect, even deference, that his images convey seems not unrelated to this posture. By way of contrast, the intrusive gaze of the more contemporary single-lens reflex camera requires the photographer to drill in on his or her subject as photographs are "taken." In Rogovin's work, though, the photographs seem "given," and in a deep sense they are. This suggests a tension central to how work is pictured in the modern age: how, in such an individualistic, artist-subject dialogic mode, can the broader world of work and culture be engaged, much less uniquely and powerfully represented?

Rogovin's intuitive resolution of this tension became a third, formal defining axis, one that combined the social and the aesthetic in his major projects: his photographs are not presented as autonomous objects, but are explicitly parts of series organized by a distinctive formal portraiture concept and grounded in place and social context. These series emerged gradually, and almost accidentally in his work at first. But as they took shape the serial concept drove the arc of Rogovin's photographic career.

Two central photographic ideas propel Rogovin's serial focus. Remarkably, while each is strikingly simple, rarely in the history of documentary photography has either been deployed with such consistency. The first emerged as Rogovin began travelling to mines and factories, photographing individual workers at their worksites. He initially took some pictures of people actually at work and in action. But increasingly he came to focus on formal portraits: the worker pauses while at his or her workstation or on break, faces and engages Rogovin and his camera, and the portrait is given/taken. Later, Rogovin began asking if he could visit the worker at home and take a parallel picture there. For these, the worker would dress as she or he pleased, choose the specific location, and decide who and what to include in the picture.

Paired portraits, work and home, usually exhibited side by side—this became the series concept. Sometimes resonant, sometimes contrasting, the differences and complementarities draw viewer interest and curiosity. This was not a wholly original concept, but Rogovin deployed it more extensively, more self-consciously, and with more sustained documentary intent than had been done previously. Sometimes, as in *Working People* (1976–9), the series mixed work types and geographic locales, with the split context of industrial work/home serving as organizing principle. Over time, substantive focus and geographic specificity became more central. As Rogovin's industrial work and his earlier 1962 to 1971 photographs in Appalachia became noticed internationally, he began receiving invitations—often from unions—to visit a particular country to photograph coal miners there. The resulting series includes photographs taken from 1982 to 1990 in Chile, Cuba, Germany, China, Zimbabwe, Scotland, Mexico, and Czechoslovakia, in addition to the United States.[14] In the photographs, the work miners do is very similar in each country, as are the mine settings; the presentational rhythm of home and work portraiture remains a constant. But the home settings and postures vary widely. This tension between consistency and variation in the lives of workers who are not "just" workers is profoundly felt as the series moves the viewer around the globe. Workers are always seen through the lens of paired portraits that are relentlessly idiosyncratic and specific yet evocatively general in their insights.

While widening the geographic lens for miners, Rogovin narrowed it for steelworkers, focusing increasingly on his home in Buffalo, New York. In 1987, Rogovin took new portraits, giving the project a "before and after" posture, and bringing both oral history and portraits into range as modes for representing and engaging a transition in the life of an American industrial city and its people.

This led to the project that evolved into *Portraits in Steel*, a 1993 book and exhibit produced with oral historian Michael Frisch, one of this chapter's coauthors. *Portraits* combines Rogovin's Buffalo steelworker home-and-work, before-and-after portraiture from the late 1970s and late 1980s, with extensive oral histories of some of the same portrait subjects conducted from 1989 through to the early 1990s, following the closure of every Buffalo facility in which Rogovin had photographed.[15]

This temporal dimension and its social-political valences appealed to Rogovin as a strategy for examining deindustrialization and its human and community impact. It also roots the photographs in an aesthetic curiosity about change-over-time. This grew into a central thematic thread in Rogovin's serial photography that reached its fullest expression in his photographs of residents in a six-square block area of a very poor sector of the city near his former optometry office, a zone of social complexity and extreme marginality beset by unemployment, drug traffic, street crime, gangs, and prostitution. These were portraits of the same people, usually in the same place, taken at four different points over four decades from the 1970s to the early 2000s.[16]

Through these two broad organizing ideas—paired home and work, and change over time—each series engages with and represents workers and poor people through portraiture, rather than documenting work or worklessness directly. Rogovin's mastery of portraiture "pictures work" perhaps more insightfully than had his images centered on documenting work and workers in action more directly. The central contrast of work/home portraits in the *Working People* series offers a straightforward interpretive message. But through the follow-up portrait in *Portraits in Steel* and in *The Mining Photographs,* and the steel oral histories, this message is darkened and complicated by the unfolding social context of steel deindustrialization and the global circuitry of coalmining.

These worker portraits are to some extent artifacts of documentary contingency. Rogovin had been permitted to photograph steelworkers only in a subset of Buffalo area steel facilities, most of them not major rolling mills. He was often limited to photographing in break rooms, or in spaces removed from workstations. The same was certainly true in his international travels where he was able to photograph miners, but not their work underground. In the domestic portraits, there were few structural constraints of this sort, although Rogovin faced one of his own creation: he asked portrait subjects to determine how and where they wished to be photographed at home.

This built-in-contrast between the home and workplace portraits seems straightforward enough: in a social realist mode, the work photograph documents the power, scale, demands, and constraints of the sites, and bounds the worker's identity and agency within that world's limits. Rogovin's social sensibility also leads him to emphasize the strength and dignity of workers and the work they do, notwithstanding the oppressive conditions and physical demands of that work, or the broader contradictions of what was soon to become an industry in decline. Rogovin's work photographs inevitably embody this tension between worker pride and skill, and worker oppression and victimization. Meanwhile, his home photographs document the complex subjectivity of a skilled working class whose relatively well-paying jobs have, for a time, supported a middle-class lifestyle and its proud display.

FIGURE 2.5 Milton Rogovin, Untitled, 1976. (Doris McKinney, 1976). Courtesy Center for Creative Photography.

But if work is more than oppression and constraint, home is not simply the opposite. This complication is encountered experientially as viewers move through Rogovin's photographs. In some instances, the home picture seems more dimensional, with the work picture appearing more constrained. But often the individual seems more alive in the work photograph, and more constricted in the image taken at home. In *The Mining Photographs*, what concentrates viewers is the tension between commonality and cultural variation and revelation, as seen mainly but not exclusively in the domestic images.

This complexity becomes more challenging in the steel series, when follow-up photographs picture the homes and lifestyles that the collapse of steelwork had rendered precarious. This elusive contextual dimension lies well beyond Rogovin's own discussion of his work and his approach, which—following the Brecht poem

FIGURE 2.6 Milton Rogovin, Untitled, 1976. (Doris McKinney, 1976). Courtesy Center for Creative Photography.

he loved to recite—articulated a social vision and commitment while generally avoiding discussion of his photography as such. Rogovin often represented his compositional choices as situational consequences rather than the result of his intention. But, as so often, there may be a great deal more to the work than what the artist is willing to articulate.

Rogovin's photograph(s) of Doris McKinney (Figures 2.5, 2.6, 2.7) suggests the extent to which Rogovin composed and shaped his photographs to express what he has sensed about the personal and social context within which his individual subjects, their work, and their homes are situated. His treatment demonstrates how, through a unique mode and approach, his photographs "picture work" with a depth that more direct photographic engagement might not achieve.

The industrial portrait is a powerful study of a woman pausing at work. Its composition focuses on stance and conveys strength and confidence. Strong on detail, the image invites curiosity about who this woman is, what she is doing,

FIGURE 2.7 Milton Rogovin, Untitled, 1987. (Doris McKinney, 1976). Courtesy Center for Creative Photography.

and her role in the overall curve of steel production. Because the oral histories for *Portraits in Steel* began by asking the subject to comment on Rogovin's original paired work and home photos, the interviews are especially helpful in deepening the context of those images, measuring this against the impressions viewers may have from the image alone. In this case, McKinney comments with pleasure that "Most of my friends that saw this picture, they'd say I look like I was from outer space. But at that time, I as working at Republic Steel and I was a burner, so this is my burning outfit."[17] They rarely notice the detail most significant to her: "And the reason the hat's sitting so high is I guess because I had my hair rolled up. [laughs]. Because, you know even though you're working in a man's job, doing a man's job, when you take off all of this here, you still want to be a woman."[18] The two home photographs suggest the tensions between McKinney's responsibilities as a single mother of two rapidly growing boys and her more independent identity as a woman steelworker.

Details in the photographs hint at further complexity. Consider this story McKinney tells about almost losing her steel mill job—or rather stories, since she actually gave two versions of it: First, when talking about the work photograph, she relates that she had been a single mother on welfare when presented with an opportunity to work at Republic Steel. Towards the end of her probation, the foreman told her that she would be fired if she didn't do better with the heavy burning torch she is holding in Rogovin's photo. She describes what happened then:

> And you say, going from two – let's see, I think how much I was making, maybe three hundred a week, and the thought of going back to the welfare and making three hundred a month—the whole weekend I cried and I cried. When I walked in there Monday, I could pick the torch up and walk with it and anything else. Because it was psychological, you know. I knew that I did not want to go back to living like I was. And if there was any ounce of strength within me, and if other women could do it, I can't see why I couldn't, and so I did.[19]

Later, when pointing out the framed diploma visible in the home photograph, McKinney retells her own story. In this version, she describes how welfare enabled her to obtain a community-college certification as an occupational therapist's assistant, but that upon graduating she could not afford to take a low-paying job in that field. Reluctantly, she took the job at Republic Steel instead:

> It was a step forward because it was a good, high-paying job; it was a step backward because it was not the kind of job I wanted to do. So it was very depressing for me ... [But] we had been deprived a long time, and the money outweighed the experience. And who was to say that the other job was going to work out? So, once I took the job at Republic, you know your whole mentality has to change in order to keep a job, you can't continue to see yourself doing something else, just doing this temporarily. No—you got to be all or nothing. I thought you could keep up with reading, and keep up with your AJOTs, Journal of Occupational Therapy, you know. But you can't keep up unless you're actively participating in it. So then you finally make up your mind, you say, "Well, as long as I'm going to be at the job I'm going to do my damnedest to keep it, and get some of the things I want, and if the time comes, then so be it, I'll go from there."[20]

These two stories are different and the same. The welfare mother terrified of returning to poverty and the college-trained paraprofessional conquering her disappointment about being in a manual-labor job are the same woman, facing the same moment of truth. The contrasting images and self-presentations embodied in Rogovin's photographs speak to this complexity and singularity.

In this example Rogovin has documented and engaged workers whose identity is so nuanced and contingent it can only be apprehended through the unfolding layers of expression in a complex narrative—or through art, in this case the art of photographic portraiture. More generally, the photography of Milton Rogovin speaks to the determination of twentieth-century artists, as discussed throughout this chapter, to "picture work" in all its subjectivity and social complexity, through a broad range of constantly evolving artistic forms and modes.

CONCEPTUALIZING WORK

Beginning in the 1960s and continuing in different forms into the work of today, many of the global artists of the 1960s and 1970s who were loosely, and often contentiously, grouped under the appellation "Conceptual" began marshalling seemingly dry documentary evidence—artless photographs, reports and statements, statistics, sound recordings—as the material for their art. While their use of such nonexpressive materials did not determine the political nature of their art, for many conceptual artists it opened up opportunities to deploy a language and an aesthetic often associated with government bureaucracy as well as the documentary tradition to make work that was critical of existing political systems, including the experience of workers. A few key examples help illustrate this development.

For more than forty years, Mierle Laderman Ukeles (American, b. 1939) has dedicated herself to raising awareness of social justice issues and the representation of labor. Based on the increasing sense of injustice over the unacknowledged and uncompensated work that she and other women did to maintain the home, she wrote her *Manifesto for Maintenance Art 1969!* which argued for a kind of general confederation between women and maintenance workers. In light of the rampant political activism and calls for change that surrounded the worldwide protests of 1968, her *Manifesto* opened with the following observation about such unglamorous work: "after the revolution, who's going to pick up the garbage on Monday morning?" However, despite the necessity of such labor, Ukeles observed that "The culture confers lousy status on maintenance jobs = minimum wages, housewives = no pay." Her litany of domestic labor while written from a feminist point of view offered a universal critique:

> clean your desk, wash the dishes, clean the floor, wash your clothes, wash your toes, change the baby's diaper, finish the report, correct the typos, mend the fence, keep the customer happy, throw out the stinking garbage, watch out don't put things in your nose, what shall I wear, I have no sox, pay your bills, don't litter, save string, wash your hair, change the sheets, go to the store, I'm out of perfume, say it again—he doesn't understand, seal it again—it leaks, go to work, this art is dusty, clear the table, call him again, flush the toilet, stay young.[21]

Ukeles followed this manifesto with a series of actions based on her resolution that "women's work" merited being seen *as* art, rather than being seen as the work she had to finish in order to make art. Whether by ceremonially scrubbing a piece of New York City pavement, or by drawing attention to the often-overlooked work of a museum's guards, Ukeles's *Maintenance Art* projects created indelible images of overlooked labor. Since 1977, Ukeles has been the first and only artist in residence in the history of the New York City Department of Sanitation. This unpaid residency provides her with an office/studio where she creates artworks that connect the often-overlooked role of maintenance work with the public sphere. For *Touch Sanitation Performance* (1979–80), her first project during her residence, Ukeles visited all of the fifty-nine sanitation districts and shook hands individually with each of the 8,500 employees (Figure 2.8). During the eleven months this project took to complete, Ukeles repeatedly expressed gratitude, saying to each worker, "Thank you for keeping New York City alive." While each of these works was performative, they exist after the event as art only through its documentary evidence: photographs, statements, and videotaped footage.

FIGURE 2.8 "Handshake Ritual" with workers of New York City Department of Sanitation. Mierle Laderman Ukeles, *Touch Sanitation Performance: Fresh Kills Landfill*, 1977–80. Courtesy the artist and Ronald Feldman Fine Arts, New York.

Photographer and political activist Fred Lonidier (American, b. 1942) puts labor struggles at the forefront of his art in work that draws overt connections between art and social practice. In *The Health and Safety Game* (1972), Lonidier documents on-the-job injuries in panels comprising photos, documents, and interviews (Figure 2.9). The majority of his subjects are blue-collar workers represented anonymously through disturbing photos of their sometimes-gruesome injuries, medical records, and other personal accounts. Placed alongside the photos are statements, often brief, documenting the workers' accounts of how they felt management had strategized to avoid accountability and compensation. Each panel gives the impression of being a newly declassified medical report, or evidence in a legal dispute over health coverage. The subject of Lonidier's project is the "game"—the juggle to manage risk and blame, a balancing act in which the injured worker has often been the loser—referenced in the work's title. Unlike the works of many of his peers, Lonidier did not design this and many other installation projects specifically for the gallery or museum setting. He travelled the installation around to union halls where its message about worker's compensation had a more immediate relevance. While mirroring the clinical tone of those charged with evaluating the validity of such claims and associated requests for compensation, Lonidier's work is the opposite of dispassionate; it is a fervent indictment of the personal losses employees can suffer at—and for—work.

Artist, filmmaker, and widely influential photography theorist Allan Sekula (1951–2013) was a friend and sometime collaborator with Lonidier on the West Coast of the United States. One of his first mature works as a young artist was *Aerospace Folktales* (1973), a thinly veiled autobiographical analysis of the effect of unemployment on his father, an aerospace engineer, and on the rest of his family. His father had lost

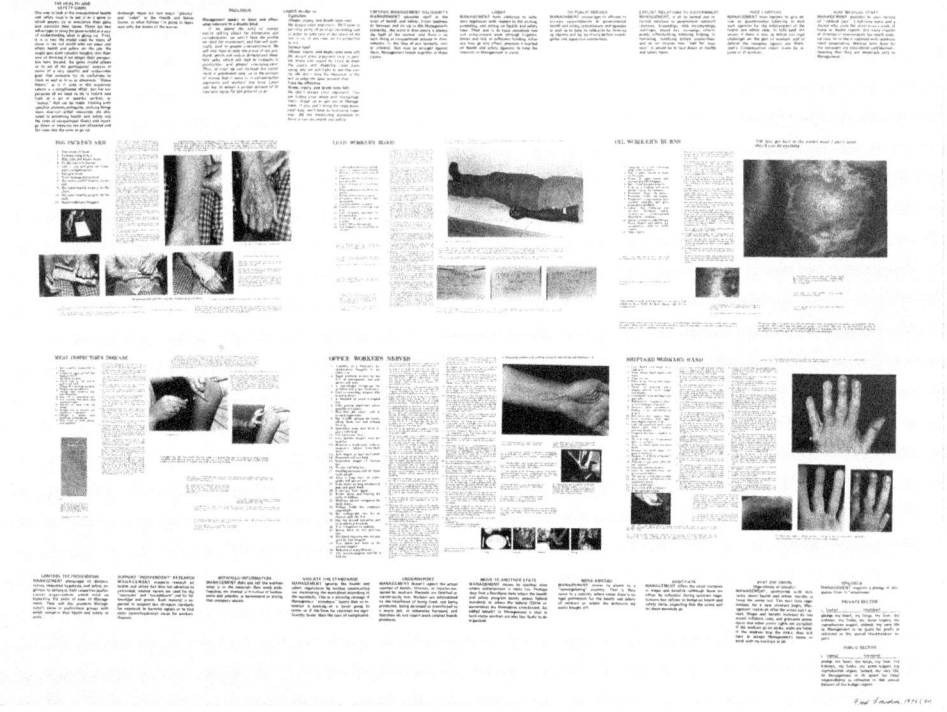

FIGURE 2.9 Fred Lonidier, detail from *The Health and Safety Game*, 1976. Courtesy the artist; Essex Street, New York; Michael Benevento, Los Angeles; and Silberkuppe, Berlin.

his job to cutbacks toward the later years of the Vietnam War. Sekula's story unfolded through documentary materials such as black-and-white photographs paired with texts and audiotapes of interviews. But the work took the form of an installation. The audio recordings playing in the background color the way viewers read the photographs, and together present a highly personal portrait that is about the nature of subjectivity in documentary itself. The performative documentary format allowed the easily ignored, commonplace experience of job loss and culpability to carry greater meaning, as seen in this example from his father's narrative:

> Interview with the Engineer ... Perhaps the major difficulty that I have encountered is being able to contact people who might have knowledge of positions which you could fill. Many times, you were side tracked by receptionists, office personnel, clerical staff, and so forth, especially if you visited a corporation or business establishment or government agency. Letter writing is not as effective either, because many times people would not take the time to thoroughly scrutinize and evaluate the potential of a man's background. And they would maybe read one or two sentences, and jump at a conclusion, "This isn't the person we want," and throw it in the wastebasket, or file it ... There is a demoralizing reaction on the part of the individual experiencing unemployment. At first, he might feel very confident that he has something that will impress a potential employer. And as time goes on and when he is faced with refusal after refusal, he begins to doubt, and then that doubt turns into what you might call a discouragement. You just don't care whether you are going to continue on any

more looking for a job—it is a futile waste of time. And it takes a terrific amount of persistence, you might say, or call it intestinal fortitude.[22]

As in this excerpt, the documentation in *Aerospace Folktales* balances the family's frustration and sense of loss with their powerful desire to normalize their experience, and, even, their feelings of guilt for somehow being caught up in the economic circumstances that had precipitated it. As the critic Manfred Herms has noted, with *Aerospace Folktales*, "it becomes apparent that for Sekula political radicalization and the creation of a multi-faceted narrative are not mutually exclusive, but interdependent."[23] Sekula's art and theoretical writings embodied what Sekula called "critical realism."[24] In the later years of his life, he dedicated himself to a study of the oceans, and making perceptible through art and documentary film the usually invisible power of the maritime economy as an engine of globalization.

The three examples from the work of Mierle Laderman Ukeles, Allan Sekula, and Fred Lonidier illustrate that the association of the conceptual photography movement with a "dematerialization" of the traditional object of art can obscure its materiality. Many conceptual artists used such minimal means to represent the material nature of the global economy, embodied as it is in the very real experience of workers.

WORK IMMERSIVE

In more recent years, numerous artists have used film and video installations to evoke the experience of workers and to move from the influence of documentary or conceptual art towards a critical approach that upends the human expectation of narrative itself. Artist and filmmaker Steve McQueen (British, b. 1969) created a paradoxically out-of-body embodied experience for viewers with his 2002 film *Western Deep*. The twenty-four-minute, twelve-second film was recorded using only the ambient light available within the TauTona goldmine in South Africa, three miles underground. The artist describes his political approach to the subject matter: "Politics will take care of itself. I'm interested in people who are involved in the situations that politicians create."[25] From the terrific rumbling of the elevator making its way to what feels like the center of the earth, to the punishing existence of the black miners at the bottom of the shaft in exploitative postcolonial labor conditions, McQueen's camera lingers on often inexplicable situations that are the norm for these workers; they labor in darkness, they have their temperature taken, they perform seemingly compulsory calisthenics. The power of cinema is here marshalled not in favor of fiction, nor exactly as part of a traditional documentary narrative, but to create an often-abstract sensory experience of another that is wilfully obscure and fragmentary. In the depiction, viewers can only glimpse this vision of a hell underground. As the critic T. J. Demos has argued,

> *Western Deep* allows audience and image to touch, thus engendering an empathic culture between forms of difference that nevertheless maintain their separateness. We—the viewers—are placed in a relationship with an outside world, but not from the safety of an objective position; rather, we approach the other by becoming other. It is precisely through this complex negation of self and other, this staging of a compassionate encounter with difference, that McQueen's *Western Deep* models new forms of being and belonging in the world. This force of becoming represents the promise of *Western Deep* and is a sign that, against the cruelty of what it documents, it is a film of hope.[26]

FIGURE 2.10 Installation view of Harun Farocki's *Workers Leaving the Factory in Eleven Decades*, 2006. Courtesy Harun Farocki, GbR in *Overtime: The Art of Work*, Albright-Knox Art Gallery, Buffalo, New York, March 8–May 18, 2015. © Image courtesy Albright-Knox Art Gallery Digital Assets Collection and Archives, Buffalo, New York. Photo: Tom Loonan.

CONCLUSION

In 2006, just over one hundred years after the debut of the Lumière brothers' film, the Czech-born German artist and filmmaker Harun Farocki (1944–2014) presented his video installation *Workers Leaving the Factory in Eleven Decades* (Figure 2.10). This installation—twelve video monitors arranged in a row and each playing a looped film clip—resulted from Farocki's own fascination with the 1895 film. He was not the first artist to return to this pivotal moment at the birth of documentary filmmaking. Indeed, Allan Sekula made an homage to the Lumière Brothers' film in the form of both a photographic series and a slide installation. *Untitled Slide Sequence* was comprised of photographs he took of workers leaving an aeronautics plant in California in 1972. The Lumière short was also the inspiration for Sharon Lockhart's film *Exit (Bath Iron Works, 7–11 July 2008, Bath, Maine*, 2008), among many other artists' works.

Farocki first approached the Lumière film through a more traditional single-channel documentary format, but the twelve-channel version marked the artist's own transition, as he began more formally bridging the world of documentary filmmaking and installation-based video in galleries and museums. On one level, Farocki's subject is the way the worker finishing an assigned shift and returning to life outside the factory was treated throughout the history of cinema. But after exhaustively researching countless hours of film stock over the course of a year, Farocki edited down his choices, selecting representative clips from eleven decades between cinema's birth and the year 2000. Rather than joining the clips sequentially, he looped each one on a dedicated monitor that played simultaneously with the others.

Surveying Farocki's installation, one perceives how factory gates—these barriers between everyday life and work, between apparently free and commodified time—have been the site of so many conflicts, protests, and even revolutions. However, mainstream cinema does not readily turn to labor as a subject and, when it does, it paints a very selective picture of the experience of workers. As Farocki writes, "The first camera in the history of cinema was pointed at a factory, but a century later it can be said that film is hardly drawn to the factory and is even repelled by it. Over the last century virtually none of the communication which took place in factories, whether through words, glances, or gestures, was recorded on film."[27]

Farocki's first selection is the entire Lumière film. He presents the next films chronologically, left-to-right, each an endlessly looped fragment lasting from only a few seconds to several minutes. He includes a few nonfiction films: unknown footage of factory gates from the Moscow National Film Archive dating to around 1912 and a French documentary by Jacques Willemont *La Reprise du travail aux usines Wonder* (Resuming work at the Wonder factories, 1968). The majority of clips chosen by Farocki, however, are fiction films: scenes from D. W. Griffith's *Intolerance* (1916), Fritz Lang's *Metropolis* (1926), Charlie Chaplin's *Modern Times* (1936), Michelangelo Antonioni's *Il deserto rosso* (1964), and Lars von Trier's *Dancer in the Dark* (2000). As Farocki describes his choices in this work, he argues that the way the location "in front of a factory" is treated in global cinema illustrates the progressive marginalization of representations of work through the course of the twentieth century:

> When it comes to a private life of a film's character, which really only begins after work, the factory is relegated to the background. In Fritz Lang's *Clash by Night* (1952), one sees Marilyn Monroe on the assembly line, coming out of the factory, and one hears her talking about it. But the existence of factories and movie stars are not compatible. A movie star working in a factory evokes associations of a fairy tale in which a princess must work before she attains her true calling. Factories—and the whole subject of labour—are at the fringes of film history.[28]

These two approaches to the representation of workers leaving the factory, one by the Lumière Brothers, and the other by Harun Farocki, provide an exquisite frame for looking back at the incredible breadth of ways work has been pictured for the last one hundred years. The first depiction naturalizes a "work/life" divide, taking as a given the way work structures the hours of our waking life and, indeed, our own identities. The second absorbs a century of mostly mainstream representations of the subject and uses the medium of cinema to critique itself for failing to find room for the intimate, human side of labor. It treats the medium of fiction film as documentary evidence for this critique and, like most of the best art that pictured work during the last century, it uses the power of documentary film and photography to challenge the lure of fiction. Farocki makes visible the fictional narrative so prevalent throughout the history of cinema: work is what one must stop doing in order to start living. His choice of subject matter was particularly relevant at a moment when factory gates appeared, to many in the West, no longer as an active site around which a social working life is constructed but instead as a shuttered reminder of deindustrialization. Like most of the artists discussed in this chapter, Farocki pictured work in order to insist on the intimate, personal, and therefore political way it constitutes our daily lives.[29] The first decade of the twenty-first century has seen the powerful entrenchment of new myths enabled by the blend of truth and fiction within today's economic narrative of contingent, at-will, automated, and internet-based labor. In the face of this, picturing what work looks like—whether in image or narrative, documentary or fiction—has never felt more urgent.

CHAPTER THREE

Work and Workplaces

RICHARD A. GREENWALD

INTRODUCTION

Work and workplaces have come full circle in the twentieth century. The three case studies presented below demonstrate the changing nature of work and the workplace, as well as certain perennial questions that remain with us today. Work in the garment industry started in small shops, sweatshop, and homes, and then entered larger factories. Those factories moved from large northeastern American cities to the global south to escape regulation and find cheaper labor costs—trying to preserve the sweatshop production system. One reason they could do this was the creation of the shipping container, which revolutionized shipping, shrinking boarders and reducing shipping costs, making offshore production economically feasible. This shift in shipping transformed the docks, making longshore labor more skilled at the same time that it reduced the number of workers needed. Economic displacement continued into the twenty-first century, with the further erosion of full-time, nine-to-five jobs, creating a growing army of freelancers. Workers in the new millennium were as insecure and precarious as the garment workers of the early twentieth century.

GARMENTS

On July 7, 1910, the cloakmakers' "Great Revolt" began, as almost fifty thousand workers in New York City's ladies' garment industry walked off their jobs. As work ground to a halt throughout the city, diverse actors moved to reshape the future of industrial relations. Involvement came from many fronts. Noted reformer Louis Brandeis left for New York, taking with him a draft labor agreement that would forever transform industrial relations and the garment industry. This draft included several ideas, the most important of which was the request that the union give up its demand for a closed or union shop. Brandeis told those involved that they were witnessing an important moment in history, the birth of a new system of industrial relations. Brandeis's proposed settlement called for a novel approach: an industry-wide agreement, a limited form of industrial democracy, a "preferential shop," health and safety regulations, a grievance mechanism, and an industry-standard wage policy.[1]

The Protocol established "a kind of industrial self-government" that Brandeis had been trying to establish for some time. Brandeis, a student of British Fabian socialists, was trying to find stability, efficiency, and hope in the heart of the most chaotic and brutal industry in the western world. As much as industry and technology seemed to advance, the garment industry in the United States and the UK stayed stuck in the nineteenth century.[2]

The protocols were the first effort to bring a chaotic and primitive industrial workplace into this modern era. There were three parts to the protocol. First were the normal labor contract issues of hours, wages, and paid holidays. In this regard, the protocol was better than most contracts of the day, clearly better than garment workers ever saw. The second part involved features unique to the garment industry: abolition of charges for electricity and supplies; the establishment of shop committees to establish a just piece rate; and, most revolutionary, a Joint Board of Sanitary Control—a committee made up of representatives of both the union and the association who would oversee working conditions. The third and most important part of the protocol was the implementation of Brandeis's conceptions of efficiency and industrial democracy.

The centerpiece of Brandeis's program for industrial democracy was the preferential shop, the ban on all strikes and lockouts, and the establishment of grievance and arbitration mechanisms. Crucial was the last clause and agreement on the preferential shop, which in effect recognized the union shop indirectly. As garment industry expert Benjamin Stolberg states, "The clause was as effective, for the union's purpose, as if the full closed shop had been adopted" because the union could always supply workers.

A central aspect of the protocol was the attempt to rationalize, standardize, and Taylorize the garment industry. All work stoppages would be eliminated. Work would continue as grievances were arbitrated. As a tripartite agreement between labor, management, and the public, the protocol steered the industry into the modernity of an industrial consumer society. In exchange for giving union leadership some authority, the protocol mandated industrial self-management. In essence, the association expected the International Ladies' Garment Workers' Union (ILGWU) to police its own members for the benefit of the industry. The union was to supply "efficient" workers and ensure continuous and rational production. If the union could do this effectively, workers would benefit. By controlling its own members, the union brought to industry what the manufacturers could not: stability and rationality.

One measure for the protocol's success could be seen in both the unionization that followed and its quick spread throughout the industry in American manufacturing centers such as New York City, Rochester, Philadelphia, and Chicago. Bringing industrial hygienists, reformers, shop owners, and workers together, the protocol contributed to the larger discourse on the role of work in the newly forming consumer society and on the rights of management and workers in an industrial society. The ILGWU, in partnership with the manufacturing association, hit on a novel way to organize the industry and thereby spread the protocol to all sectors of the garment industry: an orchestrated general strike. Both sides embarked upon a coordinated effort to quickly and painlessly rationalize the industry. First, the association provided the union with a list of all member shops. The union, in turn, pledged to pressure all nonmember shops to join the association. Lastly, both agreed to a general strike as a device through which to organize both workers and employers in the industry. The association stated that "unless the union ... as a result of the 'general strike' enrol[ed] in its membership the bulk of the workers in the industry" the agreement would certainly fail. Thus, these strikes were from their inception a tool to organize not just the workforce, but the entire American garment industry. By the early 1920s, the protocolist system was firmly established in the northeast sector of the economy.

To many industrialists and self-identified reformers on both sides of the Atlantic the protocol was a magic bullet, an inoculation against class disruption and an "uncivilized" economy.[3] Blind to the realities of the day-to-day functioning of protocolism, the public soon moved on to other concerns. While on the surface, the protocol seemed to be functioning as planned, problems were smouldering beneath. The protocol mechanisms were bureaucracy embodied. The Arbitration Board sped up the centralizing mission of the new labor system that the protocol had unleashed. It took almost all authority from workers and the shop floor and placed it in centralized and regulated bodies dominated by industrial experts. This led to an increase in wildcat strikes, which became a predominate theme in the industry.[4] As important to workers, the increased costs of manufacturing, the increase in worker volatility and wildcat strikes, and the improved transportation system led to an increase in "runaway shops," factories that left the unionized regions for nonunion places such as New Jersey and Pennsylvania.[5]

FIGURE 3.1 Garment workers in the N.M. dress shop in New York, 1943. Marjory Collins. Photo: Courtesy Library of Congress.

FIGURE 3.2 Bangladeshi garment workers, during a protest march in Dhaka on July 28, 2010. AFP Photo/Munir uz Zaman. Courtesy Getty Images.

By the 1930s, the flight of capital and dispersion of the industry led the unions and their liberal allies interested in fighting against the scourge of the sweatshop to focus on federal law rather than unionization. The fight for the Fair Labor Standards Act (FLSA) of 1938 came out of such a political push.[6]

The FLSA, while an important piece of legislation, did not solve the industry's problems. By the 1940s, runaway shops were the major issue for the union and the industry. These shops did not operate under the same safety, health, and labor laws as the shops under the protocol system. Therefore, they could undercut costs and continue to drive down the industry. Sidney Hillman, president of the Amalgamated Clothing Workers' Union, and presidential advisor, blamed the flight on birth of the so-called right to work states. The runaway shop was the critical development in the decline of the industry. Shops moved from New York City to New Jersey, then Pennsylvania, South Carolina, and by the 1980s the Caribbean, Latin America, and then Asia.[7]

As manufacturing moved offshore, so did the sweatshops. As the physical sites of work became less tangibly visible to those in the older industrial cities, college students and concerned consumers tried to bring attention to the abuses in the industry. But, the abundance of cheap products made at far remove increasingly blinded consumers—many themselves children and grandchildren of garment workers—of the connections between work, production, and consumption.[8]

WORKING THE DOCKS: LABOR, MANAGEMENT, AND THE NEW WATERFRONT

To many, the depiction of longshoring, the waterfront or dockworkers in Elia Kazan's classic 1954 film starring Marlon Brando and Eva Marie Saint, *On the Waterfront*, conjures images of either a corrupt, quaint lost world of manly men or modern overpaid workers. Kazan's film depicted the world of the New York City docks in the 1940s and 1950s as a rough and tumble, often violent and thoroughly corrupt site. Little was heard of dockyard workers in succeeding decades though, until a 2003 lockout/strike waged by West Coast dockers. The entrenched Hollywood version of these workers, however, cast them as unchanged from the 1950s: indeed, averaging over $100,000 per year (excluding benefits) at the time, their strike made them easily vulnerable, especially in tough economic times, to charges that they were greedy, selfish complainers. Yet the docks of 2003 were nothing like the piers of the past and told a vastly different story.

The number of dockers in the New York Metropolitan area decreased from a high of 35,000 in 1954 to 2,700 by 2000. Yet the tonnage that moved through the Port of New York increased from 13.2 million tons of cargo to 44.9 million in the same time. That is, the workforce decreased by 95 percent while productivity per docker increased by a whopping 3,118 percent. The numbers were similar on the West Coast as well as in major ports in the industrial world. For instance, in 1950, the 100,000 dockers on the West Coast were reduced to only 10,500 in 2015. And the West Coast dockers were even more efficient than their East Coast brethren. In 1969, it took five hundred men three months to unload a 900-foot-long cargo in the second decade of the twenty-first century, it took ten men twenty-four hours. This transformation made dockers some of the most efficient workers in the United States.[9]

While the number of dockers decreased, the average salary for dockers increased. The *Washington Post* estimated in 2002 that the average salary of a full-time West Coast docker was between $105,278 and $167,122, while the average part-timer's salary was $70,000. The average benefit package for dockers averaged $45,000 per year. Longshoremen had achieved what most blue-collar workers could only dream of: they had preserved a middle-class wage (and then some, some might say). They have also transformed docking from an unskilled craft, to a technological skill as most twenty-first-century dockers manipulated technology rather than toted bales or pulleys. In the process, they had seemingly conquered globalism. To American unions, globalization is a nefarious force that has wiped out the jobs of millions of well-paid blue-collar workers. But, according to the *New York Times*, "the members of one union [this applies to unions of both coasts] have played the global-trading system as well as any international investor … globalism has been nothing but a blessing."[10]

Of course, a key piece to this story was that the number of such men had precipitously declined, and the occupation had become a shell of its former size and one stripped of its robust, manly image. But it is a story with two important parts: one, how technology—in this case, how the containerization of shipping—displaced longshoremen; and two, how in the wake of containerization, the workers nonetheless managed to win handsome annual salaries with little or no work. How did this happen? How did unskilled workers negotiate such salaries and benefits? Why would management accept six-figure salaries for its workers? Why would they pay the salaries of workers idled by technological advance?

The pivotal moment for the industry, whether on the east or west coasts of the United States or in Liverpool, Le Havre, or wherever ships docked, came in the late 1960s and early 1970s with the advent of containerization. Prior to the 1960s, almost all the goods that were shipped (or transported) were loaded and unloaded at the pier by hand. This was the era of "break-bulk shipping." Under this system, truckers or trains delivered goods. The goods were unloaded by dockers and "checked" by another group of workers called checkers. Once checked, dockers would then load the goods on pallets to be "stuffed" into the hold of a waiting ship. It was hard, backbreaking work with constant risk of physical injury. Upon arrival, dockers would "unpack" the ship, checkers would check and it would be loaded onto waiting trucks or trains. This system was terribly labor-intensive and highly inefficient. It could take weeks, or even months, to unload a fully loaded ship. It was so unwieldy that it was almost impossible to control or impose order. Shippers accepted theft (pilfering) as a standard business expense; workers traditionally treated it as a perk of the job in partial recompense for the brutish work. In any case, dockers' unions, because they controlled the strategic economic location of the piers, could close down the entire industry costing shippers millions per day. Therefore, shippers and their associations often "bought" labor peace through labor contracts rather than risk a lengthy strike. Moreover, unions learned that a "quickie" strike could get what they wanted. The labor situation on the docks was volatile and explosive; it was absolutely unpredictable—something unacceptable for business. Periods of peace were followed by coast-wide strikes that crippled the industry.

The shippers' answer, containerization and intermodalism, dramatically transformed the industry in the 1960s. Containerization was an example of a "simple" technology, but one with major ramifications. It was simple because it involved placing goods in a box. Rather than load and unload goods by hand, goods would be loaded into containers and the containers would be loaded and unloaded by cranes. Because the containers could go between ship, truck, and rail, efficiency was found in the removal of redundant labor (loading and unloading). Containers allowed fewer workers to (un)load more goods cheaper and more quickly. Because the transition from ship to truck or train was seamless, it launched a new more unified (inter)national transportation system: intermodalism.

At first, the adoption of containerization was slow. What went into containers tended to be high-cost items (most likely to be stolen) or goods that could be easily damaged. Most everything else either went "break-bulk" or on specialty ships (for steel, grain,

FIGURE 3.3 Container cargo freight ship working crane bridge. Courtesy Getty Images.

etc.). The main reason for the slow adoption of this new technology was that US federal maritime subsidies defrayed the high labor costs. Indeed, both Sea-Land and Matson—the two companies who took the lead in containerization—did not receive federal subsidies of this nature because, as international firms, they steered clear of the strings attached to such subsidies. In short, there was little incentive at first to make the costly shift towards containerization. The first company to introduce "full" containerization was Pan-Atlantic Steamship Corporation (later renamed Sea-Land Services). In April 1956, it introduced complete container service from New York to Puerto Rico. Yet, by 1966, only 3 percent of the general cargo going through the Port of New York was on containers. In 1966, however, Sea-Land signed deals with three hundred European trucking companies and thereby became a major challenger to the European market. Containerization had arrived. By 1970, 12 percent of New York's cargo was on containers and the use was growing quickly. By the mid-1990s, 2.3 million containers would be handled in the Port of New York alone. And it is crucial to remember that once a ship had containers loaded in one port, the receiving port had to adapt the same technology to unload. What began in New York quickly became a transformation of global shipping and dockyard workplaces and workplace culture.

Containerization transformed the work as well as the industry in important ways. Because shipping costs were cheaper than freight or trucking costs, ships in the "break-bulk" era paid many port calls, inter-shipping goods from port to port. But containerization transformed all that. It reduced the cost not only of shipping, but of trucking and transportation in general. Containerization meant that ships could now visit one main port and truck goods elsewhere. Why now go to Boston, Philadelphia, and New York when you could go to New York and truck the goods elsewhere. Containerization also reduced the time a ship spent in port from 60 percent of its time to under 10 percent. Oceangoing ships only made money when they were oceangoing, so the less time they spent at port, the more money they made. This put ports into competition with each other, as ports were bypassed, losing both business and work.

How would workers and their unions respond to these changing conditions that threatened their very existence? How would they protect their jobs? Here the story of New York in the 1950s and 1960s is illustrative of a larger pattern in the industry, both in the United States and in Europe. The East Coast union, the International Longshoremen's Association (ILA), developed a comprehensive strategy to protect both their livelihood, the jobs that remained, and the ports in which they worked. This strategy involved developing a coast-wide "Master Contract," additional new work rules, and finally, a Guaranteed Annual Income (GAI) system to "take care of" workers displaced by technology. According to the terms of the GAI, no new workers were to be hired, but all existing workers were guaranteed an annual salary; they had to show up for the daily shape-up where a few would be called to assist on the docks with the container technology. For most, though, the manly business of loading was replaced by card playing to while away the days. In short, rather than resist the new technological changes, the union embraced them, and in the embraces steered them in a direction that was mutually beneficial to both labor and management. They traded the acceptance of new ways of working more efficiently for job security/protection for their members. Starting in the late 1960s the dockers' unions negotiated further cradle-to-grave benefits as part of the GAI. In other words, workers who lost their jobs because of technology (and productivity, since both were intertwined) were paid an annual salary with comprehensive benefits anyway.[11]

Though the policy at face value flew in the face of free-market thinking, it had a logic that appealed to both shippers and dockers. By accepting automation, new technology, and work-rule changes, dockers took salary, benefits, and security in trade. The increased productivity (see above) more than paid for the increases in labor costs. According to one official of the Pacific Maritime Association, the trade association of the West Coast shippers, the labor costs which averaged slightly more than 1 percent of the average cargo value of the ship represented "negligible" costs. And labor was satisfied, too: as Steve Stallone, a West Coast docker union spokesperson, said, "The question shouldn't be, 'Why does this group of blue-collar workers earn so much?' The question should be, 'Why shouldn't blue-collar workers be able to share in the benefits of increased productivity? Why shouldn't blue-collar workers be able to earn a lot of money too?'" In short, the unions believed its workers deserved to share in the profits earned through their increased efficiency. Dockers had ensured the continued profitability of their industry through productivity gains that had ensured a healthy industry and protected their jobs. They now claimed their just reward.[12]

The GAI met the needs of many out-of-work dockyard workers but those who did get called in for daily shape-up still had concerns. So, the New York ILA further responded to containerization with threefold concerns. First, they wanted to protect their jobs on their docks. Second, to protect their jobs from running to other (cheaper) ports, they needed an East Coast industry-wide contract. And, lastly, containerization put into question what was longshoremen's labor as more "stuffing" and "unpacking" of containers was done in-land. The union needed to find a way to address this and define as many jobs as theirs as possible.

In 1958, the ILA boycotted "shipper-stuffed containers." Shipper-stuffed containers were containers that were "stuffed," or loaded, in-land in violation of the contract—companies not in business in 1956 and were only shipper-stuffing containers to avoid using ILA members. In 1959, the union demanded the right to stuff and load all containers at the pier with union labor. Management said it had the right to do what it wanted to take advantage of the new technologies. Eventually, President Eisenhower invoked a ninety-day cooling-off period under the Taft-Hartley Act of 1947.

In the 1959 contract, the New York's ILA exchanged the use of any and all containers for sole authority to load and unload all containers. The New York Shipping Association (NYSA) agreed to pay the ILA a royalty for containers stripped and stuffed away from the pier and ILA labor. This was no cut-and-dried matter, however. Many containers came to the pier fully loaded at the point of manufacture and ready for loading. But, what about partial loads? Under this rule, businesses that wanted to ship a partial load of goods (not a full container) had to ship the goods to the pier and have ILA members load it. If they had the stuffing done off-site, they risked having the container unloaded and restuffed by ILA members at a considerable cost. In an effort to escape this clause, many businesses simply moved their operations away from the docks—what the ILA did not know they could not enforce.

The issue came to a head in 1968 and 1969 as the ILA forced the NYSA to accept a "Rules on Containers," or "50-Mile Rule," as part of the 1969 contract. The contract gave the ILA jurisdiction to stuff and load any and all "consolidated Full Containers," or partial containers, coming from within a fifty-mile radius of an ILA Contract Port. It also allowed the union to strip and reload containers stuffed by companies beyond the fifty-mile radius who moved there solely to avoid the contract. This meant that the ILA investigated containers, slowed trucks, and could slow loading of suspect goods. If a container was found in violation of the rule, the ILA could unpack it, restuff it and fine the company $1,000. All these provisions and tactics—shows of might by the workers—effectively slowed down the delivery and raised the transportation cost considerably.

The 1968 to 1969 strike was remarkable because it lasted one hundred days and crippled the industry, costing hundreds of millions of dollars. The staggering cost led to the NYSA to give into the ILA's new rules. The New York locals had in effect forced almost all North Atlantic ports to accept the new rules in an effort to protect their local jobs—those of a much-diminished workforce. The NYSA also had a vested interest as well. It wanted to protect their own businesses, which were threatened by inland consolidators and warehousers. In short, the new union rules were good for both labor and business.

FIGURE 3.4 The Levee, New Orleans, Louisianna, c. 1900. Courtesy Library of Congress.

But these rules had consequences. To receive the GAI workers had to continually seek gainful employment, which meant going to the hiring hall looking for work when everyone one knew there was little or no work. This had two major impacts. First, it challenged notions of manliness. Longshoremen had defined masculine physicality, like Marlon Brando in *On the Waterfront*. But cranes, lifts, and eventually GPS removed the need for pure strength. While the job's technological skills increased, its identification with strength and toughness declined, and the shift threw longshoremen's identity into turmoil. Also, the GAI led to a generational cleavage in the workplace. Older workers protected their livelihoods at the expense of younger workers, who had fewer protections and whose benefits were not as strong. These older workers, who gathered at the hiring halls, soon had little connection or contact with the younger workers, which weakened the union.

CONTINGENT, TRANSIENT, AND AT RISK: MODERN WORKERS IN A GIG ECONOMY

By the end of the twentieth century, garment production had increasingly moved to Southeast Asia and Central America and was increasingly a less visible part of the workplace of industrial metropoles. In hiding products and displacing labor, shipping containers performed another kind of illusion. A new form of labor, however, has become a major site of the late-twentieth- and early-twenty-first-century workplace: the rise of the freelancer. In what was one of the most fundamental economic shifts of the past fifty years, the nine-to-five, forty-hour-week job with benefits and some security fast gave way to the many seemingly new technologies such as the typewriter, the compact disc, and VHS tape.[13]

By 2015, more than 30 percent of all Americans work contingently as free agents, contractors, day laborers, consultants, or are self-employed. These workers do not

FIGURE 3.5 Young man doing a freelance job from his home office in Berlin, Germany. By lechatnoir. Courtesy Getty Images.

have long careers with companies that provide employer-based benefits, such as health insurance, sick time, retirement plans, and paid time off. Nor are they unionized or protected by most state and federal labor laws. In the global economy with transnational corporations that rely on outsourcing and foreign back offices, this phenomenon is also worldwide. Communication technologies also make it possible for people to telecommute, to work from home, tethered by a computer and telephone to customers, colleagues, and managers, who can interact and, through computer technology, supervise and oversee their work. Finally, the home as workplace offers new freedoms and constraints on workers: they can more easily organize their time to meet personal needs, but their isolation can be lonely and limits collective responses to problems.

A 2016 cover story in *Bloomberg BusinessWeek* entitled "The Disposable Worker" describes the future of work as it appeared to its editors: businesses were "making the era of the temp more than temporary," as firms were outsourcing many more functions to consultants and freelancers, who had no legal standing or stability. For Fortune 500 companies, so called permatemps, freelancers, and consultants were often the first choice for getting work done. While good for business, because they limit risk, the new freelance army faced mighty hurdles. They lived assignment to assignment, "gigging." They have no security and like one freelancer with whom I spoke stated, their health plan is "Let's hope I don't get sick."[14]

Welcome to the gig economy, the world in which more and more Americans work on a contingent basis as a permanent way of life, where nine-to-five jobs were increasingly a thing of the past for many. For nearly a generation, this was something that affected only factory or service workers. But, in the twenty-first century the so-called middle class had come to resemble the working class in terms of risk and economic burdens they carried. One could say, in all honesty, we are all workers now.[15]

HOW DID WE GET HERE?

In 1956, William Whyte's *The Organization Man* described a major shift in the way the modern world works and thinks about work, America was becoming a nation of white-collar workers leaving behind its blue-collar roots. Whyte, a sociologist whose book catapulted to the bestseller list, captured the angst and compromises that accompanied the mid-twentieth-century world of the white-collar workers. Most had been raised with a blue-collar ethos rooted in the Great Depression, and many still clung to what Whyte called an antiquated attitude toward work that would get them nowhere. Whyte argued that the Protestant work ethic, which was the predominate ethos of the previous one hundred-plus years, was dead by the 1950s. He identified a new social compact that had recently developed but was previously not, he said, defined: "By social ethic I mean that contemporary body of thought which makes morally legitimate the pressures of society against the individuals. Its major propositions are three: a belief in the group as the source of creativity; a belief in 'belongingness' as the ultimate need of the individual; and a belief in the application of science to achieve the belongingness."[16]

Most Americans seemed content in trading some individuality for increasing economic security—especially following almost a generation of depression and war. While Whyte worried that we as a society gave up too much in our new corporation-based culture, sacrificing our sense of being individuals, the system he named became the socially accepted norm. Yet, for all his concern, what was centrally important to Whyte was his naming the system. In naming it, Whyte facilitated a comprehensive public discussion of this fundamental shift. The name he gave it, "the organization man," entered our lexicon and became shorthand for that era's professional, middle-class worker (and for the mindless office work they did). Whyte's thesis also provided the basis for the description of this work culture. It remained so pervasive that many reviewers of the TV series *Mad Men* used the phrase to describe the office culture depicted in the show.

The rise of the freelancer and the home as workplace for the unattached employee or self-employed marked a yet-unnamed later transformation in the way modern men and women both worked and thought about work at the end of the century. For the new workplace engaged a replacement social ethic. Unlike the shift in the 1950s, which was traditionally depicted (albeit erroneously) as solely a male thing, women were a major part of the micropreneurial-class story of the freelancer sector.[17] Micropreneurs processed an entrepreneurial spirit, but on the micro-scale, where what was being sold was their personal skills. This sense that *they, their skills,* were the business made the work culture very difference: they less saw themselves as exploited workers than as entrepreneurs needing to hustle. And not surprising, perhaps, a well-established industry of seminar and workshop leaders, authors, and other gurus emerged around freelancers claiming to have the magic bullet for their success.

But in the micropreneurial age, security was fleeting. Work was based on assumed risk, flexibility, and a perpetual hustle. This led many of them to internalize their economic insecurity. Rather than blame an economic system as structured against them, many blamed themselves. If only they worked harder, faster, smarter they would have more security. Moreover, these new workers were less inclined to be loyal to any firm or business and did not trust institutions or large organizations, or leaders. They valued independence and creativity as much (or perhaps more than) financial success (maybe because many did not have it); they blended work and life rather than balanced them; and they engaged in a perpetual hustle from gig to gig. But this mind-set, in addition to the structural aspect of the isolated workplace, inhibited their collective organizing, though loose communities of freelancers nonetheless did come together around needs for mutual support.

Management gurus such as Tom Peters champion work embodied by the twenty-first-century freelancer as a heady cocktail of flexibility, risk, and smarts. What was good for business, however, did not always turn out to be good for the new economy's workers. The business press, led by *Fast Company, BusinessWeek, Fortune, Harvard Business Review, Inc.*, the *Wall Street Journal*, and others, heralded this shift toward flexibility as nothing less than the embodiment of the American entrepreneurial spirit. Yet social analysts such as Robert Reich and Barbara Ehrenreich told another story, declaring this a signal of American decline.[18] And while the decline was muted in northern European countries with strong benefit programs and welfare systems, the rise of the privatized workplace came at a price for worker collectivity everywhere. Moreover, flexibility was a two-way street: for instance, a worker could adjust his or her schedule to meet family needs, but a boss could also call upon them at any time—24/7.[19]

The various sites of the freelancer's workplaces—whether at home or in a local café at a computer, highlights the place of the public sphere is freelance work.[20] The public debate in the 1950s and 1960s over the role malls played (public commons or private retail property) in American society, ironically the era of the organization man transformation, seriously engaged with the complicated definition of public/private space. That debate looks simple in comparison to the post nine-to-five world. Many workers in the twenty-first century came to think of commercial spaces, such as cafés and bookstores, the same way people used to think about the town square: as public commons. Freelancers working in such spaces expected not only free and uninhibited access, but also certain amenities, such as clean restrooms, air-conditioning, and Wi-Fi. The army of laptop-tapping, latte-sippers working in the corner café was not a quaint blip of recently unemployed job-seekers or college graduates, but instead became a permanent feature of the new American workforce. The closure of a neighborhood café, changes in library hours, or charges for Wi-Fi had an economic impact at least as momentous as that of coffee sales. Such changes could displace a growing contingent workforce. Hence, Starbucks in 2015 returned to free Wi-Fi, de facto recognizing the important role the space plays in the economy as a new workspace. In outfitting libraries with Wi-Fi, local governments also came to realize the importance of this mobile workforce.

The shift from nine-to-five jobs to a gig economy brought with it a new work ethic that valued multitasking, embedded communities of workers, the blending of leisure and work activity, and the creativity, independence as well as money as comeasures of success. On one level the shift involved a return to a craft sensibility, a world of "makers" and technologists-inventors. In flexible scheduling, the work also replicated the time discipline of the preindustrial world. To older workers, they might seem lazy because they do not keep traditional hours. Yet they constantly worked, as defined blocks of time were meaningless for them. They might work all night to free time for personal needs during the morning. This squeezing in, mixing or blending completely blurred the lines between the social world and work. Most accept this quickened pace because they got some enjoyment out of work by finding ways to make a living doing things they were passionate about. The freelancers were, thus, combinations of nineteenth-century craftsman, outworkers, and high-tech gurus, living and working in a transitional zone between two coherent systems of work or economic regimes.

CULTURE MATTERS

But fundamentally, while cast as micropreneurs, white-collar freelancers were workers, albeit hidden for the most part in workplaces that did not look much like the factories and workshops of lore. To be sure, much in their personal life—from their work and community culture to their education, race/ethnicity, community, status, and above all economic and cultural expectations—separated them from their contemporaries engaged in the largely suffering if not failing blue-collar sector. But in the new economy, a collar did not signify class the way it once did. The new divide was between the salaried and the freelancer rather than blue- and white-collar, or between creative and noncreative classes or groups of freelancers. And it was the freelancers as a group who increasingly came to shape the way modern men and women in twenty-first-century industrial societies came to view work and therefore class relationships. In short, how freelancers saw themselves signalled much about modern industrial culture as well as where it was heading in the new millennium.

LISTENING TO FREELANCERS

Two interviews with freelancers illustrate the constraints and freedom under which they work and highlight the culture that animates their workplace. The first was James, a 27-year-old photographer from Brooklyn. A graduate of Bard College, James was a tall, serious young man, who had dreamt all his life of being an artist. When interviewed in 2016 about his work-life it was hard for him to sum it all up without writing it down on paper. He was doing what he loved; he was creative; and he did not have to have a corporate job or wait tables to support his passion. He worked as an assistant to a relatively famous photographer for an hourly wage one or two days per week. He also worked in an art gallery a day a week. And, he "took independent work" on the side, as he told me, shooting PR photos for bands and B-list celebrities. In addition, he worked as a set photographer for film and television production companies in New York City. During the interview, he counted the number of hours he worked in a typical week as hovering slightly over sixty on "a good week." Sometimes he had nothing, and he meant nothing—no work whatsoever. Last year his income was under $40,000. He said he lived dorm-style, like so many other young freelancers, with three roommates in an apartment in Williamsburg, Brooklyn. He had no health insurance, retirement benefits, or savings, but he hoped to "get some soon." Yet he seemed happy and successful, and he said he felt lucky. He was pursuing his passion and making a living at it. Asked if he felt exploited, he looked at me with a puzzled face as if he had never heard the word. But asked if he could imagine a time when he had security and wouldn't have to work so many hours, he spoke instead of mobility: he believed that if he could hone his skill and improve his portfolio, he would advance. He took personal responsibility for his economic position and did not speak of his work as a grind; he did not speak of limited opportunity; in his view, any inability to advance would be a personal failure, his fault, not glass ceilings in the social system.

A second interview with Sara Horowitz,[21] the indefatigable founder of the Freelancers Union (FU), told a somewhat different story. Horowitz, who had a picture of Sidney Hillman, founder of the Amalgamated Clothing Workers' Union, in her office, specifically used the word union to name her organization. When I asked why she choose the name union for her organization she replied it was because that was the name that worked best in focus groups. The FU may not be a union in any traditional sense, but Horowitz felt she knows it as one and knows what she wants it to be. As of 2016, the FU had over 140,000 members and dedicated itself to providing health insurance, retirement plans, and political advocacy. Their promotional material states:

> Independent workers make up 30 per cent of the nation's workforce. We are freelancers, consultants, independent contractors, temps, part-timers, contingent employees, and the self-employed. Despite our contribution to America's economy, we're often left out of the social safety net. Most freelancers cannot access affordable insurance, are taxed more than traditional employees, and have limited access to protections such as unemployment insurance, retirement plans, and unpaid wage claims.[22]

Horowitz sees a main part of her mission as educational outreach, meeting her members where they live and work, and carrying them forward as crucial to the work of FU. Horowitz's own grandfather was a garment worker union leader and in this educational focus she sees herself drawing upon his inspiration. Her hope is that once in the FU new economy workers will come to the various educational outreach workshops. And her work has had some early success. Because of its size and vision, FU become a political player in New York City, where it is headquartered in a chic Dumbo loft, with a Political Action Committee, get out the vote efforts, and intensive lobbying efforts. In the 2010s it helped change city and state tax codes to be more favorable towards freelancers. But can it truly organize these workers, and build a true union out of them?

As suggested above, freelancers' uniquely new workplace conditions complicate organizing. Unlike autoworkers in the 1930s, freelancers do not work in large factories that can be targeted by organizational drives at the factory gates. Rather, they are disparate collections of often unconnected individuals. Reflecting the generally privatized workplaces they inhabit, what seemed to offer a new political sensibility. Typically a movement that eschews leaders, many of the freelancers were leery of organizations and leaders. It remains to be seen if their new workplace culture inhibits collective action or if a structure emerges to speak to these their social concerns and labor conditions.

CHAPTER FOUR

Workplace Cultures

ANDREW PERCHARD

INTRODUCTION: STUDYING WORKPLACE CULTURES

In the song "Factory", released as part of the 1978 album *Darkness on the Edge of Town* album, Bruce Springsteen reflected the centrality of industrial work to many neighborhoods, towns, and cities across the United States at the time. One of Springsteen's bleakest albums, *Darkness* was released against the backdrop of the loss of around 22.3 million US jobs between 1969 and 1976, with the closure of some one hundred thousand manufacturing plants between 1963 and 1982.[1] The Freehold, New Jersey, native drew heavily on the experiences of his family and hometown, which had experienced the closure of the A. & M. Karagheusian Company's rug factory.[2] "Factory" reflected the ambiguous nature of industrial work; it underpins both economic and social survival while threatening life and limb. Springsteen's factory is also a highly gendered space, a masculine world of industrial labor. Springsteen's factory presents the industrial worker, like those in Sherry Lee Linkon and John Russo's memorable study of Youngstown, *Steeltown USA*, as both "powerful and powerless."[3] Above all, the workplace culture of the factory is situated at the heart of community and family.

Springsteen's song-writing has been filtered through the formative experiences of his working-class New Jersey youth, reflecting the fragility of the economy upon which his parents, family, and neighborhood relied. He witnessed the outflow of capital and people from the area he grew up in, the decline of the Jersey seashore, and the simmering racial tensions and the 1970 Asbury Park "riot."[4] As Springsteen has revealed, his mother, a legal secretary, was the main breadwinner while his father moved from one insecure manual job to another. So, when the mature Springsteen came to read Dale Maharidge and Michael Williamson's 1985 *Journey to Nowhere: The Saga of the New Underclass*, prompting him to pen his ballad "Youngstown", he already had an empathy with the subject matter. Springsteen's canon of work—spanning a forty-year career—is replete with references to the conflicted nature of work and to the centrality of working culture. His songs have provided the soundtrack to profound change in American society and the workplace. The youthful Springsteen captured the autoworker seeking to reassert his individuality and skill by reconstructing cars to race in the street after the daily alienation of the assembly line ("Born to Run", "Racing in the Street"). Into middle age Springsteen's songs reflected the struggles faced by many across the industrial heartlands of America confronted by plant closures and the outflow of capital and people ("Born in the USA", "My Hometown", and "Youngstown").[5] Springsteen's indignation at these closures—and the 2007 financial crisis and property foreclosures—were channelled into his furious 2012 "Death to My

Hometown", a song laying bare the havoc and ruination visited on former industrial communities across the United States, while evoking the rhetoric of the "robber barons."

For Springsteen, this malaise is key to contemporary US cultural and political struggles: "I believe there's a price being paid for not addressing the real cost of the deindustrialization and globalization that has occurred in the United States for the past 35, 40 years and how it's deeply affected people's lives and deeply hurt people to where they want someone who says they have a solution."[6] Springsteen's *oeuvre* touches on central themes within this chapter of the changing nature of work and workplace culture in the twentieth and twenty-first centuries. Though Springsteen's voice is unmistakably American, his treatment of workplace alienation, uncertainty, and industrial closures resonate across time and place. The conflicted nature of work and of industrial loss theme appear in popular culture in other nations: in Scotland, for example, from the songs of Matt McGinn to the Proclaimers and Runrig; and in France, from the music of Renaud to Franck Magloire's novel, *Ouvrière*.[7] They speak to the first of the chapter's themes, that of the changing nature of work and workplace cultures. The chapter focuses on the *zeitgeist* of the loss of industrial jobs, the erosion of workplace identities, and the "precarity" of the jobs that replaced these. Secondly, it addresses another theme in Springsteen's songs—the contested nature of the workplace and the alienation of workers. Finally, the chapter considers the cultural significance of industrial closures.

Why does deindustrialization merit so much attention in the study of twentieth- and twenty-first-century workplace culture? In 1921, around 60 percent of the US and UK workforces were occupied in manual labor, with administrative, professional, and service jobs accounting for roughly 25 percent of those employed. By the turn of the twenty-first century, this was reversed; manual labor in the UK and US economies accounted

FIGURE 4.1 "Here in Youngstown": Bruce Springsteen visiting the abandoned Jenny blast furnace, 1996. Photo: Dale Maharidge. Courtesy Dale Maharidge.

for 31 percent, with professional, public administration, and service jobs providing 69 percent, of employment. A similar pattern of transformation in employment was seen in France, Germany, and Italy.[8] In 1950, manufacturing still accounted for the largest share of employment and GDP of any single sector within the economies of North America and Western Europe. By the twenty-first century, it had been largely replaced by the service sector in all but the lowest income economies.[9] Industrial work and culture was central to many national economies and societies worldwide. Why does nostalgia for industrial culture persist when it was often dangerous and dirty work? As one former foundry worker at Harvester International's Louisville plant in Kentucky put it: "When Harvester shut down, I was devastated but yet—God I was so happy. It was just such a hell but, yet, it was my income, it was my life. Every emotion that you can feel I went through it ... I'm glad that I don't still work there, but, man, I wish I still worked there."[10]

To understand the significance of deindustrialization—initially coined to describe the Allies' postwar stripping of Germany's industrial power but popularized from the 1970s to describe closures in mature industrial economies—it needs to be located within the wider context of workplace-struggle over time.[11] What does the act of deindustrialization involve? Economists have typically explained deindustrialization in terms of the transition from an industrial to a service economy in the Northern Hemisphere, with globalization moving such jobs to the global south.[12] However, a burgeoning literature has captured the significance of the profound social and cultural legacy of deindustrialization; in Jefferson Cowie and Joseph Heathcott's memorable words, looking "beyond the body counts" of job losses.[13] As Johoda and colleagues remarked in their influential 1938 study of the Austrian textile town of Marienthal: "When we try to formulate more exactly the psychological effects of unemployment, we lose the full, poignant, emotional feeling that this word brings to people."[14] The loss of workplace culture is of profound importance to that. The full poignancy brings us on to appreciating a deeper understanding of workplace culture.

Deindustrialization was neither a new phenomenon nor localized. In the last twenty years, scholars have illustrated the damaging effects of British and Dutch colonialism on indigenous textiles manufacturing in eighteenth- and nineteenth-century India and Indonesia.[15] This process was reversed in the twentieth-century jute industry when the trade was relocated from Dundee, Scotland, to Kolkata, India.[16] Between 1922 and 1939, the New England economy lost 67 percent, 56 percent, 35 percent, and 31 percent of jobs in cotton textiles, textile machinery, boots and shoe manufacture, and woollen and worsted textiles respectively. These jobs principally went to low-wage producers in the US south.[17] Jefferson Cowie's seventy-year study of Radio Corporation of America (RCA), meanwhile, mapped RCA's capital relocation from Bloomington, Indiana, south to Memphis, Tennessee, and finally to Ciudad Juárez, Mexico. As Cowie observes, there is nothing new about capital flight in the bid to find cheaper and more compliant labor elsewhere. However, the pace of that has changed, facilitated by free-trade agreements like North Atlantic Free Trade Agreement (NAFTA), further restricting the negotiating power of workers and trade unions to lobby government to prevent such practices.[18] This is part of a longer, global history of capital flight, and the offshoring of jobs—from Argentina, through the industrial heartlands of Canada, France, Germany, the UK, and the United States, and more recently the former Soviet bloc and China. In the 1990s alone, the collapse of industry in northeastern China left an estimated thirty million workers unemployed, with the country's steel province, Hebei, expected to lose 60 percent of its steel companies by 2020.[19]

The offshoring of such jobs has been linked to another key theme in this chapter, that of control over the labor process. As anthropologist Jane Collins has put it: "spatially dispersed production regimes and casualized bonds between employers and workers erode the local conventions and practices that formerly structured and, to some extent, regulated employment."[20] Deindustrialization is part of longer-term contests over the labor process, weakening the moral bargaining power of workers.[21] Industrial jobs losses were also significant because of the scale of them. While these jobs could be dangerous, they were relatively well-paid and unionized, affording workers some benefits and protection against arbitrary victimization and industrial hazards. In Western Europe and North America, this was accompanied, especially from 1950 to 1975, by relative social security. Many of the jobs that have replaced them are nonunionized, poorly paid, and precarious. The erosion of workplace rights from the 1970s in countries like the UK and United States, as key industrial jobs were lost (and trade union membership fell), is now felt across most sectors of the economy.[22] As Barbara Garson wrote after the 2007 financial crisis: "Good jobs disappeared into bad jobs so deftly that hardly anyone has noticed the switcheroo. Soon enough the zombie jobs that replace the real ones will move among us as if they were normal."[23]

For political economist Guy Standing, the replacement of "industrial citizenship" with "precarity" has become the modern *zeitgeist*. For Standing, as for Springsteen, this is inextricably linked with globalization, which undermined the social gains extended from the workplace after the Second World War. Meanwhile historical sociologist Tim Strangleman views the endurance of "industrial citizenship," of occupational culture, as a longer running theme, drawing a line between social identities after deindustrialization to the experiences of crafts affected by the Industrial Revolution as outlined by the social historian E. P. Thompson.[24] For Strangleman, the disruption of relatively secure and protected employment with "precarity" has contributed to a "critical nostalgia" for industrial work and culture.[25] So while deindustrialization and the "precarity" of employment (and erosion of workplace culture and rights) are not the only significant themes in the twentieth- and twenty-first-century workplace, they are overriding and enduring ones.

Deindustrialization has also exercised a profound effect because of its extension of cultural norms and signifiers beyond the workplace and worker into the fabric of the life of the community and society. In 1959, as Springsteen turned ten, American sociologist C. Wright Mills observed: "Neither the life of an individual nor the history of a society can be understood without understanding both. Yet men do not usually define the troubles they endure in terms of historical change and institutional contradiction."[26] The following year, Welsh cultural theorist Raymond Williams articulated the importance of understanding "structures of feelings," "as record of our reactions, in thought and feeling, changed conditions of our common life."[27] Mills and Williams made vital contributions to our understanding of how societal change was felt and experienced. Springsteen's songs reflect an appreciation of both, capturing at a crucial time the experience of workplace and wider social change. Springsteen's songs, like those of other songwriters, also reflect a "cultural circuit" in which his upbringing then resonated with the shared experiences, and collective memory, of many who heard them, subsequently permeating into popular culture.[28] Linkon and Russo brilliantly capture Springsteen's evocation of the destructive force of capital flight and offshoring, alongside the betrayal felt by individuals and communities in Youngstown, Ohio, as they watched their workplaces dismantled for scrap, their jobs exported, and their communities unravel.[29] In some countries, that collective loss has been translated into a national narrative and influenced political change. In Scotland, where industrial culture was absorbed as part of the DNA of the nation, deindustrialization has been absorbed into the national story. This was encapsulated in the Proclaimers' 1987 song "Letter from America," combining the powerful themes of outward migration, deindustrialization, and national decline. With the contraction of such work, the lexicon of deindustrialization was understandably absorbed into national narrative. When the iconic Ravenscraig steel mill closed, in 1992, one of the country's foremost bands, Runrig, captured the narratives of laid-off steelworkers and the changing politics of the country.[30] While campaigning for a devolved Scottish parliament in the late 1990s, journalist Neal Acherson noted: "Scotland's industrial landscape also became archaeology ... These ways of working had long ago become part of Scotland's self-definition. Now a third identity-question was added to 'When was Scotland?' and 'Who are we?' It was: 'What do Scots do?'"[31] Acherson, Runrig, and the Proclaimers, were articulating the "structures of feeling" of communities and individuals affected by deindustrialization, bringing "biography and history" together, and reflecting that in the national narrative. Here, workplace culture is explored against this backdrop of change. This chapter places deindustrialization and capital relocation, the workplace specter of the twentieth and twenty-first centuries, within the longer-term context of contests over control of the workplace, seen through occupational identity and culture. This chapter demonstrates that strong occupational cultures and networks endured over time within industrial jobs and crafts. This could be equally true of certain firms, sometimes linked to specific sectors (such as aluminum production), which exercised a profound impact on culture within the workplace and community.

WORKPLACE CULTURE

Sociologists Paul Chalfont and Emily LaBeff characterize culture as "everything that is socially learned and shared by a group of people in a society."[32] In this chapter, workplace culture is considered as organic, manufactured, and contested. Occupational culture could be shaped by the nature of work as a result of the physical and locational challenges—such as in the case of mining, fishing, and in sectors like aluminum production or logging—by industrial politics, trade unions, and craft practices. Organizational norms and behaviors, as well as systems and rules, also shaped workplace culture. This was, as in the case of the examples of scientific management methods, through supervision, and time and productivity targets, including rewards, or changes in working culture, as through the Human Relations (HR) school. In other companies, it could be through industrial welfarism, or "paternalism." Large organizations have exercised a profound effect not just on those who work within them but on society at large. Organizations are not simply the repositories of wider cultural attitudes in host societies but consciously shape attitudes through the appropriations of symbols and values, and their manipulation of these.[33] Workplace culture also emerged through craft practices and trade unions. Culture in the workplace was complex and contested, affected by the type of work, location, gender, ethnicity, and race.

While Springsteen's voices are unmistakably American, a similar story was reflected elsewhere. The uncertainty that Springsteen captured in the voices of working people around him as he grew up reflected earlier sentiments that social historian Edward Palmer Thompson sought to capture in his history of the transformative effects of industrialization on working people in eighteenth- and nineteenth-century England, *The Making of the*

English Working Class. Thompson's work explored the experiences of those most affected by the Industrial Revolution from obscurity in a narrative that privileged and promoted technological progress driven by prescient entrepreneurs:

> I am seeking to rescue the poor stockinger, the Luddite cropper, the obsolete hand-loom weaver, the "utopian" artisan, and even the deluded follower of Joanna Southcott, from the enormous condescension of posterity. Their crafts and traditions may have been dying. Their hostility to the new industrialism may have been backward-looking. Their communitarian ideals may have been fantasies. Their insurrectionary conspiracies may have been foolhardy. But they lived through these times of acute social disturbance, and we did not. Their aspirations were valid in terms of their own experience: and, if they were casualties of history, they remain, condemned in their own lives, as casualties.[34]

Thompson wrote this while teaching in adult education, in the late 1950s, in areas that were experiencing the effects of industrial contraction in textiles and coal mining.[35] For the trades of the English industrial revolution and West Yorkshire workers affected by industrial change, as for Springsteen's car worker or unemployed Ohio steel workers, the themes of alienation and struggle recur within occupational culture and identity. As Strangleman has observed of industrial identity and deindustrialization over the long *durée* through his revisiting of Thompson:

> We can conceive of industrial workers seeing their livelihoods destroyed by industrial change, new technology and market forces as inhabiting a similar space to Thompson's "poor stockinger, the Luddite cropper, the obsolete hand-loom weaver, the 'utopian' artisan." Their latter-day equivalents might be the "poor redundant steelworker, the obsolete textile operative and the laid-off coalminer." Thompson was describing the experience of disembedding and the attempt to resist this process, or possibly to re-embed the newly detaching market economy in a moral order, albeit a modified one.[36]

Here, complexity in workplace relations and culture has been overlain periodically in Europe, Japan, and Latin America by the political economic contexts of authoritarian political regimes. For example, fascist Italy initially adopted a more laissez-faire approach to labor policy. This was superseded after the mid-1920s with the 1927 Labor Charter, with an emphasis on controlling all aspects of public life, the setting of standards on working conditions, accompanied by Fordist methods as part of fascist drives for a modern economy.[37] In Nazi Germany, the Deutsche Arbeitsfront (representing employers and employees) supplanted trade unions by imposing the illusion of cooperation; as Catherine Epstein observes: "In practice, however, employers always retained the upper hand."[38] With the exception of some reflections on apartheid South Africa, this chapter eschews analysis of workplace culture within authoritarian regimes.

Workplace culture did not always begin and end at the factory gates. In the case of certain occupational communities, such as mining, "anticipatory socialisation"—"the sense of the proximity to industry and the labour of others"—situated inherited craft or occupational traditions at the heart of the family.[39] In his account of a childhood in the Welsh coalfields, Einion Evans recalled: "I was conversant with the pit vocabulary since my childhood ... I knew about the underground locations and the tools, and also the names of some of the men."[40]

FIGURE 4.2 Growing up in the shadow of the winding wheel: gala day float, Loanhead, Midlothian, Scotland, 1920s. Courtesy National Mining Museum, Scotland.

For Scottish miner Tam Coulter:

> Ma maternal and paternal grandparents were mine workers. Ma mother worked on the surface … when she was a young girl. Then she went to a different job after that but she did work on the pit top … [I] left school on the Friday, started on Saturday, because ma dad worked in the pit, and the procedure then was, yir dad got you a job.[41]

For Evans, occupational culture bled into the community, it was absorbed as a child until the spatial and physical specifics of mining became intuitive. For Coulter, mining culture was blended with genealogy. Domestic socialization and parental discipline extended to the colliery, and vice versa. This initiation continued when Coulter started at the pit:

> yer dad got you a job that was helping to support the household plus the fact, if the manager couldnae hold, fire, sort you out, he told yer dad. And so the pressure came on him and ma dad said tae me, "Ye' so and so that ye' are, ah've worked so many years in this pit never had nae bother until you started."[42]

Similar sentiments were evident across the British coalfields.[43] Coal mining exhibited strong traditions and structures in the coalfields of Western Europe, and in the coal mines of Appalachia, too.[44] In mining, such socialization was embodied by spatial awareness and experience underground. Historian Joy Parr notes: "Our bodies are the instruments through which we become aware of the world beyond our skin, the archives in which we store that knowledge and the laboratories in which we retool our senses and practices to changing circumstances. Bodies, in these senses, are historically malleable and contextually specific."[45] As Scottish miner's leader Michael McGahey put it: "Well, o' course, the point

FIGURE 4.3 "Anticipatory socialization" in the coalfields: Cubs visiting Lady Victoria Colliery, Newtongrange, Midlothian, Scotland, 1970s. Courtesy National Mining Museum, Scotland.

aboot it is one must recognize the na'ure of the industry ... Because they know and recognize they're in a struggle wi' Mother Nature, and she does nae give her treasures verra kindly. And in the struggle wi' Mother Nature they're dependent on one another."[46] The physical dangers, and embodiment, of mining were embedded into occupational culture. The nature of that work, the industrial politics arising from coalfield contests over control, informed a sense of collective behavior and the "moral economy" of such communities.[47] This embodiment, and reliance on workmates, is illustrated through the remarks of Scottish mine manager, Bill Marshall: "Now to compromise safety, the guys, I was talking about, working on top of a conveyor, they werenae stupid. They knew the dangers and eliminated them with their skills. The skill of their eyes, their hands, and to watch what was going on around them ... It was just a culture, a feeling you have."[48] Marshall's testimony makes equally apparent the importance of physicality and masculinity:

> As an under-manager myself, I always tried to be straight with men. I was a hands-on guy. If there was a bad roof or something, I wasnae feart of getting mucked aboot 'cos I wouldnae ask anybody to do what I wouldnae do maesel'. That was ma' culture. So I put maesel' in harm's way a few times ... You got guys who relied on different ways of doing it—they delegated. But when it got hot, I didnae delegate, I was there. That was my way, but I'm no the kind of guy that says, "No, I want you to go and do it. You use your judgment to do what you need to do and I'll stand back."[49]

Such a strong occupational identity and culture was reflected in a distinct sense of status by miners and managers in the British coalfields.[50] Coulter evoked this powerfully, while illustrating the distinctions within mining communities:

> Once you were a producer, ah think it's maybe like something similar tae the animal kingdom, now the lion has tae get the grub first. Ah think once yi' wir a producer and handing in, contributing more tae the household, you got maybe a wee bit better treated than a younger brother or whatever, you know or a sister ... We thought we were the best in the world. We were the elite.[51]

Such testimonies reflected the gendering of the "other"; mining culture in Britain was stridently masculine, enforced after the 1842 Mines and Collieries Act, ending women and children's employment underground. While Coulter acknowledged that his mother worked at the pithead picking coal on the tables, underground was a male sphere. Similarly, retired miner Alec Mills stated: "I was a coal miner and proud of it. A man's man, a miner's man."[52] For Bill Marshall, his fellow managers who failed to demonstrate their physical claims were symbolically emasculated: "I know other under-managers, a couple, who really got money for doing nothing, nothing—they just sat back and let it happen ... And there was one of them and he was reviled by the men ... He had an office underground and the men used to go up and piss on his door."[53] Similar distinctions were visible in the testimonies of British engineering managers between those who had come up from the occupational traditions of the shop floor and those who had joined the firm directly at a managerial grade.[54]

The role of women within mining communities varied. In Britain, women were legally prohibited from underground work and worked on coal sorting tables, and in colliery canteens and offices. They were also central to the pursuit of industrial struggle.[55] France and Sweden restricted women from working underground in coal and iron mines in 1874 and 1900 respectively. In Japan, as late as 1920, there were sixty-six thousand female miners until a ban was introduced in 1933, and then again between 1939 and 1947, and in India until 1928, with a brief return between 1939 and 1947.[56] In the United States, women were employed underground in Appalachian mines, and fought prominently within both the workplace and the community for recognition.[57] In 1982, at a moment when mining was in serious decline, there were 2,500 US female coal miners.[58] US female coal miners' narratives also reflect an "anticipatory socialization" into coal mining, as well as the embodiment of the working environment. Pennsylvania miner Ethel Smith, who started working with her father underground at the age of fifteen, remembered, "My dad never said anything special to me about being a girl. He'd just say, 'Let's go children' ... My dad had worked us children at so much, at so many hard things, that it just seemed like another job to me."[59] Nevertheless, as another US female miner, Alice Crawford, recalled, mine supervisors where she worked used her workload to try and increase productivity among male miners by challenging their masculinity. These attempts at control failed, as Crawford's male colleagues respected her as a worker and refused to be drawn into attempts to undermine solidarity.[60] Above all, in these narratives of mining communities, one finds the distinction between insiders and outsiders.

The endurance of these divisions continued into the twenty-first century and could be seen in the distinction between those that worked in the industry and those that had not. In mining, this physical reliance on workmates translated into strong ties of loyalty, often expressed in military metaphors: "Ah think ... because of the nature of work and the nature of lifestyle we could at least hold our own ... because we're hardy buggers and we fought, ah dare say something like soldiers."[61] For Scottish miners Carl Martin and Rob Clelland, these social networks and loyalties, forged underground, endured throughout their lives. For Martin, "Miners are a different breed ... If I had my life over again I'd still like to be a miner 'cause as I say, you'll get companionship amongst miners."[62] Clelland reminisced: "Once ah wis in the pit ma social friendships or whatever you want tae call them just snowballed, you know. It was a big deal tae me."[63] Such loyalties masked variations and divisions too. In certain parts of the Scottish coalfields, sectarian religious differences and traditions could be evident on a daily basis.[64] In South African mines, racial segregation was embedded in colonial South Africa's mining regulations before apartheid. These regulations privileged the safety of white mine workers over their African counterparts from 1911.[65]

Similarly occupational socialization played an important role in the shipyards of the Clyde, Scotland, and Tyne, England.[66] Shipyard traditions were strongly linked to extended social networks and status. In Northern Ireland, and on the Clyde (into the 1960s), jobs in shipyards often operated a religious bar, with Catholics prevented from working in certain firms and trades.[67] In contrast, on the interwar Clyde docks, Irish Catholics and Presbyterian Highland Scots made alliances; solidarities were built out of shared experiences of land agitation movements in rural Ireland and the Highlands and Islands.[68] In European and North American steel making, "anticipatory socialization" was also evident.[69] Anthropologist Christine Walley evokes this, and the impact of deindustrialization, around Chicago's steel mills:

> Early one morning when I was fourteen years old, my mom entered my bedroom and shook me awake. "Don't worry," she said quietly, "it'll be OK. They called the ore boat back, but it'll be all right." I wondered why we should be worrying about an "oar boat" being called somewhere but drowsily accepted her reassurances and went back to sleep. In retrospect, I imagine my mother on that chilly March morning both trying to reassure me and seeking comfort to face what was ahead, even as she couldn't quite bring herself to tell me what happened. The real news was that the recall of the ore freighter from the middle of Lake Michigan meant that Wisconsin Steel, the mill in Southeast Chicago where my father worked as a shear operator, had shut down.[70]

The loss of occupational status following closures was abundantly evident among UK and US steelworkers. As encapsulated in the words of one Scottish steelworker: "How do you tell fifty-year-old steelworkers to sell tartan scarves to Americans?"[71] Like coal mining, so in steel, workplace loyalties afforded greater protection against dilution of trades while providing flashpoints with managerial prerogatives. These traditions and status were suffused with a strong sense of masculinity. In the more mixed occupational environment of Lancashire textile towns, socialization was equally evident; as Elizabeth Roberts observed, children had it "transmitted to them": "a working-class culture, a complete design for living and a set of rules to be learned about 'proper' behaviour."[72]

On the British railways, the craft traditions, strong company identities (prior to nationalization), and patrician management left their mark in distinctive occupational cultures. Here too socialization and familial networks played an important role in the career path on the railways. Similarly, specific craft traditions were highly embedded. Nationalization forged an equally strong organizational identity and culture throughout the rail network. When that was threatened, with outsiders bought in to manage, this led to clashes between different occupational cultures.[73] This mirrors clashes in the coal industry between "outsider" and "insider" managers.[74]

Strong organizational cultures can be read both as a continuance of earlier traditions but also a reflection of the failures of coercion, and of the adaptation to the realities of the fight for control over the labor process. Some employers explicitly recruited through families, using the discipline of the family to regulate the pattern of behavior of young workers. The motivations were not exclusively motivated by the wish to control, or respond to, growing labor power during periods of the twentieth century, but in some cases by a wish on the part of some employers influenced by their religious and or moral beliefs to encourage more cordial relations. These were often reinforced within a strong organizational narrative. The embedding of organizational and occupational culture within communities added to the sense of loss of these workplaces.

The ecological reach of the workplace extended into surrounding communities, whether out of necessity—such as the logging towns of the Pacific Northwest or in the copper belt of Zambia—or the initiatives of companies to embed themselves into the firmament of local society (through company housing, school boards, sporting clubs, and the metering of time by the factory whistle or horn).[75] These workplaces and occupational communities also illustrated divisions along ethnic, gender, and racial lines. Company control and ecological reach even took the form of naming company towns after corporate patriarchs, such as Arvida, Québec, named after Arthur Vining Davis, the founder of the Aluminium Company of Canada's US parent company Alcoa, or Henry Ford's "Fordlandia" in the heart of the Amazon.[76] Such was the case in the strong organizational narratives evident in the aluminum industry. The global aluminum industry provides illustrations of the ecological reach of company culture into communities and divisions, what historian Brad Cross has characterized as an "aluminium civilization."[77] In these occupational settlements companies policed their workforce and socialized their families. This was intrinsically linked to the requirement for stability in industrial relations, where a 24-hour stoppage could cause substantial damage to electro-metallurgical equipment. The reliance on proximity to hydro-electric power for smelting meant that most aluminum companies built company towns in remote areas—such as the Scottish Highlands, the Vallée de la Maurienne in the French Alps, Saguenay in Québec, and Kitimat in British Columbia. Similarly their upstream mining operations in Ghana, Guyana, and Jamaica, were often remote. Workplace paternalism and hierarchies were reflected in the sociospatial divisions of the company villages of French company Alais, Froges et Camargue (subsequently Aluminium Pechiney), and the British Aluminium Company (BACo), in the French Alps and the Scottish Highlands respectively.[78] In Arvida, Alcan smelter management was dominated by Anglo-Scots Canadians with French Canadians mostly occupying shop floor positions. In the community sociospatial divisions reflected ethnic and religious distinctions between "Anglo" Presbyterians and Francophone Roman Catholics.[79] In MacKenzie-Wismar, British Guiana (Guyana), and in Gold Coast (Ghana), Alcan and BACo respectively strictly policed racial divisions, separating Guyanese and Ghanaian bauxite miners from predominantly Anglo-Saxon white management.[80]

Differences between company cultures also led to heightened social tensions; as Sandy Walker, an engineer at the Lochaber smelter in the Scottish Highlands, recalled after BACo's merger with Alcan:

> That's when the divide came and it was a massive divide, massive. I don't blame the people who Alcan employed as managers, it's probably just what they were told to do as the ethos of managing a plant, but however, it destroyed the whole community, aspect, of being employed there ... whether that was being dictated to from Canada

I don't know, but any thoughts of ... paternalism that was all gone ... you were just literally a number then.[81]

While occupational regimes shaped workplace culture for coal, steel, and shipbuilding, workplace culture association with the firm, played a larger role in aluminum. The "structures of feeling," arising from occupational networks, were sharply exposed when it came to the closure of plants with strong identities, expressed in terms of betrayal and the breaking of a social and moral contract. As Johnson Controls employee Danny Mann observed after the closure of its Kentucky works: "There was no loyalty in corporations at all. I knew that, but you would expect a little bit of, you know, kindness or understanding. I work with my hands for a living. I'm a blue-collar worker and I'm proud of being that. If it wasn't for blue collar this country couldn't be what it is."[82] A similar sense of betrayal, arising from a strong sense of workplace culture forged by company culture and narratives, was evident among employees at industrial workplaces in Europe and North America.[83]

Workers, and communities, sometimes sought to contest company control. Cultural resistance in a range of rural and urban environments may be manifested in a range of forms from sabotage to evasion, as well as in language.[84] In BACo's Highland settlements, workers and local communities both accepted and contested the company's attempts at control. Employees subverted the company's use of a language of rights and loyalty during industrial disputes, as well as over closures and environmental impact.[85]

Companies' attempts at embedding organizational workplace rules and norms reflected long-running attempts to ensure compliance and control over the labor process, as well as social engineering. This was particularly visible in the scientific management and the human relations movements from the early twentieth century, as well as in some of the underlying reasoning behind "welfare capitalism."

"COOPERATION IN INDUSTRY": CULTIVATING THE "HUMAN FACE" OF INDUSTRIAL CAPITALISM

In May 1921, John D. Rockefeller wrote to his industrial relations advisor about his new ideas for enlightening workplace relations:

> I finally adopted a title COOPERATION IN INDUSTRY. The word "Cooperation" does not suggest to my mind as it does to yours, a relationship with Profit Sharing ... I felt it a safe title to use and really a safer one than DEMOCRACY IN INDUSTRY, which to my mind would more generally be regarded as indicating control rather cooperation by Labor with Capital.[86]

Historian Howard Gitelman concluded that Rockefeller's support for the HR School was not, "as he claimed, 'a fair deal for the working man'," but rather: "His interest in employee representation can most charitably be characterized as one of industrial peace at any price, save unionization. He did not care for the workers or their welfare but only for their acquiescence."[87] In their analysis of Mayo's influence on human relations, Kyle Bruce and Chris Nyland refute the portrayal of the HR School as a benign attempt to overcome the crude control of scientific management initiatives: "The Human Relations school was in fact a right-wing and decidedly undemocratic innovation that was developed in response to the demand from organized labour that workers be ceded an active and significant part in management decision making."[88]

The HR School was a reaction to worker resistance to the imposition of scientific management methods. As measures to control time and workplace traditions in the nineteenth century had met with resistance, so in the twentieth, workers and trade unions opposed scientific management through strikes, industrial sabotage, and subterfuge.[89] As with later industrial action, female workers led these contests, such as in the Singer Strike of 1911 in Scotland or those against the Bedaux system at textile factories and Rover in the English Midlands in the 1930s.[90] Brazilian and Indian workers also led successful campaigns in the 1920s and 1930s to reject the imposition of scientific management methods.[91] Managerial attempts to change working practices—and the deskilling and anomie associated—lay at the heart of the US steel strike of 1959, and auto-plant strikes and assembly-line guerrilla warfare in the United States and UK between the 1960s and the 1980s.[92] In apartheid South Africa, companies deployed scientific management to erode control over the labor process, coupled with coercive racial laws and the surveillance of the state. Nevertheless, mining unions still mounted industrial resistance, and took a prominent role in the broader anti-apartheid movement.[93]

Like scientific management and the HR School, "modern welfare capitalism," even if "a kinder, gentler sort of paternalism" in the United States was motivated by employers' priority to confront the labor power notably in the interwar era but, as seen in Google "play pens" in the twenty-first century, continued well after that. For firms like Kodak and Sears Roebuck: "the Wagner Act, which along with labor's newfound strength, made it more difficult for employers to resort to force majeure when threatened by an organizing campaign. Coercion did not disappear, but large non-union companies had to rely on persuasion to carry more of the load."[94] In interwar Chicago, welfare capitalism gained traction over trade unionism because of ethnic divisions. However, as the Depression took hold, the experience of welfare capitalism raised expectations of social provision and informed Congress of Industrial Organizations (CIO) campaigns.[95]

As it had been for Taylor, Ford, and Rockefeller between the wars, so workplace culture, as a touchstone of productivity and control over the production process, became a major preoccupation of a postwar generation of scholars, managers, and policy-makers.[96] The growing voice of the labor movement, and the social contract arising out of the war economies of Britain, Canada, and the United States, and the postwar period in Western Europe and North America, fuelled by the boom years, saw the integration of a range of legal frameworks and mechanisms for the governance of industrial relations. As ongoing industrial disputes demonstrated—over control of the assembly line, craft demarcations, and the attempts to assert managerial prerogative—this was an uneasy peace at times. Nevertheless, changing global economic conditions after the OPEC crises and Dollar devaluation, and a shift in the political economic climate in the UK and the United States with the elections of Margaret Thatcher and Ronald Reagan in 1979 and 1980 respectively, and subsequently Brian Mulroney in Canada in 1984, saw an assault of employment rights and forcefully reasserted employer prerogatives. These attacks also coincided with sharp contractions in traditional industrial sectors, programmes of public-sector divestment and liberalization, and deregulation of financial markets.[97] In Latin America, the dominance of military dictatorships and other draconian governments by the late 1960s drove trade unionists and labor activists underground or into exile. In some cases, such as Chile, this was accompanied by aggressive liberalization of the economy.[98]

RUINATION: THE AGE OF DEINDUSTRIALIZATION

Several years after the release of Springsteen's *Darkness*, in 1981, *New York Times* journalist Iver Petersen observed as a silent vigil of former autoworkers watched from their US-made vehicles as their former workplace, Detroit's Dodge Main auto plant, was razed to the ground. Dodge Main was just one of the large car plants that lent Detroit the name of "Motor City." All the drivers witnessing the demolition had a different story to tell about their memories of working in the plant, each one intensely personal. A security guard on site, quizzed by Petersen, pointed out the significance of the event that was unfurling: "There are people who walked in and out of these gates for thirty-five years. They come by and point and say, 'I worked at that window up there', then they pick up [a] brick or a piece of stone and go away." Historian Steven High has underlined the wider significance of these events:

> These autoworkers had spent their lives working in the assembly plant and in the process had forged strong attachments to people and place. Workplace communities were remembered strongly that frigid day. The story unfolding outside the gate at Dodge Main has been repeated in towns and cities across North America, we live in a "post-industrial" age, or so we are told. Mill and factory work no longer defines North American society and it is fast losing its saliency at the regional and local levels.[99]

The response of former Dodge Main workers to the demolition of the plant reveals the acute loss of such jobs to an area already blighted by such closures. These losses fell disproportionately on Indiana, Illinois, Michigan, Ohio, and Wisconsin, with manufacturing employment dropping by 19 percent between 1979 and 1986 alone.[100] The profound economic and cultural effects of these closures are to be seen to this day in cities like Detroit, Flint, and Youngstown.[101]

These "body counts" belied the profound impacts of deindustrialization, not just on individuals and communities but on society at large, in a material and symbolic sense. As historian Christopher Lasch has put it: "the hope that political action would humanize industrial society was replaced by surviving the wreckage."[102] "Survivors," psychologist Hank Greenspan notes, were left "confronting the reality of being 'disposable en masse', with any sense of predictable history gone."[103] Nevertheless, workplace networks also provided a wellspring of resistance to closures, some of which, such as the Upper Clydeside Shipbuilders work-in of 1971, were inspirations for other plant occupations in Scotland and elsewhere, such as the predominantly female work-in at Lee Jeans Greenock plant in 1981, and the workforce at Caterpillar's in 1986.[104] Into the twenty-first century, French workers at Rayon works threatened with closure in Ardennes and at Moulinex's plants in Normandy, engaged in bold direct action; as the protagonist in *Ouvrière* remarks: "we don't die so easily."[105]

Notwithstanding the risks of industrial work, their occupational cultures provided a modicum of security albeit only the illusion of permanence. Those jobs contrasted with the precarious, frequently nonunionized, and unskilled employment that replaced them. Frequently, these jobs were subject to far greater surveillance by employers and a lack of recourse to employee rights, such as in the "panoptican" world of the call center or warehouses where employees were tracked and timed using GPS technology. As in workplaces of the past, employees in twenty-first-century call centers have contested that control.[106] Addressing the American Sociological Association conference in 2008, Arne Kalleberg identified the "global challenge" of the "precarity" of work as a "core contemporary concern within politics, the media, and among researchers,"

FIGURE 4.4 Protesting closures: steelworkers protesting the closure of Usinor Longwy Steel Works, Lorraine, France, January 30, 1979. Courtesy Getty Images.

FIGURE 4.5 Miners embrace each other after their last shift at Kellingley Colliery, England, December 18, 2015. Courtesy Getty Images.

with "uncertain and unpredictable work" contrasting "with the relative security that characterized the three decades following World War II."[107]

CONCLUSION

Bruce Springsteen's canon of work represents what Mills defined as the "sociological imagination"—"history and biography and the relations between the two."[108] Springsteen captures the "structures of feeling" arising from the replacement of relatively secure employment and rights associated with unionization (a social contract) and strong occupational cultures with "precarity." While these changes have been associated with the economies of North America and Western Europe since the 1970s, this is a much longer global history. However, the literature covering the experiences of industrial dislocation in Asia, Africa, and Latin America is scant. Deindustrialization was part of longer historical attempts to reduce labor costs, elude regulation, and assert control. Capital flight exposed as fleeting the organizational cultures often intended to gain greater managerial prerogative over the workplace. However, workers were not passive parties. They subverted corporate narratives in their fights against closures and over environmental legacy. In the parlance of the "moral economy," workers and communities sought to defend "traditional rights or customs."[109] Yet the persistence of occupational cultures demonstrates a "critical nostalgia," in the face of a sense of powerlessness and abandonment. But while that nostalgia for solidaristic action and network has belied ethnic, gender, and racial divisions, the social and cultural effects and sense of dislocation of deindustrialization endure.

CHAPTER FIVE

Work, Skill, and Technology

AMY E. SLATON

INTRODUCTION

Eighty years after it first appeared in cinemas, twenty-first-century American college students still laugh at the opening sequence of Charlie Chaplin's cutting satire of American factory labor, *Modern Times* (Figure 5.1), as Chaplin's bumbling worker tries in vain to keep up with a speeding assembly line. They snicker and grimace sympathetically as the little laborer, finally driven to madness by the pressure and routine, pirouettes his way through the factory, dives deep into the massive geared mechanisms of the operation, and is ultimately taken away by ambulance, presumably to a rest cure that will restore his equilibrium. Has Chaplin's factory worker lost his sanity, or his work ethic? Of course, in modern industrial working lives, these might easily be understood as the same thing. Chaplin understood in 1936 that the ordered working life must run in sync with the machine, and students watching the film in 2016, many of whom have already held jobs in fast-food outlets, warehouses, or accounting firms, recognize the equation. Their productive lives have been and will be shaped by, paced by, and they might say, guaranteed by the smooth functioning of machines.

The modern relationships among industrialized work, skill, and technology are captured for many observers in the idea of automation: the transference of productive tasks from human to machine. Chaplin might not be surprised to see the levers and dials that remotely controlled the speed of his assembly line now replaced with software, any more than callers in the twenty-first century are surprised when a phone call to a business or doctor's office is not only greeted but completed by an automated voice. The idea that automation has increased its presence in places of work over the last century and will continue to do so is utterly naturalized in modern developed nations where employers and economic analysts often see efficiency and desirable scales of output (of both goods and services) to be facilitated by the removal of decisions and tasks from the hands and minds of humans.[1] Others, however, question whether that removal is desirable from the vantage point of society. Many labor advocates and working people maintain, as Chaplin might, that automation has dehumanized the experience of work, contributed to wage declines, and eliminated jobs. They face counter-arguments in managerial claims that automation has greatly enlarged the global economy over the past century, eliminated many dull and dangerous jobs and allowed new levels of precision and complexity in the operations of manufacturing, service, medical, and military sectors.[2]

Those differences of opinion reproduce judgments on industrial capitalism as a whole and, for most historians, the different outlooks usefully capture the differential social positions of owners, administrators, managers, and workers that are long familiar

FIGURE 5.1 Charlie Chaplin as the American factory worker driven to madness in Chaplin's film *Modern Times*, 1936. Courtesy Getty Images.

to readers of critical literature on work under industrial capitalism.[3] Historians have associated the division of labor and segmentation of capitalist labor markets that accompanied industrialization with historical cases of social inequality, clearly mapping such organizations of work onto demarcations of class, race, gender, and geography, and we now understand, onto historical instances of violence.[4] These patterns of human privilege and suffering as summarized by historians of automation such as David Noble some time ago demonstrated how the control of production by machines in most instances arose from pervasive managerial disregard for worker well-being.[5] As industrial employers as a whole attained the ability to determine the value of labor, that disregard thoroughly shaped the material conditions of work, including but not limited to deskilling; automation was merely an elaboration of the kind of subordination already being enacted by the miner's pick and powered lathe.[6]

Devotion to mechanization among owners, managers, and investors spread from the nineteenth century through the twentieth with automation. With the rise of computing since the mid-twentieth century, even the most extensive and intricate of production decisions became detached from human operators. For example, skeleton crews came to run water-treatment plants and robo-calling telemarketing firms, while programmers developed algorithms for tasks ranging from disease diagnosis to speech writing.[7]

In each successive generation of cutting-edge managerial planning, the surviving positions consisted of relatively fewer jobs involving high-level executive functions and many more centered on severely specialized and repetitive tasks. Since its outset

FIGURE 5.2 Computer terminals at the headquarters of the Washington Suburban Sanitary Commission, Laurel, Maryland, c. 1980–2006. Photo: Carol M. Highsmith. Library of Congress. Public domain.

industrialization has increasingly cast the whole human worker, a person capable of intellectual growth and open-ended experience, as an expendable feature of the production economy, rendered so as an inhumane capitalist ideology deployed technology to its own ends.[8] In Marx's phrase, through the division of labor, "the worker becomes a fragment of himself."[9] A review of notions of optimized distributions of skill and the technologies of production involved in those distributions since 1920, provides a picture of how technology shaped the course of the following century, its variable impacts on different social groups and how, in turn, workers responded to technological change.

This chapter focuses on the social intersections that have accompanied industrial labor, broadly defined, in the United States since 1920, a location and time in which the inequitable nature of wage labor and the concomitant cultural functions of identity are especially pronounced. Moving through three periods roughly defined (the interwar decades; wartime and postwar years; and finally, the civil rights era and subsequent decades), this chapter follows Americans in their places of work as an ostensibly democratic polity carried out deep differentials in economic opportunity, from factory to building site to cargo dock to cleanroom. Many of these differentials occurred as, in historian Eileen Boris's words, "employers structured work to take advantage of sexual divisions and gender ideologies."[10] Ideas of race, age, disability, LGBTQ identities, and other ascribed categories have similarly shaped experiences of work. The US case is not interchangeable with others, but as its industry frequently led the way with twentieth-century technologies, and as these technologies increasingly functioned on a global scale, the US case offers an especially powerful example of the ways in which productivity and the opportunity to work enact social privilege and penalty.

While customary historical depictions of modernizing industry appropriately associate worker alienation with enlarged scales of production, these enactments also occurred in settings based on traditional production methods, in enterprises that were little capitalized, or in those that in other ways ran counter to the model of mass production. To reserve the term technology for initiatives of mechanized manufacturing or other capital-intensive means of production ignores the work of street vendors or truck farmers, and also waitresses or nursery school staff. Such a narrowed definition may render such people as appropriate subjects of sociological or anthropological study but outside the realm of modern technology-based work.[11] There is in fact no labor without technology, and historians have helped to problematize the very demarcation of some occupations as more or less technological than others, a demarcation that can hide significant features of the labor experience. This broadened view of the work and technology terrain allows for an understanding of how enslaved, indentured, and other bonded forms of labor, seemingly far from the world of automation or high-tech processes, also produce worker capacity (a conjoining of ideas of identity and meaningful action), today as in the past.[12] Indeed, histories of colonialism and slavery have begun to retrieve technological knowledge and practice from production operations once categorized as "unskilled." Cognitive competencies once unseen have thus become visible.[13]

The aim of all of these scholars is not to conflate intellectually rewarding labor with numbingly routine or punitive work through time, but to question which kinds of work appear to contemporary observers (or to historical audiences) to engage the intellect and which do not. From what cultural values do such appearances derive? Paid work performed in industrial operations or within the home; and tasks of child and elder care, farm work, or other forms of labor undertaken outside the wage systems of many nations, all invariably reflect the coproduction of people and technology. "Skill," the attribution that sorts workers into those more or less deserving of reward and opportunity, can be analysed as residing at the conjunction of those objectives. This chapter proceeds from that vantage point, aiming to disrupt the ease with which popular discourse on technology invokes industrial employment as a corrective to economic and social inequities, instead providing a critical, structural understanding of the world of work itself.

SOLIDIFYING STRATIFIED LABOR

The regular transfer from humans to machines of decisions such as how to position one part onto another in an industrial assembly operation, how to set the cutting edge on a machining apparatus, or how to measure ingredients in chemical- or food-processing operations transformed work throughout the first half of the twentieth century across the industrializing world. Nowhere was this more clearly the case than in the United States. The trend accelerated with the advent of widely affordable computing after 1970 and has continued at breakneck speed in the new millennium.[14] For those consigned to machine- or, increasingly, software-controlled jobs, opportunities to exercise creativity and assert one's autonomy were profoundly constrained, and the possibility of learning new or unpredictable things severely limited. Workers on "higher" levels of employment (indisputably a normative term) experienced relatively less constraint, but there was no sense that all persons could or should expect maximally creative or independent experiences in their working lives; indeed, some persons were led by employers to expect the opposite, as differing human productive capacities were felt by cultural arbiters to be real, natural, and unavoidable.[15]

Assembly line production introduced by Henry Ford before the First World War would dramatically transform work; but no less transformative was an emerging technology of scientific management that would focus on the worker. By 1920, US companies ranging from auto makers to insurance brokers had found that the systematic management techniques of Frederick Winslow Taylor promised tightly linked enhancements to productivity and profit on one hand, and ascriptions of worker identities and competencies on the other. In articulating the notion of "the right man for the job," who could be a person of high ability or low depending on the work needing to be done, Taylor worked to demonstrate the economic necessity for all "kinds" of persons, the existence of every level of capacity, if modern industry was to operate efficiently. Neither training nor pay was appropriately expended on those at the lower end of the spectrum; those of detectable but limited ability would be put to preplanned and routine physical tasks; and true managerial sensibilities and responsibilities would be instilled in those of the highest calibre.[16]

Taylor's "scientific selection" of workers for different tasks proceeded at all junctures from deeply gendered and racialized ideas about human difference. Women, Taylor believed, were more dexterous than men, and thus suited to fine manual labor; persons of German ancestry were naturally penny-pinching compared to those of other ethnic groups and thus would be responsive even to small pay rises. Each category of person was suited to a particular kind of work and supervision under a particular management structure.[17] The optimized economic functionality attributed by Taylor and his followers to divided, closely managed labor arose from a worldview in which some people were innately inferior, and thus undeserving of varied, rewarding, or autonomous labor.

Taylor would not have been nearly so popular both in the United States and in Western Europe had he not captured long-held racist, ethnocentric, sexist beliefs of many American and European industrialists and experts in other fields.[18] But in the work of Taylor and his followers, the elision of any values-driven notions of efficiency offered a particularly incisive instrument of social control and one held to be above moral reproach.[19] This approach, predicated on the idea that empirical understandings of employee inclinations might help employers achieve greater output from their workforces, found new purchase as a managerial mind-set after the First World War.[20] An expert body of social-scientific knowledge emerged to support the physiological, engineering, and process design expertise already established by Taylor, Ford, Gilbreth, and other leaders of industrial rationalization. These industrial experts pioneered America's new mobilization of social science in the name of productivity, but their appeal across the world's industrial landscape shaped the culture of work everywhere.

Western Electric's patronage of sociopsychological studies at their Hawthorne plant in Illinois offers a powerful example of this empirical address of management problems in the interwar period.[21] Under the direction of Harvard Business School professor Elton Mayo, the Hawthorn studies made explicit the problem of worker dissatisfaction with the conditions of closely managed, profit-maximizing productive labor: settings in which individual volition faced serious constraint and worker discontent, expressed in the form of union activity or general noncompliance, was increasingly evident by the early 1930s. Certainly wartime production pressures had made the risks of such worker recalcitrance newly evident to both industry and government interests in the United States. As social and behavioral sciences widely gained professional credence and applicability to industry in this period, Mayo, along with management theorists Fritz Roethlisberger and William Dickson, came to Hawthorne to analyse and seek means of influencing the motives of workers. Intricate observational studies of worker behaviors proceeded at the Hawthorne plant from 1924 to 1932, with experimental interventions—to the pacing of work, wages, and other factors—designed to help detect optimized psychological and physical working conditions.[22]

While this scientific project was unquestionably directed, in historian Loren Baritz's phrase, to "adjusting people to situations,"[23] it cannot be easily characterized as one bent on forcibly drawing workers into compliance. For one thing, Mayo's focus on employees' personalities and social networks credited workers with significant affective experiences. Whether or not one takes at face value the researchers' stated concern with employee happiness, Mayo understood expert-designed labor processes earlier conceptualized by Taylor as irresistible to workers to be a more complex prospect. But as the historian Richard Gillespie points out, the Hawthorne Experiments did represent a deployment of scientific objectivity for particular societal applications, that is, those that benefited employers in search of maximized worker output. Mayo as a rule omitted close attention to workers' voices or discounted them as the uninformed complaints of people who failed to understand the logic of the counting house and factory. He sought to offset unwanted labor conducts with strategic management techniques such as nondirective interview counselling, normative approaches cloaked in an unassailable aura of scientific inquiry. Social scientists' curiosity about the human experience of work was perhaps real and their inquiry perhaps genuinely open-ended, but the "logical and unambiguous" character of the Hawthorne "discoveries," as Gillespie makes clear, nonetheless rendered inequitable social prescriptions authoritative and brought into being ideas of human nature that were of indisputable utility to management.[24]

The Hawthorne episode reproduced social distinctions between scientific experts and their subjects consonant with those being made in industry between managers and workers. Recent critical scholarship on human resource practices and other management arenas, much of it informed by Foucault, has demonstrated the ways in which management has historically worked to win labor's compliance with such regimes.[25] This important literature cautions against seeing technology as a means only of material production; technology has historically also been deeply implicated in management and the nonmechanical "rational" technology of labor organization. This was true of the factory installation of mechanized machining equipment in 1880, set to run at one of three speeds, and of the waitress's tray in 1940, sized to carry a certain number of plates.[26] But not only simplified or divided labor was thus controlled; the following case study, centered on the entry of scientific practices into commercial construction, illustrates the sophistication with which management-deployed technologies controlled industrial work.

MODERN PRODUCTION AND HUMAN DIFFERENCE

In the first three decades of the twentieth century, the use of reinforced concrete largely displaced traditional stone and brick masonry in the construction of many civic and industrial buildings in America. Unlike those traditional building methods, concrete is based on a flow process, in several senses of the term: having been mixed in bulk, often at a central plant remote from the actual building site, it is poured into waiting forms to harden in place. Older building processes involved artisans possessing all levels of knowledge and skill, from the most junior assistants through accomplished senior crafts persons. The use of commercial concrete by contrast permitted building firms to employ a bifurcated workforce including ranks of low-paid, little-trained men under the direction of a few much more highly paid, more highly trained supervisors.

Most highly trained of all was the handful of degree-holding engineers on each project who now served to test cement and concrete as these materials were being used on the worksite. The college curricula and professional publications of these engineers held vast amounts of detailed mathematical and technical information. But in the workplace, much of their work devolved onto extremely subjective practices, including feeling samples of wet cement with their hands, or making measurements with the simplest of calibrated instruments, some the equivalent of kitchen sieves and measuring cups. These were not ad hoc practices, but procedures dictated in commercial specifications that the engineers and their clients produced collaboratively. There is little evidence that those on the worksite without college training could not have developed such facilities, such "skill." Yet in the regime of labor authorized by the engineers and the company leaders, only the hands and eyes of the engineer on the construction site could be trusted to serve as quality control. That which the laborer did, however similar to our eyes, was not inspection; the tester, not the test, assured the presence of reliable knowledge.[27]

This work, then, was shot through with the conceptions of human difference on which industrial management ideologies had been built. Engineers in America in the 1920s were rarely Catholic, predominantly native-born, and virtually none were of what the dominant culture saw as of nonwhite heritage. Laborers in the building trades, meanwhile, were rarely Protestant, often foreign-born, and in some US cities almost entirely of southern European heritage, an "ethnic" status often equated by the native-born with something

FIGURE 5.3 Pouring concrete in construction of Umatilla ordnance depot, Hermiston, Oregon, 1941. Photo: Lee Russell, Library of Congress. Public domain.

other than whiteness.[28] All of these people were male, but only the engineer could make such tests, and "Tony the Italian," as one engineering textbook personified the building trades laborer, was not to be trusted with quality control judgments. The material practices and knowledge deployed in commercial labor settings, and the identity of practitioners on all levels, were thought to be mutually confirming.

WARTIME WORK: CRISIS, CHANGE, AND STASIS

Following ideas of skill, labor, and identity in the United States through the Second World War and postwar reconversion allows us to see which of the entrenched social relations of work yielded to these labor crises and which were maintained—to test, in other words, the nation's commitments to occupational opportunity and justice. In the very broadest terms, ideas of gender, race, and ethnic difference that had long shaped occupational opportunities budged as women and minority Americans found some modest new employment opportunities during wartime, but as the historian Jennifer Light makes clear, "the meaning of 'wartime labour shortage' was circumscribed even as it came into being."[29] Postwar conditions tested these national democratic commitments still further.

The start of the Second World War found a great many Americans entirely accustomed to the idea that persons of male and female gender belonged respectively in heavy or light, and highly paid or lower paid industrial positions, and segmented across racially determined occupational opportunities. This was a system in which the dominant culture saw work through a binary idea of human genders and biological conceptions of race. Meanwhile, the intersectional implications of identity brought multiple disadvantages to, say, female workers of color.[30] Strong associations of men and women with different kinds of labor shaped virtually all American industries, across manufacturing, construction, and extractive sectors, from their inception in the nineteenth century. Historians tracking postwar resumptions of gendered employment patterns have shown that the wartime idea that women might reasonably take on physical tasks normally done by men, such as heavier assembly work or the operation of heavy machinery, or cognitive labor such as engineering and mathematics, was a temporary deviation. Federal limits on male employment eroded employer resistance to hiring women, as in the auto industry, but wage differentials persisted throughout the war and the notion of "temporary seniority" for women made it clear that essentializing notions of gender held sway.[31] In her study of the limited opportunities granted to women in wartime computing operations, Light emphasizes that, "the geography of women's work settings changed, but the new technical positions did not extend up the job ladder."[32] What is more, in the case of many educational and employment opportunities that opened to women (say, in wartime engineering and mathematics training programs in the aviation industry), government authorities and private institutions denied eligibility to black women.[33] And, not unrelatedly, as newly disabled veterans returned from war, ideas of wartime heroism did not outweigh customary ideas of altered bodies as unemployable.[34] The war may have brought a new sense of collective national labor needs but it did not displace deeply discriminatory ideas of human differences.

Following the Second World War, management and the rank and file in the auto industry shared what sociologist Ruth Milkman identified as a significant ambivalence regarding women's right to postwar jobs in the auto industry, and other sectors displayed similar resistance.[35] Analytically unifying the gender bias displayed by management and by male autoworkers, however, hides structural impediments to maximized labor

FIGURE 5.4 Women working on Second World War aircraft assembly, c. 1950s. Photo: George Marks. Courtesy Getty Images.

opportunities. With enough jobs to go around, male workers might have maintained traditional patriarchal prejudices, but would have had little immediate economic reason to insist on women's exit from industry during reconversion. Management, on the other hand, had little economic interest in maximizing the number of employees in any enterprise, especially if the economic marginality of certain communities seemed inevitable or natural. Women and minority communities found new opportunities in wartime and learned to master not just routine assembly jobs, but complex technological systems such as those used in aeronautical engineering or munitions production. The change did not, however, indicate that a comprehensive democratic reform was sweeping the nation; rather, social stratifications in America were barely coming into question even as the nation fought fascism abroad. Perhaps not surprisingly, the urgencies of war also did little to interrupt long-standing management associations of maximized efficiency and productivity with shrinking wage costs, as the case of automation and mechanization in postwar shipping operations demonstrates.

LONGSHOREMEN AND THE CHANGING PORT

The early growth of container-based shipping systems in American ports through the 1950s, 1960s, and 1970s transformed the handling of commodities ranging from cars and appliances to chemicals and foodstuffs. This was a mechanization effort that displaced some of the most powerful worker collectives in the nation: the longshoremen who had created vastly influential unions (and, significant to their opponents, often left-wing unions), and strong social communities, on both coasts. In the 1930s, the men who handled cargo as it moved between land and ships played a major economic role in the national economy. As had been the case for generations, the global transport of a huge range of industrial and agricultural products relied on the bodily strength and fortitude of American longshoremen, and especially after the 1920s, union-devised work rules closely protected the health, safety, distribution of work, and wages of these workers. In the 1950s, however, shipping industries and the producers who relied on them, empowered by anti-union postwar state policies, turned to an ambitious program of mechanization. Standardized shipping containers did not pervade American or global ports for several more decades. But the trend towards labor-saving, machine-based handling of cargo after the war's end heralded a new idea of efficiency among the shipping concerns: huge magnets now lifted loads of pig iron; bulk cargos could be moved by conveyor. The longshoremen faced a drastically altered employment landscape, even as the fully reconfigured ports and intermodal infrastructures required for container use remained some years off.[36]

Marc Levinson has described this episode well. The longshoremen reacted to the imposition of rationalizing technologies strongly as both their security and their control of working conditions came under threat, although not always with a clear and unified response. Some unions held out against the ports' modernization. The Mechanization and Modernization Agreement of 1960, a landmark decision, however, represented by contrast a moment when automation found favor among influential union leaders—a sense that new machines need not bring their benefits only to management. Levinson and Seonghee

FIGURE 5.5 Container facility at Harbour, Oakland, California, c. 1980–2006. Photo: Carol M. Highsmith, Library of Congress. Public domain.

Lim both describe that optimism as misplaced—and self-servicing as it privileged union leaders and seniority—and conclude that this agreement profoundly disempowered the longshoremen in the short and the long run by giving priority to owners' conceptions of efficiency. The port workers' traditional control of conditions at the point-of-production eroded as employers cut hours, increased mechanization and productivity expectations at the same time, and in all ways paved the way for containerization.[37] Historians have concluded that the union leaders' move exemplified a broader national shift of many unions from an emphasis on shop floor resolution of grievances to a reliance on complex bureaucratic processes of perhaps questionable value to workers. In their account of what they title the "jobless future" of automated society, the sociologists Stanley Aronowitz and William DiFazio note that computers along with just a handful of human operators almost entirely run containerized ports in the twenty-first century, but they demonstrate that containerization—and later technologies of work—came about through a long-established pattern of decisions that "ordinarily favoured management."[38]

The drastic shrinkage in employment opportunities for longshoremen since the 1980s (their numbers dropped in New York alone from fifty thousand to two thousand between the 1950s and the 1980s)[39] was, in fact, part of a much wider set of economic changes in the settings where they had once built their careers and communities. The giant cranes, staging yards, and tractors that accompanied container use made sense for developers of a dramatically changing industrial landscape who had little concern with maintaining traditional distributions of economic opportunities. The deindustrialization of New York City, for example, proceeded rapidly in the ten years following 1967, as immense facilities in New Jersey and Pennsylvania offered container-friendly options for producers and brokers of all kinds; that an entire employment sector also left the city seems to have mattered little to corporate decision-making or civic economic policies.[40]

THREE STEPS BACK

The 1980s saw a series of global trends that profoundly weakened the influence of labor and promoted widespread deskilling. The technological capacities of workers worldwide, already facing devaluation as mechanization and automation continued their twentieth-century incursion into manufacturing and shipping, now encountered what David Harvey describes as a concerted political project "to re-establish the conditions of capital accumulation and restore the power of economic elites." Any hopes of socialist alternatives to the "social compromise between capital and labour" that may have arisen on the left during the postwar period now ended.[41] At the same time, influence that unions may have held in national economic debates faded, in Kristine Mitchell's words, "in the face of increasing capital mobility, the rise of multinational corporations, and government dependence on international borrowing."[42] With the elections of Reagan and Thatcher, industries ranging from telecommunications to coal mining encountered a combination of privatization and deregulation as the interests of business found government support and workers' influence receded in both private and public arenas.

If Taylorization had moved many executive or conceptual functions required for production operations from workers to managers, this new labor regime often removed those functions from the productive workplace altogether. Draconian job cuts in this period, as Bart Cole and Christine Cooper describe, meant that skills and tacit knowledge associated with established workforces were often entirely lost to industry, with significant consequences beyond unemployment.⁴³ In the case of UK coal mining, for example, the mechanization of coal-face operations meant not only that traditionally skilled miners lost their jobs, but that the coal-face knowledge of managers, focused on nonmechanized mining, had little relevance. As British policymakers favoring a new energy mix, based on imported coal or a greater emphasis on oil, sought to argue for the innate inefficiencies of the UK coal industry, the evident obsolescence of managerial knowledge likely aided in that case.⁴⁴

Similarly, during the privatization of Britain's railway industry during the early 1990s, the turn from long-standing maintenance workforces to complex structures of subcontracted labor brought serious safety problems. New companies formed expressly for the purpose of seeking such railway maintenance or renewal contracts and often employed workers with no "intimate knowledge of signal function and track layout." As Cole and Cooper write, even managers in such new enterprises had little experience to draw on; failures and accidents mounted.⁴⁵

These regrettable consequences for workers and consumers were not incidental byproducts of the new rationale of privatization and supply-side government planning. The rise of Thatcher-Reaganism in the UK and the United States constituted not simply an economic reconfiguration but a backlash against inclusive social politics of the preceding reform era. In America, the Great Society, the War on Poverty, and other reform movements of the 1960s, which occurred in parallel with culminating moments of the long civil rights era, set the stage for this backlash. These reform movements brought increasing awareness of national economic inequities, and a focused address of gender, racial, and other forms of bias in America, which by the 1970s, resulted in legal protections in housing, education, and hiring. The changes heralded an end to some historic patterns of bigotry and economic marginalization for women and other minority communities in the United States, and activism among other historically disadvantaged groups including persons of LGBTQ identity was on the rise. Yet white ethnic workers resented developments they saw as disadvantaging them. Reagan and Thatcher, and rising tides of conservative political parties across Europe, built on these attitudes to win support for new technology-based organizations of work that favored employers.

In the post-1980 era, the rapid introduction of electronic technologies for information storage and retrieval, automated telephone communications, and the calculation labor required of virtually all business operations both controlled the low-wage, minority-dominated work found in American service industries and subjected professional-technical workers to cheap global back-office markets.⁴⁶ The broad field of industrial logistics shifted rapidly to mechanization and automation after about 1990, with product distribution, once dependent on ranks of warehouse workers and inventory specialists, now involving relatively few employees. Inexpensive computing power added still more viability for foreign back offices and mail-order consumption, further reducing employment possibilities for those of middle and lower socioeconomic status.⁴⁷ The sense of social compact that had motivated inclusive economic and social planning of the civil rights era seemed to be dissolving in a climate of probusiness neoliberalism.

Not all gains in minority rights across the United States were lost in this period, but changes in technology and labor since 1980 elaborate the glass ceilings, false promises, and other manifestations of the post-1980 climate of technological change and social stasis that limited opportunities for many women and minority workers. The combination of technological developments and increasing competition from rising markets such as China and India in this period produced conditions in the United States in which those traditionally least able to claim economic opportunities found still less occupational traction.[48] In the post-1980 era, called "post-racial" or "post-gender" by some observers, admission to an occupation or job was rarely overtly denied on the basis of an individual's ascribed identity, but limits to full occupational participation were common. This was true at the highest levels of education that might reasonably be expected to guarantee economic attainment, such as the professoriate.[49] But instances of race or gender discrimination on the lower economic rungs reveal the global structural conditions that produced unfair and precarious distributions of opportunity for great numbers of laboring people. As Aronowitz and DiFazio demonstrate, "the increased participation in an occupational sector by women and minorities is often an indicator of falling wages in that occupation."[50] The interconnected categories of lower wage work and persons of perceived lower capacity continued to characterize work in industrializing nations of Europe, the Americas, the Far East, and Australia a century after Taylor's treatise.

The persistence of this inequality rested in the continued resonance of notions of male and female aptitudes or proclivities as discreet and naturally occurring (and the belief that male and female persons are of two natural, necessarily identifiable types). These ideas continued to frame the unpaid and paid work in the twenty-first century that occurred within households, a setting in which remuneration and rights historically fell far below those expected in other places of work even on the lower rungs of the economic ladder, such as factories and farms.[51] The use of paid servants faded from middle- and upper-class American households in the early twentieth century, but the care and feeding of children, adults, and elderly family members actually grew in scope and became the purview of family members, and disproportionately, female family members.[52] When this work was performed by nonfamily members for pay, as when nursing, home care, childcare, or cleaning personnel were employed, it produced a pattern of profound disadvantage for such personnel. Such jobs involved low wages, few benefits, and little security. This was a pattern highly resonant with a long history of women's industrial labor in the home: low-paid, unregulated, and not infrequently illegal work of sewing, assembly, or clerical tasks performed in one's own household, often on a piecework basis. As Boris observes, "The history of homework regulation reveals the ways that concepts of womanhood and manhood, visions of proper home life and childhood, and the persistent ideological separation of home from work have structured state policy."[53] Her analysis highlights the extremely porous lines between public and private spheres, licit and illicit business operations, and personal and cultural identities.

A second set of demarcations between those deserving and undeserving of economic opportunities shaped by the new spatial reach of technologies played out against the backdrop of globalization since 1980, as American (and European) firms chased lower wage labor pools from hemisphere to hemisphere. The managerial ideal that employers must periodically shake loose of localized labor pools to avoid the "development of habits, wage structure, or seniority," was an old one, but as Jefferson Cowie explains in his history of the Radio Corporation of America (RCA), new comfort levels with capital migration meant that any floor to wage, safety, and security standards could be dismantled. RCA's assembly operations were predicated from the 1960s on increases in line speed and shop floor discipline; training could be minimal and line workers often felt disadvantaged by these conditions. While this regularization of production served the logic of profitable manufacturing, it reflects the imbalance of power that also makes sense of offshoring: no one worker or community is owed opportunity by the employer and more tractable, less costly workforces can always be reasonably pursued. RCA accordingly moved its television plants within the United States and to Mexico over the second half of the century. Cowie notes that the moral and political aspects of capital migration are hard to pin down: "How can one weigh a group of people who get good jobs against another group that lose them?"[54] Yet it seems somewhat selective to ignore the racialist and nationalistic logics that enable American employers and policymakers to accept the problematic wage structures and working conditions found in these "foreign" locales (conveniently labelled as such to deny any logic of worker collectivity across borders).

Cowie's history illustrates that industrial capitalism itself and the technology of work discipline have a morality that is subject to critique. The following case suggests that even capitalist expansion efforts focused on the use of technology to create new jobs have promoted unequally distributed benefits, placing different participants at different levels of potential attainment.

THE MULTIPLE FUTURES OF TECHNOLOGICAL INNOVATION

The creation of nanotechnology associates and certificate programs at the start of the millennium offers one example of attempts to fill an industrial "skills gap" that some observers see afflicting the US high-tech sector more broadly.[55] Visitors to a US Department of Labor website in 2016 that describes the qualifications, day-to-day responsibilities, and salaries for over one thousand occupations, including work in new nanotechnology operations, could browse the site by accessing a category called, "Bright Outlook." The listings in this category represent areas in which employment for Americans was predicted to grow in the coming years including "Nanotechnology Engineering Technician" and "Nanotechnology Engineering Technologists."[56] Visitors to the website would not find listings for job openings, but rather a collection of possible futures among which they might choose, such as the work of technician or technologist in nanoscale manufacturing firms. In a sector identified by the government to be thriving, the citizen who seeks a secure and remunerative career will find his or her own "bright outlook." One nanofocused educational consortium suggests several dozen communities across the country where a viewer could obtain specialized postsecondary training centered, for example, on the subatomic scale materials and processes now used in the computer, electronics, pharmaceutical, and other sectors.[57] Since around 1995, advocates offer, federal education and education research funding has supported the creation of nanocentered programming in community colleges and other sub-baccalaureate settings intended to prepare students to be nanotechnology workers.[58] One federally supported project foresaw massive job openings in the field. Their site signalled jobs in the field that would employ on the order of "nearly one million workers by 2015." "US market value of projects using nanotechnology," it noted, "is estimated to be $1 trillion or 5% of the GDP by 2020."[59] Filling the projected technology-produced job gap required the coordination of technical education and economic planning, however, about which less was said or promised.

While the Department of Labor website and some reports advocated for nanocentered educational funding,[60] there remained inconsistent evidence that those obtaining two-year technician credentials would easily find jobs in so-named nanotechnology industries within the United States; indeed, what industries would actually make up the national nanomanufacturing sector itself remained unclear.[61] While in some isolated instances community college nanotechnology programming closely matched regional labor market needs, this was by no means universally the case.[62] Crucially, this sort of "mismatch" (already a loaded term, in implying that the system if properly operated would in fact allow for matching) is not best analysed as an error, or as a misreading of employment data on the part of those who sponsor two-year nanotechnician training programs. A broader picture must be considered.

For one thing, the notion of a misreading fails to explain the complexity and extent of efforts by some educators and policymakers to expand opportunities for those Americans who they believed were unlikely to complete four-year college programs. Yet, even if such jobs for community college graduates did exist, they would not solve all the problems accompanying the transformation of work. The national education-for-work initiative that has played out in the United States since 2000, for instance, predicated on bringing some learners to readiness for technician positions through two-year degree programs, associates (however inadvertently) certain racial and minority populations with putative limited intellectual and productive potential for the world of high-tech industrial work. In 2016, persons of minority background disproportionately attended community colleges in America but in very little literature was that pattern questioned as possibly reflecting discriminatory social structures.[63] Few policymakers embraced the idea that America should maximize the number of its citizens attending four-year colleges. Contemporary movements to reduce student college debt placed the blame on misguided students who should not have aspired to four-year degrees (rather than on overpaid university administrators and extortionate institutional health care costs).[64] Educators generally remained less equivocal in their support for vocational and technical schools, which offered terminal credentials and entry to low-status and typically lower-wage manual workers.[65] Many advocates of updated technology-focused associates degree programs insisted that "opportunity" remained unquestionably their organizing principle. But, as educational historians Steven Brint and Jerome Karabel found some thirty years ago, community colleges often operated on the basis of "softly lowering student ambitions" to fit labor market conditions, and thus promises of unlimited upward mobility for graduates were not often realized.[66]

The GI Bill and other government grant systems from earlier eras notwithstanding, the hope or promise of education for high-tech jobs labored with historic class blinders to the provision of higher education in the United States. Implicit in early-twenty-first-century generalizing claims of uplift-through-learning, in which a new knowledge sector ostensibly would impart benefits to all citizens without distinction, were means of differentiating among individuals. This determination of the student or worker's likely value to the economy has been a central project of capitalist labor systems. Management scholar Barbara Townley usefully identifies this valuation as a function of knowledge systems more broadly, as described by Foucault.[67] In modern higher education, for example, the individual learner constitutes a self that is seen not to possess "an irreducible internal core of meaning," but rather to be continually formulated by, in Nicholas Rose's terminology, "the expectations targeted upon it."[68] In the case of two-year, four-year, and graduate institutions, education ascribes differing innate endowments that direct that learner to a "suitable" kind and level of occupational preparation, a project buoyed along by the culture's wider categorical trust in techno-scientific activity as a means of personal security. To be sure, inventive and energetic instructors violate this apportionment by introducing open-ended inquiry into their sub-baccalaureate teaching. The severely limited resources and tremendous workloads of community college instructors do not incentivize this kind of teaching, however, even if research show it to improve the employment prospects of students it reaches.[69]

CONCLUSION

The case studies described above, all drawn from the years between 1920 and the present, show some significant continuities in the role of technology in work with earlier eras in American history and with the global settings that followed similar commitments to rationalized, ever larger systems of industrial production. Automation, the veneration of machine over human in places of work, and the many other uses of technology that have constituted modern managerial regimes have never been things that just "happened to workers." Rather, employers, educators, and economic policymakers posited that different people naturally came to have different life experiences. The project of technology, in this dominant ideology, confirmed a (perceived) natural order in which some persons were naturally in a position of social and economic dominance over others, while that order in turn gave meaning to technology. In short, technology did not implement some preexisting social system and social values did not determine the human encounters with material labelled "technology" and "work"; rather technology, work, and human difference all made sense of one another.

Causally interleaving how historical actors' commitments to mechanization shaped their own and others' social experiences, the feminist historian of technology Judith McGaw has provided an exemplary gendered account of how technology engages with the culture of work. In her account of industrializing New England paper-making firms after 1800, neither social ideologies regarding labor nor technological processes necessarily came first; rather, each rendered the other legible for historical actors in different moments.[70] Many generations into the national project of wealth accumulation through industrial modernization, American enthusiasms in the twenty-first century for Science, Technology, Engineering, and Mathematics (STEM) education and technological innovation, as means of "raising all boats" through the cultivation of talent and the invention of new goods and services, provide one clear example of social ideology preceding technological change.[71] STEM advocates placed great faith in technology, even as STEM projects, in their valorization of technology and engineering, stubbornly tended to resist any redistributive reform. Such advocacy ironically often remained in the mainstream of traditional popular associations (seen in the work of Taylor and much scientific management) of "types of people" with "types of work." Eighty years after construction firms sorted concrete workers' abilities along lines of ethnic background, elite technologists of the modern era continued to distinguish that what the white intellect mastered in the research lab was "engineering," while that which the African American intellect mastered was something else.[72]

Whether future technologists and reformers will interrogate the reification of technology that has dominated developments of the last hundred years remains unclear. One powerful strain in contemporary industrial societies emphasizes the salience of gender, race, disability, sexuality, and other such ascriptions in how work and technology organize social life. Others question these categories as artificial social constructs that themselves make discrimination possible. But if those discriminatory categorizations are to lose their efficacy as means of economic and political marginalization, the notion that "types of work" correspond to "natural" abilities (manifest in racial, ethnic, and gendered terms) must be displaced. This requires society to understand that wage inequalities and different levels of safety, security, or creativity in the workplace do not inhere in different productive tasks. The production of those differentials must instead be understood as a choice that can be exchanged for a more equitable approach to labor.

CHAPTER SIX

Work and Mobility

NIMISHA BARTON AND ANDREW HAZELTON

The domestic and international movement of peoples shaped labor markets and work regimes across the West after the First World War. In the United States, employers and policymakers constructed internal and external migration systems in response to shifting labor imperatives and racialized citizenship. Economic transformations toward labor-saving technologies in manufacturing and the continuing movement of rural peoples to cities closed off legal immigration while simultaneously generating alternative immigration via guestworker programs or undocumented entry. Meanwhile, the texture of migration experience in Europe differed in key ways. War, revolution, political violence, and ethnic conflict roiled the continent and stimulated forced migrations throughout the century. The unceasing tumult left continental Europe devastated and short of necessary labor to rebuild it. Guestworker programs also took shape in Europe against the background of colonialism and its aftermath.

In spite of the different contexts for Europe and the United States, capitalism's steady expansion spurred the appearance of similar labor migration regimes. Employers, policymakers, and politicians in both America and Europe constructed migration systems governed by a similar ethos: use nonwhite laborers temporarily to plug gaps, then dispose of them when finished. However, impermanent migration regimes paradoxically led to permanent residence with political, social, and cultural ramifications for host countries.

Policymakers and employers created bifurcated labor regimes that integrated white European immigrants but rejected nonwhites. These regimes used nonwhites as unskilled, temporary, deportable workers. Gender and family concerns informed these determinations: American and European policymakers believed women and families encouraged migrants' permanent settlement—for better or worse—depending on current needs. Consequently, late twentieth-century lawmakers shaped family and welfare policies with an eye to labor and immigration policy. As Western states introduced and expanded immigrant family reunification policies in the late twentieth century, they increased the visibility of nonwhite families. In turn, xenophobic far-right political movements gained strength in the new millennium. In Europe, the preponderance of Muslim immigrants and the increase in terrorist attacks by Muslim militants gave this xenophobia a pronounced Islamophobic cast. In the United States, the dominant nativist strain opposed the presence of Mexicans and their descendants.

This chapter explores the emergence and development of labor migration regimes in the West. Case studies in America and Europe illustrate the racialization of immigrant labor by examining three significant periods: the interwar period (roughly 1920–40), the postwar boom period (through the mid–1970s), and the post-recession period (roughly 1973–present). Following the First World War, the United States significantly curtailed European migration. By 1920, France became the West's immigrant destination as a result of American immigration restriction and labor shortages that predated the war. France provides an excellent example of the state-capital collusion that gave migrant labor regimes their illiberal cast. In both France and the United States, governments and employers used nonwhites to provide cheap, temporary labor to employers who claimed that labor shortages threatened production.

As migration regimes took shape over the early twentieth century, gender, sex, and familial norms of host societies emerged as central considerations for policymakers. In Europe, states regarded reproductive immigrants as worthy of integration. By contrast, American policymakers viewed immigrant fertility (especially among nonwhites) as a threat to the national fabric. The Great Depression threw these gendered, sexed, and racialized labor regimes into stark relief: in both France and the United States, European laborers demonstrating reproductive sexuality were allowed to stay while nonwhites (and in France, non-reproductive persons, too) were deported.

In the post-Second World War period, the West experienced an economic "Golden Age" that spurred the rise of large, coordinated state-managed guestworker regimes to meet real or claimed labor shortages. In Europe and the United States, states, societies, and employers welcomed white, skilled migrants and their families. By contrast, they offered nonwhites temporary guestworker programs designed to admit unskilled, racialized males as easily controlled and disposable labor. In other words, postwar western states solidified the bifurcated labor migration regime that classified skilled whites as permanent residents while relegating unskilled nonwhite males to temporary and ill-regulated guestworker programs. In Europe, the history of imperialism as well as postwar decolonization informed the structure of nonwhite labor regimes. Moreover, the colonial and postcolonial context added virulence to the racialization of a nonwhite, postcolonial labor force steadily concentrating in Europe. In the United States, a racialized Mexican labor force was subjected to rigorous controls, controls so onerous that they incentivized undocumented migration, which in turn compounded racist characterizations of Mexicans as criminal and exploitable.

Following the economic crisis of the 1970s, Western European states attempted to halt migration and repatriate single, nonwhite males. But states also introduced family reunification policies that allowed foreign men to bring their families to Europe—policies that increased the visibility of nonwhites long designated as "unassimilable" and "undesirable." In the United States, the growing population of undocumented immigrants, reforms that provided legal status for them, and existing policies that favored family reunification for legal residents fed an anti-immigrant backlash. Therefore, despite western states' and societies' rejection of nonwhite labor, family reunification policies exposed a central paradox of guestworker regimes: host societies expected foreign workers to provide cheap, unskilled labor without arousing political, social, or cultural reaction. This position became untenable as immigrants' dependents arrived in Europe and the United States amid late-twentieth-century economic dislocations. With each economic downturn, right-wing politicians capitalized on growing discontent among westerners who often attributed their woes to the "immigrant problem" in their backyards.

TOWARDS THE DEVELOPMENT OF ORGANIZED LABOR MIGRATION

Prior to the First World War, migration in Europe was a local affair. From the seventeenth through the nineteenth centuries, Europeans traversed short distances in response to local labor markets and seasonal manpower demands in agriculture. In the eighteenth century, rural industrial production created a rural proletariat, but by the nineteenth century, the rise of machine production in large urban centers accelerated the formation of an industrial proletariat drawn from the countryside. As rural areas deindustrialized, peasants took to developing cities for waged work. But jobs were sex-specific and shaped the economic opportunities afforded to men and women as workers. For instance, domestic work and textiles remained the province of women and often spurred their migration.[1]

European migration patterns also shifted in the nineteenth century as migrants traversed greater distances on a grander scale in response to shrinking opportunities at home and growing empires abroad. As continental population growth outpaced growth in economic opportunities, men and women left for the Americas and Oceania where they found work. Moreover, imperial powers—Great Britain, especially—exported populations to build empires. European settlement colonies grew around the globe—the Portuguese in South America and Africa, the Dutch in Asia, the French in North Africa, and the British seemingly everywhere else (Figure 6.1). Indeed, the United States began its history as a settlement colony before becoming an independent state during the age of revolutions.[2]

From the mid-nineteenth century onward, American migration and immigration were characterized by strong reaction to the movement of peoples, especially when

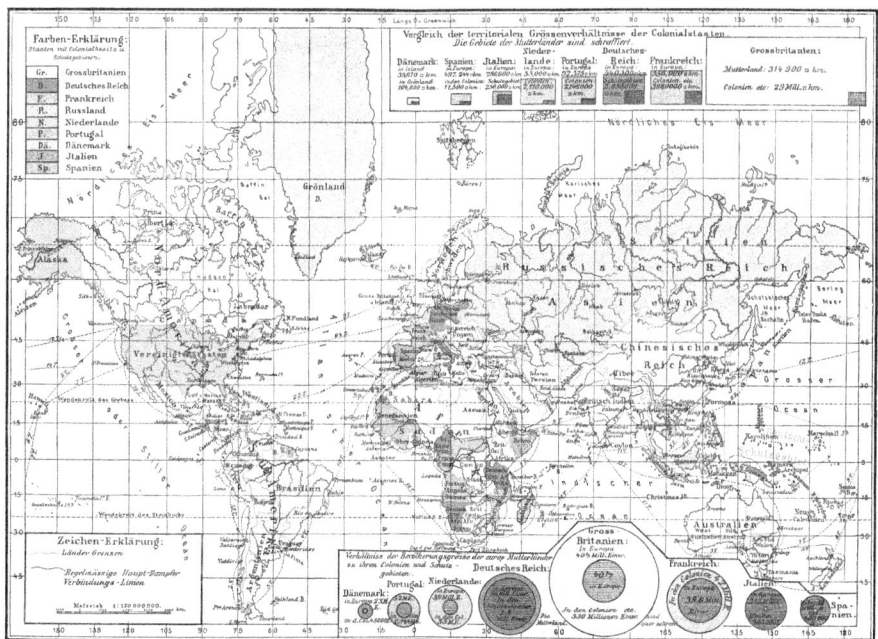

FIGURE 6.1 A nineteenth-century map of the world depicts the spread of European dominion across the globe. Courtesy Falkensteininfoto, Alamy.

that movement coincided with economic competition. In the late nineteenth century, millions of rural people both domestic and foreign moved to major American cities for industrial employment. Racial and ethnic differences between native-born Americans and immigrants led to restrictions on the latter in immigration policies and even the definitions of citizenship itself. Racially restrictive policies first targeted Chinese immigrants in the American West. In 1882 Congress passed the Chinese Exclusion Act banning Chinese immigration and barring Chinese from naturalizing, the signature achievement of decades of anti-Chinese activism by native whites. In California, large agricultural concerns switched to Japanese or Filipinos, the latter exempted from racial restrictions as subjects of America's empire. Meanwhile, a revolution and decade-long civil war in Mexico pointed toward the future of racialized labor migration in the United States.

The fortunes of European immigrants changed as American policymakers expanded racial exclusion principles to Europeans after the First World War. As immigration from Northern/Western Europe declined and that from Southern/Eastern Europe increased, native-born Americans among labor, Progressive, eugenics, and other movements feared the effects on wages, democracy, and racial and national unity. They got their chance to legislate restrictions against Europeans as the immediate wartime refugee threat combined with long-term trends in production away from unskilled labor and toward labor-saving technologies. The Immigration Act of 1917 imposed literacy tests to weed out the poor and uneducated and the 1921 Emergency Quota Act and 1924 Immigration Act effectively closed America's "golden door" to Europeans. The laws limited European immigration and shifted what remained toward the supposedly whiter races of "old" Europe. Overall, the changes to immigration law virtually eliminated southern and eastern European immigration and privileged northern and western Europeans.[3]

American immigration policy in the late nineteenth and early twentieth centuries proceeded from two assumptions: that immigration should meet economic need, and that American citizenship and the right to permanent residence was race-based. Now that mass production had transitioned away from unskilled labor, nativist arguments gained traction amid the postwar geopolitical upheaval. However, as Congress closed the door to Europeans so "assimilation" could begin, it simultaneously granted quota exemptions to the Western Hemisphere, a nod to Southwestern employers who relied on Mexican labor. In Europe, prospective immigrants would have to look elsewhere.

Since 1789, France had served as a refuge for political exiles fleeing oppression. But as French birth rates declined over the nineteenth century, a widespread and deeply rooted populationist rationale among French statesmen, lawmakers, employers, politicians, and citizens produced a powerful "pull" factor for migrants set adrift between 1880 and 1940. Early in the Third Republic (1870–1940), French deaths outnumbered births for the first time. A few decades later, the First World War (1914–18) decimated the French male population. Indeed, in the 1920s only immigration drove population growth. Thus, the relatively open migration policies of the early twentieth century responded to populationist fears that the nation would disappear if France failed to import more people to serve as laborers and soldiers, fathers and mothers, essentially "producers" and "reproducers" of the nation.[4]

Immigrants came to France from all over Europe and beyond. As early as the 1880s, the pogroms of Eastern Europe and the Balkan nationalist conflicts stimulated migrations of Eastern European and Ottoman Jews. By the First World War, the entire continent churned with movement: subjects fled civil wars and revolutions in the former Russian, Austro-Hungarian, and Ottoman empires; citizens fled intemperate regimes in fascist Italy,

Germany, and Spain; soon Jewish refugees fled Nazi Germany's expanding Lebensraum. Throughout, French industry and agriculture benefited from nineteenth-century patterns of frontier migration from neighboring countries such as Belgium, Italy, Switzerland, Spain, and Luxemburg. In short, a motley assemblage of political and economic refugees flocked to France during and after the First World War, and employers and the state cooperated to integrate these white laborers into economic sectors that needed them.

Prior to the First World War, foreign workers labored in industries French workers had deserted, including metallurgy, chemicals, masonry, construction, and mining. These were mostly unskilled and unpleasant jobs. If, before the war, foreign workers had served as a supplement to the French workforce, during and after the war, immigrant workers were indispensable. The state organized sustained industrial labor recruitment in coordination with employers to keep munitions factories operating smoothly throughout the war. France's importation of Italian, Spanish, and Portuguese farmworkers also reflected the state's need to compensate for the lost manpower that had been called to the front. After the war, despite the return of demobilized soldiers, labor shortages hampered French reconstruction and economic development. Consequently, employer-initiated and state-supported organizational efforts to recruit foreigners continued throughout the 1920s.[5]

Industrial and agricultural employers collaborated to create state-backed foreign labor recruitment organizations that sought European migrants, offered them enticing work contracts, furnished them with necessary paperwork, provided them with transportation to France, and inserted them where labor demand was greatest: colonial and Chinese laborers went to docks and military construction; Spanish, Portuguese, and Italians to agriculture; and Greeks, Armenians, and Italians to industry—more specifically, wartime munitions factories.[6] The largest conglomerate of French employers was the Société Générale d'Immigration (SGI), and SGI efforts in the 1920s prompted large numbers of European migrant workers to arrive and reconstitute their families in France. A commercial immigration company, the SGI was controlled by coal and farm interests responding to labor needs in the post-First World War years. Poland, Austria, Czechoslovakia, and Yugoslavia constituted the four "principal countries of emigration"—the heartlands of the former Austro-Hungarian Empire. Thus, French employers and the state cooperated to create an organized migrant labor regime in France under wartime and reconstruction circumstances.

While white European migrants faced a state- and employer-directed labor system, nonwhite laborers faced a paramilitary labor regime that used them brutally to fill economic gaps before dispensing with them. During the war, more than 222,000 workers from French North Africa, Indochina, Madagascar, and China labored in munitions factories. To prevent discord between French and colonial workers the state created a disciplinary surveillance system to monitor colonial and Chinese men, the Colonial Labour Organisation Service (SOTC). The SOTC grouped colonial workers into battalions arranged by nationality, assigned them employers, and made arrangements for housing, transportation, and food. The French state also used the SOTC to prevent racial conflict and to derive maximum productivity from nonwhites.[7]

While French employers and the state partnered to channel both whites and nonwhites into specific economic sectors, nonwhite and colonial workers were subject to an illiberal labor regime that sought to direct, control, and surveil them more aggressively than Europeans. Moreover, while European laborers remained in France after the war, the majority of colonial workers and soldiers were rapidly, forcibly repatriated come 1919.

Though many colonial and Chinese workers continued migrating to France after the war, they remained in low-paid, hazardous trades and, unlike European migrants, French naturalization and citizenship policy did not welcome them. Thus, the migrant labor regime in France reinforced the racial boundaries of the French national community.[8]

Migrant labor systems in France were both raced and gendered, mirroring labor patterns in the greater economy. Frenchwomen gradually deserted lower paying jobs in favor of more lucrative and respected white-collar work as secretaries, nurses, and store clerks. The increasing pool of immigrant women in France filled the gap Frenchwomen left behind. Before and during the First World War, women formed part of the foreign workforce that seasonally migrated across borders, especially along the Italian and Swiss frontiers. Moreover, immigrant women counted among the foreign farmworkers that employers and the state directed into agriculture. Some also found work in munitions factories during the war, along with Frenchwomen and colonial workers. That said, many French capitalists considered foreign women—Spanish and Greek, especially—ill-suited to factory labor. For instance, officials frustratedly noted that foreign women underproduced Frenchwomen by 20–50 percent on identical work.[9] After the war, immigrant women continued laboring in feminized sectors of the economy including agriculture, domestic service, textiles, and family-owned businesses.[10]

One last factor shaped the developing twentieth-century French migrant labor regime: a commitment to reproductive sexuality. The relatively open-door French policy between 1880 and 1940 corresponded to what contemporaries viewed as a dire population crisis. During the 1920s, the state not only sought to institute labor policies serving economic and employer needs, but also constructed population policy via naturalization, citizenship, and welfare laws that facilitated the rapid absorption of procreative foreigners into the nation. These laws privileged immigrants who exhibited a reproductive sexuality—large families; heterosexually married couples; and foreign widows with numerous children. The Great Depression exposed this populationist logic. Despite the 1930s economic crisis that devalued immigrants as laborers, the ongoing population crisis continued the need for immigrants as reproducers. Thus, in the 1930s, France expelled and repatriated foreigners who did not meet procreative criteria—above all, foreign bachelors and immigrant women who committed reproductive crimes (i.e. "pederasty," abortion, infanticide, etc.). During the Depression, the state had no need of laborers, and it certainly had no need of those unwilling to contribute to France's demographic future.[11]

In the United States, policymakers and state actors simultaneously embraced European immigrants and their family members while holding Mexicans at arm's length. Although the 1920s immigration laws severely restricted European immigration, they created new policy questions regarding so-called illegal aliens. Activists, ethnic associations, and even immigration judges critiqued blanket deportations for unauthorized entrants. Both the 1921 and the 1924 legislation privileged family reunification in issuing visas. In many individual cases, undocumented European immigrants with family ties in the United States managed to stay.[12] The story was different for Mexican immigrants. Congress repeatedly deferred to Southwestern employers by exempting Western Hemispheric nations from immigration restrictions while simultaneously extending restrictions on Mexican migrant laborers. As Mexican migration in the Southwest accelerated after 1911, immigration officials suspended literacy tests and per capita taxes when local employers and labor needs demanded it. In fact, the "Immigration Bureau did not seriously consider Mexican immigration within its purview," leaving it up to Southwestern labor markets to sort out.[13] These workers were simply "birds of passage," sojourning briefly in the United States before returning.[14]

The Great Depression exposed differential treatment for Mexicans and Europeans. In the United States, white immigrants continued to live and work freely while Mexicans who had migrated permanently were expelled, part of broader policy trends privileging white laborer-citizens over nonwhites. In California, hundreds of thousands of Mexicans and Mexican Americans were "repatriated" in a publicity campaign carried out by Los Angeles County, the state of California, and Mexico itself in a bid to reduce Mexican relief claims.[15] While European immigrants and their descendants certainly suffered along with other Depression victims, white ethnics partook in American life on mostly equal terms with native-born citizens. They built and benefited from the industrial union movement and enjoyed the benefits of New Deal labor laws, job programs, and what Michael Katz has characterized as the semi-welfare state.[16] New Deal policy, however, excluded predominantly nonwhite service occupations and agricultural labor from collective bargaining, other protections, and benefit provisions such as Social Security. Where possible, these workers sought out generally more limited social programs administered by state and local governments, not the federal government.[17] In the South, labor law did not extent to black sharecroppers, and single mothers had to petition stingy local officials who restricted the flow of federal money to them. Thus, European immigrants and their descendants steadily won entry into the new world of American entitlements from which nonwhite Americans and immigrants were excluded.[18]

In the first few decades of the twentieth century, then, France and the United States erected state- and employer-directed migrant labor regimes that typified racialized and gendered labor systems across the industrializing (and colonizing) West. Within these migrant labor systems, employers and states privileged whites over nonwhites, offering them higher wages, better treatment, and fewer restrictions. Several factors, including race, gender, and sex, served to stratify the economy. For instance, in France, white male workers stood at the top of the labor hierarchy and colonial and nonwhite male workers at the bottom; foreign female workers were relegated to traditionally feminized economic sectors; and the state demanded that all foreigners contribute both productive *and* reproductive labor to the nation, or else face consequences. The Great Depression threw this economic and demographic logic into stark relief, demonstrating that while the state did not need foreign labor anymore, it was willing to accommodate those who contributed to the nation's reproduction. In the United States, state and society also constructed nonwhite immigrants as temporary, migratory, and necessary, though they placed less emphasis on gender and familial categories. Although the 1921 and 1924 laws expanded the category of "illegal alien" by criminalizing unauthorized entry, Border Patrol did not consider Mexican immigration a problem. For them, these brief sojourners supposedly came to work and then returned. The Great Depression repatriations of Mexican families gave the lie to this myth, while European immigrants shielded from similar repatriation policies instead joined an amorphous but inclusive "Caucasian" Americanism that barred nonwhites from the political and social mainstream.[19] The logics of racial exclusion and reproductive inclusion established in the early twentieth century would cast a long shadow over labor migration policy as it evolved over the twentieth century in the West.

POSTWAR GROWTH AND EXPANDING GUESTWORKER REGIMES IN THE WEST

The Second World War drastically reshaped labor markets in the West and relied extensively on labor migrants—or "guestworkers"—to first sustain and later enlarge the global economy. As the black fog of war lifted, the West entered an unexpected period of major economic growth lasting from 1945 to 1975. In spite of—or, indeed, perhaps because of the unhappy events of the war—the postwar years were greeted warmly by all with felicitous turns of phrase—Germany's *Wirtschaftswunder* ("economic miracle"), France's *les trentes glorieuses* ("thirty glorious years"), America's "Golden Age." Yet, throughout the West, it was guestworker regimes built on exclusionary racial principles and reproductive sexual norms that powered these economic "miracles." If, during the First World War, employers and the state cooperated in national security and wartime production interests, the magnitude of economic demand during and after the Second World War encouraged closer collaboration between western capital and governments. States took aggressive roles in their national economies, directing and expanding production to meet wartime needs.

In the United States, the Bracero Program, a guestworker program created when large growers claimed critical labor shortages were undermining wartime production, provides a case in point. While European immigration to the United States during and after the Second World War continued largely unfettered, Mexican and Caribbean migrants conformed to the strictures of temporary guestworker programs. These programs sought to admit racialized, unskilled, and deportable labor forces. Moreover, the Bracero Program screened carefully for male workers with family commitments in Mexico on the belief that their families ensured their return.[20] Through an exploration of the Bracero Program, we can see the ongoing importance of race and gender/familial concerns in the development of postwar guestworker programs in the West.

Despite initial shocks in returning to peacetime economics, white Americans benefited from a postwar "Golden Age" of prosperity as middle incomes grew rapidly. Benefiting from the New Deal social contract, industrial workers joined the middle class, and housing, education, and infrastructure policies created a "virtuous cycle" of economic security, upward mobility, and robust growth unchallenged by international competition. Southern and Eastern European immigrants and their second- and third-generation kin in mass-production industries returned to employment as the federal government enlisted factories in the war effort while millions of young men joined the armed forces. Yet Mexican immigrants and nonwhites more broadly faced a decidedly more perilous situation.[21]

In US immigration policy, the McCarran-Walter Act (Immigration Act of 1952) consolidated and reformed existing policies, redefined citizenship, and embedded employment concerns in the quota system. The law retained European quotas and continued exempting the Western Hemisphere, but Congress eliminated the racial naturalization restrictions in the wake of the Second World War's fight against fascism's racist doctrines. As historian Mae Ngai puts it, this established "the general principle of color-blind citizenship" following gradual expansions of naturalization rights to Chinese, Indians, and Filipinos to strengthen Cold War alliances. The law also embedded employment concerns in the quotas. Half of each national quota was allocated to individuals with special skills the economy needed. The rest went to spouses and children of legal residents and citizens, continuing the family unification priority in immigration policy.[22]

Despite the law's preference for high-skill immigrants and their family members, the law allowed the immigration of unskilled workers, but only as guestworkers who encountered employer abuse and lax regulation. The McCarran-Walter Act's subsection (h) (ii) outlined the temporary authorization of non-Mexican guestworkers, or "H2s." According to historian Cindy Hahamovitch, "immigrant farmworkers would enter temporarily or not at all." Florida sugar growers used Jamaican H2s as a conveniently controllable workforce. Meanwhile, the Bracero Program continued well beyond the wartime emergency that created it.[23] Overall, growers easily exploited the guestworker regime because of their power over employees, budgetary constraints on Labor Department enforcement activities, and federal delegation of oversight to state and local governments. Faced with shrinking appropriations by conservative postwar congresses, Labor Department officials certified labor shortage declarations that state and local bureaucrats forwarded.[24]

The guestworker regime had safeguards, but they were rarely enforced, with disastrous effects for American farmworkers. Theoretically, guestworkers were barred where their employment would adversely affect citizens. They would receive prevailing wages that American workers accepted, and they could not work on struck farms. In practice, farmers submitted requests before the harvest began. They advertised job postings for farmworkers even earlier, listing wage rates citizens would never accept. They thus manufactured labor shortages that friendly local officials certified and forwarded to the Labor Department. The "prevailing wage" became the rate employers wanted to pay. Growers wielded near-absolute control over these guestworker programs until the late 1950s when labor, liberal, civil rights, and religious activists drew attention to abuses, demanded reforms, and the Bracero Program's end.[25] The laissez-faire approach toward guestworkers reduced wages in agriculture compared to industry. The 1930s exclusion of farmworkers from modern welfare state benefits and the heavy reliance on guestworkers meant that cheap agricultural labor partly subsidized industrial workers' prosperity by keeping food and fiber prices low. The guestworker share of the harvest workforce rose, and wages declined. Between 1951 and 1957, braceros increased from 15 to 34.2 percent of harvest labor while agricultural wages declined from 47 to 37 percent of industrial wages between 1945 and 1959.[26] Growers' control over imported nonwhite labor drove much of this decline.[27]

The Bracero Program also generated unintended consequences for policymakers by stimulating undocumented immigration from Mexico. Illegal aliens far outpaced official bracero contracts for several reasons. To start, only men could apply as braceros, leaving behind girlfriends, spouses, and families looking to join them down the line.[28] After bribing officials in interior recruitment centers, braceros were shipped north by train to border reception centers where staff performed humiliating physical inspections designed to uncover disease or applicants without farmworker calluses. Once contracted by a growers' association, braceros endured low earnings, underemployment, occupational injuries (some of which led to death), and exploitative and unsanitary living conditions. Should they protest, they faced quick deportation. Yet, despite the many hazards, many Mexicans crossed the border illegally.[29]

By the mid-1950s, newspapers, unionists, and Mexican-American activists, increasingly seeing undocumented immigration as reaching crisis levels, drew attention to large increases in illicit border crossings. Congressional Cold Warriors demanded secure borders and fretted about a fifth column of communists entering via Mexico. Ironically, some of these same congressmen had voted for the "Texas Proviso" in the new immigration law exempting illegal alien employment from criminal penalties, a measure Texas congressmen inserted to protect growers. The exemption undoubtedly contributed to the growth in the undocumented population alongside the legal braceros. In fiscal year 1953, employers hired 201,380 braceros; the same year, Immigration and Naturalization Service (INS) processed 885,587 illegal aliens, most of them Mexicans.[30]

The Eisenhower Administration responded with Operation Wetback, a border crackdown conducted over 1954 and 1955. The operation detained hundreds of thousands of Mexicans as aliens, encouraged, according to INS, the "self-deportation" of hundreds of thousands more, and shifted employment toward braceros. INS commissioner Joseph Swing cordially met with growers and pledged that if they needed a guestworker, "we will see that he gets it." Moreover, he noted, as legally in the United States, braceros were unlikely to "skip out" and could not randomly be deported.[31] Through Operation Wetback—and Operation Terror, its Los Angeles equivalent—Border Patrol claimed to have apprehended over one million Mexicans as aliens. Border Patrol averred that many of them converted their status into braceros, though the claim may have reflected the patrol's need to demonstrate control over the border.[32] With the border "secured," bracero employment increased to over four hundred thousand contracts annually. But as INS budgets shrank, apprehensions fell and undocumented immigrants from Mexico continued to outpace guestworkers. When the Bracero Program ended in 1964, growers in nonmechanized crops simply reverted to undocumented immigrants.

The following year, Congress revised immigration policy with the Hart-Cellar Act, abolishing the racial quotas. The family reunification principle remained an important part of immigration law, but it was joined by a new system of preferences for skilled professionals. The act also limited Western Hemispheric immigration and gave preference

FIGURE 6.2 Mexican migrants wait to cross the border at Nuevo Laredo, Tamaulipas-Laredo, Texas, c. 1948. Courtesy Andrew Hazelton (private collection). Photographer unknown.

to political refugees, but did so according to Cold War sensibilities. In recognition of the problems with the guestworker regime, Labor Department certification requirements strengthened protections against worker displacement by guestworkers. Overall, the 1965 Immigration and Nationality Act continued the postwar moves away from discriminatory quotas but effectively retained the ban on unskilled nonwhites. The law's explicit preference for professionals and political refugees (albeit only from left-wing states) ensured that the tired, poor, huddled masses would have to continue yearning to breathe free from their homes abroad if they wished to immigrate legally.[33]

Europe also adopted guestworker programs during this period that distinguished between whites and nonwhites. Like the United States, labor need was great in Europe after the war. Indeed, despite the nearly two million displaced persons left stranded across Europe in summer 1945, almost all were reabsorbed within a few short years due to the urgent need to rebuild European economies damaged by war and subsequent labor shortages. If, in 1950, five million foreigners lived in Western Europe, by 1980, over fifteen million foreigners resided there. European states, employers, and labor contractors recruited guestworkers from Italy, Portugal, Spain, Greece, Turkey, and Yugoslavia. In major imperial powers such as the UK, France, and the Netherlands, guestworkers also came from colonial territories in Africa, East Asia, and the Indian subcontinent.[34]

Postwar Germany provides a prime example of European guestworker programs since, like most other European countries, it first contended with a large migrant workforce after 1945 when reconstruction efforts began. Moreover, Turks recruited to work in West Germany came to constitute the largest migration stream in postwar Europe. West Germany relied on cheap East German labor immediately after the war, but the Berlin Wall halted that flow. Germany soon negotiated bilateral treaties with Turkey, Morocco, Portugal, Tunisia, and Yugoslavia to acquire guestworkers. Long-standing cordial diplomatic relations and world war alliances between Germany and Turkey made for an obvious pairing. Moreover, postwar Turkey's population growth and high unemployment made West Germany an important safety valve. In 1965, there were about seventy-two thousand Turks in Germany; by 1974, over a million. Although Turkish businessmen initially acted as labor recruiters for Germany, in 1961 the new German constitution granted Turkish workers free entry. Once again, labor recruitment organizations cooperated with states to introduce temporary guestworkers. The Turkish Employment Service processed guestworker applications, put candidates through rigorous health exams, and then handled transportation and visa costs in Germany. As in interwar France, these nonwhite workers lived in male dormitories as they saved money for remittances. By the late 1960s, employers also began recruiting Turkish women for low-paid work in electronics and textiles. Indeed, after 1967, women comprised one-third of Turkish entrants.[35]

As the example of postwar Germany indicates, while European states worked once again with employers to recruit and regulate foreign workers to rebuild, racial considerations shaped guestworker regimes after the war in magnified ways. It was a trend visible in other European countries. For instance, France recruited racially desirable workers while shunning *"indésirables"* such as Slavs, Armenians, and colonial workers. The UK also distinguished between desirables and undesirables, preferring dislocated Western Europeans; tolerating Eastern Europeans when necessary; and disdaining Jews, blacks from the Caribbean, and South Asian colonial migrants. Throughout labor-starved postwar Europe, states and employers also showed a clear preference for young, healthy, unmarried Displaced Persons; without family, so the logic went, they were temporary and deportable.[36] Thus, both racial considerations and reproductive concerns once more played a role in the recruitment of migrant labor in Europe.

In sum, in both the United States and Europe temporary guestworker programs for unskilled nonwhites subsidized and powered the economic miracle for postwar white citizens. In Europe guestworker regimes depended on nonwhite labor migration from underdeveloped economies to rebuild and power the western economy. In the United States, agricultural guestworker programs continued the trend of assimilating European-descended persons after the quotas and privileging white labor while reforming immigration in favor of skilled workers, refugees, and their family members. By bearing the brunt of unskilled, low-paid labor, nonwhites in the West enabled educated whites to take jobs in the burgeoning white-collar sector. At the very least, nonwhite labor allowed whites to enjoy a blue-collar prosperity made possible partly by cheap food harvested by cheap nonwhite labor. It is no exaggeration to claim, therefore, that nonwhite guestworkers underwrote the postwar western economic miracle. In Europe, that the push toward integration in a Common Market took place against the background of violent wars of decolonization and the subsequent racialization of the unskilled immigrant workforce would set the tone for the identity politics and civilizational "clashes" of the late twentieth and early twenty-first centuries.

RECESSION AND THE POLITICS OF FAMILY REUNIFICATION

The 1973 oil crisis inaugurated the contemporary migration period characterized by global recession, inflation, and unemployment, and the Far Right's return across the West. The reinforcing relationship of economic recession, immigration and identity politics is most visible in the popular (and populist) platforms of the resurgent Far Right—political movements premised on defending national identities and "western values" and fixated on visible "minority" immigrant communities, especially on the immigrant woman in Europe and undocumented immigrants in the United States. In Europe, the economic crisis spurred efforts to halt migration to cope with unemployment, but these efforts largely failed. Instead, states introduced family reunification policies that only exacerbated the "immigrant problem." In the United States, the oil shock, increasing economic competition abroad, trade deficits, and a decline in and outright assault on unions pushed working-class whites out of the middle class. As policymakers embraced supply-side economics domestically and neoliberal agendas globally, American industrial workers watched their jobs disappear. With few alternatives, workers took low-paid, service-sector jobs. At the same time, Mexican policies pushed millions of rural poor into the undocumented migrant stream toward the United States. Attempts to reform or manage this migration failed, leading to increased visibility of people of Mexican descent in America and an emboldened right-wing nativist response.

As the oil crisis gave way to a decade of "stagflation"—stagnant growth, high unemployment, and record-setting inflation—the failure of Keynesian economic policies to restore prosperity legitimized neoconservative economics. The Nixon, Ford, and Carter administrations, caught between the risks of raising interest rates and making unemployment worse, or stimulating spending and exacerbating inflation, struggled to formulate coherent responses. Ultimately, the Carter and Reagan administrations settled on taming inflation at the risk of persistent unemployment. The Reagan White House went further, however, championing supply-side economics that granted high earners and business and financial interests the tax cuts and deregulation the beneficiaries argued would restore growth.

The economic disaster and policy paralysis that enabled Reagan's rise also formed the backdrop for profound changes in American industry. Deindustrialization and double-digit inflation eroded working-class whites' job security and living standards. Manufacturers extracted concessions from unions in exchange for keeping factories open. But increased energy costs and international competition led employers to automation and cheaper labor, and to move production to Southern states with lower wages, tax incentives, and anti-union right-to-work laws. The 1970s represented a trading of "factories for finance," as politicians bet on deregulation and capital investment.[37] Private equity and venture capital firms restructured companies and outsourced manufacturing in the 1980s. In 1981, union resistance was dealt a fatal blow when Reagan fired striking air traffic controllers, green-lighting aggressive private-sector union-busting.[38] The case of the Radio Corporation of America (RCA), reveals these trends. RCA relocated its manufacturing plants from southern Indiana in the 1960s to lower its labor costs and escape union activism. First, it moved production to Memphis, Tennessee, before finally offshoring to Ciudad Juarez in Mexico.[39] When inflation fell and growth returned, Americans did not share the prosperity equally; supply-side economics channelled income and wealth gains upward.

American acceptance of supply-side economics reflected the rising tide of neoliberalism globally. In Mexico, American trade and investment poured in just as millions of rural people found their lives untenable. When the Bracero Program ended, undocumented immigration from Mexico accelerated. US and Mexican policymakers hoped a Border Industrialization Programme (BIP) could address chronic underemployment in Mexico by industrializing the border region, thus creating jobs for Mexicans and investment opportunities for US capital. The BIP was essential in RCA's pursuit of lower labor costs into Mexico; RCA opened its Juarez plant two years after the BIP began. However, the new Mexican *maquiladoras* adopted the latest automation technologies. Wages were relatively high, but promises of mass employment for prospective migrants never materialized.[40] Concurrently, Mexican policymakers implemented neoliberal policies opening Mexico to foreign goods and capital, undermining communal land tenure, and reducing rural development and subsidy funding, part of the price of international negotiations to restructure Mexico's finances.[41]

By the mid-1980s, accelerating undocumented immigration from Mexico stimulated vigorous debate over the immigration proposals that became the 1986 Immigration Reform and Control Act (IRCA). IRCA offered a path to legal residency for illegal immigrants who had entered the United States before 1982, remained for at least three years, and not committed crimes. It also required they pay any outstanding fines and back taxes. Roughly 2.6 million people achieved legal residency through this "amnesty." Of these, 1.2 million were farmworkers.[42] To "control" future Mexican immigration, the bill criminalized the knowing employment of undocumented workers and required employers to attest to workers' immigration status. These provisions were, however, difficult to enforce. Unauthorized immigrants often supplied fraudulent employment documents, and proving intent to hire undocumented labor was difficult. Moreover, the law did not address "push" factors sending rural Mexicans north in coming decades. And family unification—through both formal procedures to reunite legal aliens and their families and informal reunification via continued undocumented migration—soon led to acrimonious political debate over Mexican immigrants' role in American society.

IRCA served only as a band-aid response to the tide of undocumented immigrants because neoliberal policies forced millions out of Mexico. In the Western Hemisphere, the North American Free Trade Agreement (NAFTA) only increased the flow of immigrants. Promising American investment and increased foreign commerce, NAFTA destroyed trade barriers, but it decreased small Mexican producers' access to American markets or new job opportunities through US capital. Rather, these producers found themselves unable to sell their produce and livestock, even in their own backyards. American agricultural and food products crowded them out. To be sure, some mid-level producers were able to expand operations, but rural, working-class Mexicans sank deeper into poverty. Unable to survive now on their privatized individual plots and without rural subsidies and tariff protections that had been part of the Mexican social contract since the 1930s, Mexico's poor increasingly exercised their final option—undocumented immigration to the United States.

NAFTA's impacts on the poultry industry reveal the basic problems. NAFTA and similar prior policies undermined the ability of Mexican *traspatio* (backyard) chicken producers to survive the marketplace. As imported processed chicken parts from American companies like Tyson Foods flooded the Mexican market, the mostly self-sufficient *traspatio* producers could no longer generate surpluses selling their more expensive chicken in village markets. The privatization of communal lands undermined self-sufficiency. No longer able to eke out a living, this surplus population now moved permanently toward the United States along formerly cyclical migrant routes. In the United States, employers either turned a blind eye toward or actively encouraged this migration. Tyson's North Carolina poultry operations took advantage of newly available Mexican workers in its bid to defeat union campaigns among black workers. Tyson's human resources department even falsified immigration and employment documents for these imported workers, and it then intimidated its new workforce by threatening them with deportation if they disputed work rules, wages and payments, or abusive foremen.[43] The neoliberal restructuring of domestic and global economies in North America had hoped to reduce undocumented immigration; in reality, it stimulated more.

The accelerated pace of Mexican immigration from the early 1990s until the "Great Recession" of 2008 engendered a white nativist backlash in the United States against Mexicans and Mexican Americans. By the early twenty-first century, the presence of over eleven million undocumented immigrants, continuing arrivals of family members of authorized immigrants on family visas, and the increasingly visible role of people of Mexican descent in American life fed right-wing populist sentiment. It tellingly erupted at various points in the early 1990s. In 1994, California approved Proposition 187, which targeted immigrant families by threatening to deny public benefits to undocumented residents. Across the country, English-only activists fought with some success to overturn bilingual education, one of the major Chicano movement victories. In 2000, former Republican-turned-Reform Party presidential candidate Pat Buchanan denounced illegal immigrants as uneducated and likely to drain welfare funds.[44] In the 2016 presidential campaign, Donald Trump's appeal to racial fears and his demonization of Mexicans as criminals, drug traffickers, and "rapists" won support among large swaths of white, male voters uneasy over what they saw as the effects of illegal immigration.[45] In sum, in the absence of job programs for working-class whites affected most by deindustrialization, the twin processes of unmitigated globalization and labor migration from Mexico fuelled both nativist rage and the embrace of right-wing politicians.[46]

FIGURE 6.3 Supporter holds a sign as Republican presidential candidate Donald Trump speaks at a rally February 19, 2016, in Myrtle Beach, South Carolina. Courtesy Aaron P. Bernstein. Getty Images.

Similar trends emerged in Europe after 1973. Policymakers encouraged the repatriation of nonwhites (a policy that failed) while they paradoxically welcomed foreign dependents through family reunification measures. In 1973, Germany stopped recruiting workers from non-Common Market countries—that is, non-Europeans. France issued an "*arrêt d'immigration*" in 1974 and, starting in 1977, began offering monetary incentives to North Africans who returned home with their families. Only Switzerland attempted to bar foreigners and their dependents entirely. But these policies produced ironic outcomes: returning home now meant losing access to European wages, so immigrant workers asked their dependents to join them. In fact, Western Europe's generous welfare policies may have served as significant "pull" factors for foreign workers with dependents. For instance, in West Germany, the Kindergeld (generous child allowances) motivated Turkish male workers to bring wives and large families to Europe in the early 1970s. Recognizing this, Germany introduced restrictive welfare policies in 1975. To further regulate foreign workers, these measures were accompanied by restrictions on work permits. So did labor and family policy evolve in tandem to reinforce national agendas.[47]

European states paradoxically sought tighter regulation of foreign workers at the same time that they introduced family reunification policies because, barring forced deportations, they simply could not work out a definitive stop to immigration. Moreover, family reunification conformed to economic, historic, and humanitarian logics. After all, the foreign workforce played a significant role in developed economies; they did the worst, lowest-paid jobs that citizen-laborers rejected, and their wages fed consumer economies. Additionally, long-time cultural, linguistic, and historic ties bound colonial populations to the UK, France, Belgium, and the Netherlands: the empire had literally come home to roost. Finally, although postwar Europe experienced peaceful growth, conflicts directly attributable to European colonialism raged across the globe and produced political, ethnic, and economic refugees. Such conflicts included the Partition in India and Pakistan, the Rwandan genocide, and the Khmer Rouge in Cambodia. Other conflicts directly involved western states—the Vietnam War and the United States, the Kenyan Mau Mau Rebellion against the British, the Algerian War for Independence against the French. International turmoil has set more nonwhites adrift in the last three decades and, with many refugees possessing long-standing cultural ties to Europe as a result of colonialism, Europe appears a natural destination. Though not formally part of family reunification schemes and not explicitly labor migrants, asylum-seekers nonetheless contributed to the visibility of twenty-first-century nonwhite immigrant families in the West (for instance, Central American refugees in the United States or Syrian refugees in the West, more largely).

In sum, the post-1970s world churned with family migration, the result of both family reunification policies and ongoing refugee crises. From the 1970s onward, women constituted the majority of global migrants, and of the fifteen to sixteen million foreigners residing in Europe at the start of the twenty-first century, about 45 percent were women. While no "new" labor migration occurred after the 1973 oil crisis and recession, family reunification policies brought women and children, many of whom joined the workforce to survive. Like women migrants before them, they labored in domestic service and textiles and contributed to the economy further through their "invisible" work in households, as caretakers, or in family businesses. In the modern industrial economy, foreign women were the ultimate unskilled, cheap reservoir of labor.[48]

In Europe, the arrival of foreign women and families generated new social and cultural questions that spurred the reappearance of nationalist, xenophobic, far-right movements across the West. The resurgence of these right-wing movements in 2016 threatened to

FIGURE 6.4 Approximately thirty Syrian war refugee family members arrive to a Red Cross Centre on April 4, 2014 in Malaga. Courtesy Jorge Guerrero/AFP/Getty Images.

undermine the entire postwar-European order premised on integration and cooperation. Above all, these concerns centered on questions about the viability of western welfare states no longer premised on racial and ethnic homogeneity; on fears surrounding the "clash" of civilizational values; and, increasingly, on the so-called "proper" treatment of women wearing headscarves in France. Moreover, these fears and anxieties do not remain disembodied; they result in policies and programs—surveillant at best, restrictive at worst—such as the 1996 French law forbidding Muslim girls to wear headscarves to primary school or in twenty-first-century programs to "re-educate" immigrants about western gender and sexual norms in Scandinavia.[49]

CONCLUSION

After the First World War, European and American policymakers erected bifurcated labor migration regimes that comported with states' racial definitions of citizenship and considered gender and family dynamics as essential factors in migrant screening. These regimes privileged whites and integrated them and their labor into national economies but relegated nonwhites to temporary guestworker programs with poorly paid work. At the same time, gender and family concerns shaped the migration experience and informed the political and social fallout from immigrants' presence. Both states and native-born citizens believed the presence of foreign women, children, and families encouraged permanent settlement of nonwhite populations.

In the interwar period, the United States expanded the racially exclusionary immigration and naturalization policies first crafted for Asians to southern and Eastern Europeans. The American "golden door" closed and European migrants now looked to France. As it produced for the war and later rebuilt, France welcomed and absorbed white immigrants and their families, as people who could both produce for the economy and reproduce for the nation. However, France simultaneously spurned nonwhites, tracking them into dirty, dangerous, poorly paid jobs. Through regimented nonwhite guestworker programs, employers and government ensured labor discipline and that these workers would return home.

In the post-Second World War period, Europe and the United States enjoyed unparalleled prosperity as Europe rebuilt and US manufacturing dominated the globe. European-descended persons in the United States integrated into the economy and benefited from postwar prosperity, their rise into the middle class accelerated by their inclusion in the New Deal social, political, and economic order. However, policymakers maintained and expanded agricultural guestworker programs rife with abuse for Mexican and Jamaican men. These programs excluded these workers' dependents, believing families would encourage permanence. Restrictions, however, led many to immigrate illegally. US immigration law also changed in the period, moving away from national origins quotas and toward high-skill professionals and Cold War refugees. In Europe, guestworker programs—such as the one bringing Turks to Germany—continued to import "temporary" male unskilled labor, though also made room for low-paid migrant women who were content to take on jobs in traditional female economic sectors.

Following the 1970s economic crises, western nations retreated from guestworker programs in the interest of promoting native-born employment. However, the unintended consequences of decades of bifurcated labor migration regimes were unavoidable. In the United States, the Bracero Program's end and the adoption of supply-side and neoliberal economic policies in North America accelerated Mexican undocumented immigration

FIGURE 6.5 June 24, 2016: French far-right leader Marine Le Pen holds a press conference at the National Front political party headquarters during the 2016 controversy surrounding "Brexit." Photo: Vincent Isore/IP3/Getty Images.

just as working-class whites saw their jobs disappear through deindustrialization. In Europe, a halt to temporary but legal nonwhite immigration and generous social benefits encouraged migrants to stay beyond their visa and send for their families. In both cases, the increased presence of nonwhite workers and their families fed the growth of far-right political movements that characterized immigrants as dangerous criminals who undermined "pure" national characters.

A decade and a half into the twenty-first century, the impact of these movements was powerful, but their historical ramifications and future unclear. The economic dislocations of globalization in the late twentieth and early twenty-first centuries intersected with racial definitions of citizenship that targeted immigrants and their families. Anxious segments of native-born white populations across the West fixed their anger and their resentments over precarious economic and geopolitical situations on the "immigrant problem." The anti-immigrant rhetoric in 2016 political campaigns on both sides of the Atlantic revealed the vitriol coursing just below the surface. A strong "Brexit" vote to leave the European Union in the English Midlands—an area decimated by deindustrialization—and the appeal of Donald Trump to older male working-class whites in similarly distressed Midwest states put on display a visceral nativism that threatened to reconfigure western politics. Understanding and, more importantly, working through these profound changes will require careful examination of the historical division between white and nonwhite labor migration in the West.

CHAPTER SEVEN

Work and Society

ANDREW AUGUST

The 1942 report that served as blueprint for the British welfare state identified the "giants" that needed to be addressed in postwar reconstruction, including "Want … Disease, Ignorance, Squalor, and Idleness." Its author, William Beveridge, argued for health provision, social insurance, and the "avoidance of mass unemployment."[1] In a second volume Beveridge claimed that prolonged unemployment served to "kill a man's interest in life … [it] makes men seem useless, not wanted, without a country." A determination to prevent the return of mass unemployment following the Second World War encouraged Beveridge's confidence that "it is possible to have a human society in which every man's effort is wanted and none need stand idle and unpaid."[2] This focus on full employment of adult men reflects the centrality of work to twentieth-century understandings of citizenship, belonging, and masculinity.

Access to work and its remuneration determined most people's places in society. Millions of men and women struggled to make ends meet, relying on low-paying jobs, confronting periodic or persistent unemployment and facing discrimination in and out of the workplace. In the decades before the Second World War, economic crisis in Western Europe and North America exacerbated the inequality pervasive in western capitalism. After the war, governments adopted interventionist social policies that sought, and partially succeeded, to mitigate the most severe poverty and inequality. Yet differences based on class, gender, and race continued to shape access to jobs and resultant social hierarchies. From the mid-1970s, globalization, inflation, and new political approaches drove retrenchment. Commitments to full employment and social rights to adequate housing, health care, income, and education faltered. As unemployment spread, so did inequality. Families dependent on marginal and inconsistent work found themselves trapped in poverty, with limited access to education, employment, and full participation in early twenty-first-century society.

EMPLOYMENT, UNEMPLOYMENT, AND INEQUALITY, 1920–2015

In the wake of the Great War workers faced difficult conditions. The First World War accelerated rationalization and scientific management designed to improve workplace efficiency. Alongside an emphasis on speed, employers sought to reduce the need for skilled workers by subdividing processes and redefining the role of foreman. Unskilled labor was cheaper, and skilled workers' expertise allowed them some control over manufacturing. Though workers developed a variety of strategies to battle employer efforts, the balance of power clearly lay with business owners. Persistent unemployment helped undermine workers' positions. Periods of severe unemployment plagued the economies of capitalist Europe and America at the start of the 1920s and again, more lastingly, in the Depression years of the 1930s.[3]

The economic crisis in the interwar period deepened inequality, as particular industries, regions, and groups of workers faced unemployment and declining wages. The highest risk of unemployment fell on unskilled and uneducated male workers.[4] Workers in heavy industry suffered the most. For example, British shipbuilding saw an unemployment rate of 62 percent in 1932.[5] Long-term unemployment spread, and even those who remained in work faced declining wages.[6] A cotton spinner recalled, "wage reductions, 33 per cent, 7½ per cent, 5 per cent, and it was reduction after reduction after reduction."[7] One estimate of increasing inequality shows that the top 10 percent of earners accounted for 38.10 percent of US income in 1920, a figure that rose to 44.43 percent in 1940.[8] In Britain, the ratio of income earned by the eightieth to ninety-fifth percentile of earners compared to that earned by the bottom 80 percent increased from 1.96 in 1911 to 2.34 in 1938.[9]

The Second World War brought astonishing suffering to millions in Europe and also to North Americans who felt the effects of shortages and deaths of many lost in battle. Mobilization for war, however, finally jolted economies out of the interwar depression. In the UK, unemployment figures declined from 12.9 percent in 1938 to 0.8 percent in 1942.[10] US figures, while not directly comparable, dropped from 19.0 percent in 1938 to 1.9 percent in 1943.[11] War-related industries expanded on an astonishing scale. Aircraft manufacturing in Britain employed twenty thousand people in 1933. Eleven years later, 1.8 million worked in the industry.[12] Women and African Americans moved into war work in large numbers, and many women already in the workforce shifted from low-paid female occupations to better-paid jobs in industry. In 1939, only 27 percent of the insured workforce in British chemical industries were women, but in 1943 women filled 52 percent of these jobs.[13] Although the war brought a decline in inequality, discrimination against women and black workers persisted. Experiences in war work and military service inspired postwar expectations for greater racial equality in the North. A postwar campaign for civil rights built upon wartime "Double V" strategies that sought victory in the war and equal rights for African Americans. In Britain, due to an emphasis on heroic sacrifice by working-class men and women, "the legitimacy of social inequality was constantly, if subtly, challenged by the war effort."[14] British rhetoric and policy demanded shared sacrifice to a greater extent than in the United States, and the resultant questioning of inequality set the stage for more far-reaching challenges to class and other inequities in postwar society.

After a period of postwar adjustment, economic growth, the expansion of welfare provisions, and the assertion of union power combined to reduce inequality in western societies after the Second World War.[15] In France, three decades of economic growth averaging 5.2 percent annually supported conditions of full employment in "*les Trente Glorieuses* (the glorious thirty)."[16] According to Organisation for Economic Co-operation and Development (OECD) figures, French unemployment rates between 1956 and 1970 hovered between 0.8 percent and 2.2 percent. Similarly, unemployment rates in West Germany remained below 2 percent through the 1960s, and UK rates in that period reached only as high as 2.2 percent (in 1968 and 1970). Figures for the United States reveal less commitment to full employment, as US unemployment reached 6.8 percent in 1958 and 6.7 percent in 1961.[17] Even in the absence of full employment,

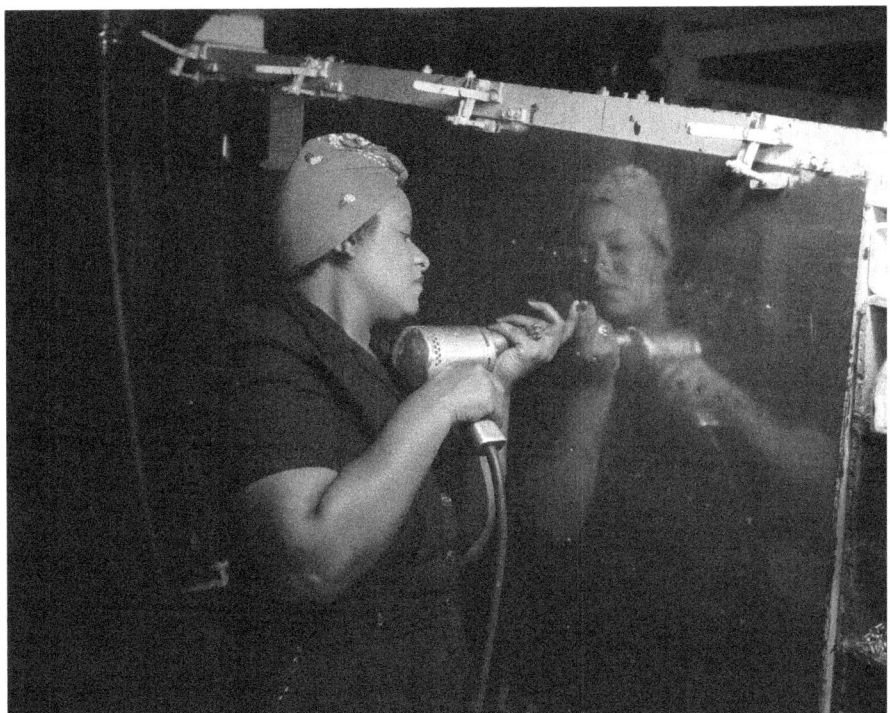

FIGURE 7.1 Worker assembling a bomber in Nashville, Tennessee, 1943. Photo: Alfred T. Palmer, US Office of War Information. Public domain.

though, strong demand for labor and union organization in the United States helped increase weekly earnings of non-supervisory workers by 62 percent between 1947 and 1972.[18] Jack Metzgar, a steelworker's son who grew up in Johnstown, Pennsylvania, recalled, "the Steelworkers' union begat all that was good in our lives."[19] In Britain, real wages increased by more than a quarter between 1950 and 1965. Higher earnings allowed workers to participate in the growing consumer economy. In the early 1960s, British workers consumed 40 percent more meat, more than double the butter, and more than 20 percent more vegetables than they had a decade and a half earlier. A 1967 survey found that most British working-class families had washing machines and over a third had refrigerators (compared to fewer than one in twenty in 1956).[20] In 1950, Americans owned 49 million cars; by 1972, this total had more than doubled, to 119 million.[21]

These changes diminished the often-striking inequality that characterized twentieth-century capitalist societies. Yet the distribution of the benefits of consumer society remained uneven. While unions helped negotiate higher wages for their members, American labor organizations often reproduced cultures of discrimination and inequality by excluding or restricting black workers. Shifts in employment toward clerical, service, and professional jobs began in the 1950s, when US employment for operatives declined by 0.1 percent and jobs for laborers increased by a paltry 0.4 percent. On the other hand, clerical employment increased by 2.5 percent, sales jobs grew 1.4 percent, and professional/technical jobs boomed with 5 percent growth.[22] Stagnation in manual laboring sectors meant that, even in 1969 when employment was relatively strong, 20 percent of American workers suffered unemployment for at least a short period.[23]

Even for workers with steady employment, the postwar boom could be a mixed blessing. In the early 1960s, a group of researchers studied "affluent" British workers created by the postwar boom. Visiting an automobile worker and his wife, an investigator found the house to be "immaculately clean, very well decorated ... full of reasonably good and very well maintained furniture." The woman, however, shared her frustrations: "everybody had to work far too hard to have any ... life at all." She also noted the high prices of food, housing, and other commodities.[24] Thus, while the decades following the Second World War represented a high point for workers in western societies, characterized by strong demand for labor, increasing wages, and relatively generous welfare benefits (discussed below), inequality persisted, and participation in the postwar consumerism often required relentless hard work.

Beginning in the 1970s, economic challenges undermined strong employment conditions in the United States and the commitment to full employment in Europe. In the United States, unemployment reached peaks of 8.5 percent in 1975, 9.7 percent in 1982, and 9.6 percent in 2009. In the UK, double-digit unemployment persisted from 1982 to 1987 and returned in 1993. The French figures peaked above 10 percent in 1994, 1996, and 1997, and French unemployment remained above 6 percent every year from 1981 to 2013. Even in Sweden unemployment rates surpassed 10 percent in 1996 and 1997.[25] Employers cut manufacturing jobs that had provided steady employment and rising wages. In 1979, for example, US automobile companies announced factory closings idling fifty thousand workers and undermining an additional eighty thousand jobs with suppliers.[26] In Yorkshire, 189,000 factory jobs disappeared from 1980 to 1986. One Yorkshire man commented: "We've got no money, we've got no jobs ... we've got nowt."[27] Following the defeat of the miners' strike in 1984 and 1985, British authorities closed coal mines rapidly, eliminating a quarter million jobs.[28] In coal villages where economic life and culture revolved around mining, a redundant miner recalled: "When they shut it was sheer devastation."[29] What job growth did occur tended to be in lower-paid, often female-dominated sectors of the labor market, in service-sector, low-end white-collar, and government work.

Amid rising unemployment and pressure from international competition, employers reduced wages, contributing to increasing inequality in western societies. In the United States, real wages peaked in the early 1970s but declined consistently through the mid-1990s and again in the first years of the twenty-first century.[30] Across sixteen capitalist democracies, labor's share of national income, a useful measure of relative equality, declined from 73 percent in 1980 to 64 percent in 2005.[31] Unemployment and falling wages affected those at the lower end of the income scale most severely. From 1979 to 1989, for example, real hourly US earnings fell by 14.6 percent for those in the tenth percentile of wages, but they increased by 6.8 percent for those in the ninetieth percentile.[32] Steep declines in heavy industry undermined communities in the north of England, as well as Scotland and Wales. In these regions, deindustrialization left long-term, even intergenerational, unemployment in its wake, while the southeast of England benefited from a boom in finance and service industries.[33]

In addition to this broad-based inequality in the workplace and throughout society, persistent patterns of inequality in the labor market based on gender and racial or ethnic differences reinforced social hierarchies. Rates of women's wage earning increased across the period, but women's earnings remained low. In the United States, for example, approximately 24 percent of women earned wages in 1930, rising to 29 percent in 1950 and 40 percent in 1975.[34] From the 1970s, amid widespread unemployment, women's participation in paid work continued to increase. In the United States, 51.5 percent of women were part of the labor force in 1980 and 59.2 percent in 2009. In the UK, 48.6 percent of women sought employment in 1980, and 58.6 percent did so in 2009. Similar increases appear in other western countries.[35] Despite this trend, deep cultural ambivalence about women's employment, gendered perceptions of skill, and a determination by male workers and employers to confine women to distinct and subordinate positions kept most employed women in poorly paid segments of labor markets.

Job segregation often forced women into work that employers and male workers defined as less skilled than men's jobs. At the Philco radio assembly plant in Philadelphia between the wars, male managers categorized women's jobs as less difficult and lighter than men's work. One woman recalled, "I used to get angry … the men got the best jobs."[36] More broadly, between 1910 and 1940, more than 85 percent of employed women in the United States worked in only ten occupations. At the end of the century more than 95 percent of secretaries, childcare and domestic workers, nursery school and kindergarten teachers in the United States were women.[37] Perceptions of skill difference persisted as well, though definitions of skill reflected gendered assumptions more than actual technical knowledge.[38] A leader of a 1968 strike by female sewing machinists against Ford in Britain complained: "we have to pass a test on three machines … why shouldn't they recognize us as skilled workers?"[39] As office jobs expanded rapidly in the decades following the Second World War, gendered job definitions proliferated. A study of banking in the 1960s found "a clear-cut sex distinction in the staff. Careers in banking are for men; the routine work such as machine-operating is for women."[40]

FIGURE 7.2 Striking machinists from the Ford facility in Dagenham, 1968. Courtesy Getty Images.

Definitions of women's work as unskilled (or "semi"-professional) reinforced gender hierarchies in society and culture, as low wages left many women dependent on male earners or facing poverty.[41] A British employer expressed a common attitude: "There are certain classes of work which are essentially women's work and should be paid ... at a rate suitable to it being women's work."[42] In the United States, women's wages averaged 57 percent of men's wages at the end of the 1920s. Little change left women's wages at 58 percent of men's in the mid-1960s. The impact of feminism and government regulation helped increase women's wages to 75 percent of men's by the late 1990s.[43] Despite some additional change in the twenty-first century, 2010 figures show a persistent gap of 18.8 percent in the United States, 19.2 percent in the UK, 14.1 percent in France, and 14.3 percent in Sweden.[44] In addition, women continued to bear the burden of unpaid household labor. American women still did 1.6 times more housework than men in 2009 and 2010.[45]

Racial and ethnic inequality at work also reinforced social hierarchies. African American men and women faced persistent discrimination that limited their opportunities to the lower ranks of labor markets. While northern cities drew large numbers of black migrants in the 1920s, employers maintained limits on the jobs open to them. Swift and Armour meatpacking plants in Chicago, for example, prohibited black workers from work on finished products.[46] In many cases, white workers approved of these limitations or resisted attempts to overcome them. During the Second World War, government pressure led to new opportunities for some black workers.[47] At the Packard Motor Company plant in Detroit, twenty-five thousand white workers struck to protest the promotion of three black men to assembly line jobs in aircraft manufacture.[48] Despite gains during the Second World War and in the postwar period, racial and ethnic disparities persisted. In 1960, while African Americans comprised 25.7 percent of Chrysler's Detroit workers, only 67 out of 11,125 skilled workers were black.[49] In 1960, the earnings of Mexican-American veterans lagged Anglo veterans across the full range of occupations. For example, Anglo veteran craftsmen earned 19.9 percent more than Mexican-American veterans in similar jobs.[50] In 2011, median hourly wages for non-Hispanic white men in the United States exceeded wages for black men by 38.6 percent and exceeded Hispanic men's median wages by 55.1 percent.[51]

Outside the United States, racial and ethnic discrimination also confined many members of minority populations to poorly paid and often low-skill jobs. A labor shortage in France led to large-scale immigration from North Africa in the 1920s. From the 1950s into the 1970s, many immigrants from former colonies and Mediterranean regions entered northern Europe, while more recent immigrants entered Western Europe primarily as asylum seekers, refugees, or labor migrants from Eastern Europe.[52] Many faced poor pay and barriers to employment in skilled work. In one Paris sugar refinery, for example, North African workers earned an average of 29.50 francs per day in 1929, while native French men earned 50.80 francs.[53] In Coventry, local unions tried to keep black and Asian workers out of highly paid jobs in car manufacture. An Indian immigrant who arrived there in 1962 recalled the difficulty getting such jobs: "you stand in a queue, see the white blokes coming from the back, getting the jobs and you was turned down."[54]

When unemployment increased, workers from minority groups suffered the most. In 1934, the unemployment rate for black men reached 40 percent in Chicago, 48 percent in Pittsburgh, and a staggering 60 percent in Detroit.[55] A black packinghouse worker in Chicago complained that, with white workers desperate enough to take on unattractive stockyard jobs, African Americans lost out: "They were hiring young, white boys, sixteen and eighteen years old, raw kids, didn't know a thing" to replace black workers.[56]

Minority groups functioned as labor market buffers in downturns from the 1970s. In the 2008 recession, black and Hispanic workers in the United States again suffered disproportionately. In 2010, the unemployment rate for white workers peaked at 8.0 percent, while Hispanic workers faced a rate of 12.5 percent and black unemployment reached 15.9 percent.[57]

Persistent inequalities in access to health, quality housing, and education overlapped with gender and racial or ethnic difference. Men and women with low skill levels and little education fared poorly in labor markets, earning low wages and facing insecurity and unemployment.[58] For example, in 1931, 21.5 percent of unskilled men in Britain were unemployed, compared to 11.9 percent of skilled or semi-skilled men.[59] In 1986, another peak year for British unemployment, unskilled workers accounted for just 3 percent of economically active men but they made up 11 percent of the unemployed.[60] In 2007, 10.3 percent of Americans who did not graduate from high school were jobless. The rate for those who had completed a college degree was 2.4 percent.[61]

The spatial concentration of those on the margins of the labor markets created zones of poverty in major cities and in regions hardest hit by late twentieth-century deindustrialization. In these areas, poverty and unemployment, poor housing, environmental degradation, poor schools, high crime rates, and racial or ethnic discrimination reinforced one another. In Detroit, for example, the number of census tracts with at least 40 percent of the population living in poverty doubled in the 1970s, and racial segregation defined many of these areas as black neighborhoods.[62] Schools in segregated and impoverished neighborhoods struggled to provide even basic levels of education to their students. A total of 25,500 black or Hispanic students entered ninth grade in segregated, non-selective Chicago schools in 1980. Of these, sixteen thousand did not graduate four years later, and of those who graduated, a significant minority read at or below eleventh-grade proficiency.[63] These areas also became centers of environmental hazards. Hazel Johnson's Chicago neighborhood served as "a dumping ground for 163 years."[64] In French cities the impoverished *banlieues* (suburban districts), housing significant populations of immigrants and the children of immigrants with low education levels, have become centers of mass unemployment and marginalization from French society.[65] In 2006, one estimate found male unemployment in these districts approached 36 percent.[66] In Britain, the combination of deindustrialization and the privatization of much local authority council housing in the 1980s left areas of poor-quality housing where those excluded from the mainstream labor force collected.[67]

WORK AND WELFARE

In the twentieth century, western capitalist societies developed welfare programs to address some of the implications of this inequality. In Britain, the United States, and France, work was central to approaches to welfare benefits and entitlement. In the 1920s, some American companies offered benefits including medical care, opportunities to purchase shares in companies, and sponsored leisure activities. Employers hoped this "welfare capitalism" might build loyalty, stabilize their workforces, and undermine union growth.[68] Many workers remained skeptical. One packinghouse worker complained: "What good was a band-aid or an aspirin when I was standing up to my ankles in cold water, freezing half to death?"[69] Once the Depression hit, much of this corporate largesse, patchy and inadequate as it was, disappeared, and a period of experimentation in American welfare began. The most lasting innovations of the New Deal era enshrined distinctions between contributory programs for privileged workers (unemployment insurance and Social Security, generally geared toward male workers) and public assistance (typically means-tested and directed at women).[70] In a debate over the creation of Social Security, Representative Robert Doughton reassured skeptics that, "the worker's right to benefits is conditioned upon his previous employment."[71] Only some workers counted in these calculations, though, as domestic servants and agricultural workers (many of them black) did not qualify until the 1950s.[72]

The postwar years saw the growth of collective bargaining and employee benefits, often driven by unions and civil rights agitation. Private health insurance and pensions spread among regularly employed unionized or salaried workers.[73] Many, though, remained without coverage. Two new programs in the 1960s developed US government provision of health care. Medicare provided health coverage for the elderly, while Medicaid offered some health benefits to the poor. The division between these programs, according to Michael Katz, "reinforced the wall between social insurance and public assistance" central to American social programs.[74] The main New Deal income assistance program, Aid to Families with Dependent Children (AFDC), expanded significantly in the 1960s and 1970s, as activists worked to reduce barriers to enrolment. They encouraged those eligible, chiefly poor women with dependent children and no male support, to "Come and learn your rights" to welfare.[75]

In Britain, persistent unemployment in the decades after the First World War challenged government policies that assumed the availability of work. The system of contributory unemployment insurance quickly broke down, and the government struggled through forty Insurance Acts between 1920 and 1934.[76] Authorities distinguished between those deserving of help and the allegedly unworthy, denying benefits to three million applicants in the 1920s, because they failed to demonstrate that they were "genuinely seeking work."[77] In the 1930s, the means test, an invasive and humiliating investigation of family resources, replaced this genuinely-seeking-work standard for those needing assistance. During the Second World War, many in Britain embraced a broader notion of individual rights and collective responsibilities. This appeared most clearly in the tax-funded universal National Health Service, but an aggressive program of council housing construction, family allowances, and a commitment to full employment also reflected the collectivist approach of the postwar British state. Contributions from workers, employers, and taxes provided the basis for most social spending.[78] From the start, though, the inadequacy of insurance payments and the persistence of the means test for those seeking benefits outside the contributory system (through National Assistance) indicated that the British system fell short of its lofty goals.[79]

The French welfare state, even more than that in Britain or the United States, revolved around employment. In the interwar period, family allowances paid by employers rewarded parents, and particularly fathers, with significant supplements to their wages. Employers controlled these benefits and used them to encourage loyalty, resist demands for increased wages, and control their workforce (as well as encourage fertility).[80] An employment-centered approach persisted after the Second World War, as the French developed a broader social security system directed to the employed male head of the family. Social insurance schemes covering health care, old age, and family allowances linked benefits (including unemployment benefits starting in 1958) to employment.[81]

The economic downturn beginning in the 1970s and conservative backlash in the 1980s, associated in the United States with the Reagan administration and in Britain

FIGURE 7.3 Minister of Health Aneurin Bevan at a hospital near Manchester on the first day of the National Health Service, July 1948. University of Liverpool, Faculty of Health and Life Sciences. Creative Commons.

with Thatcher's governments, drove reconsideration of social programs. In the 1990s, the Clinton administration built on Reagan-era criticism of the welfare system and replaced AFDC with Temporary Assistance for Needy Families (TANF). TANF included a work requirement, a five-year limit on federal benefits and wider state authority in denying benefits. New York City drove many recipients into a "workfare" program of low-wage work, without the benefits or protections of regular employment. One participant challenged this lower status: "What is it about me … that my work is different or of less value than the same work done by someone else?"[82] Welfare reform reflected changing perceptions of the system and those dependent upon it that spread from the 1970s. Politicians peddled derogatory racial and sexual messages in the image of the "welfare queen," sexually promiscuous, cheating the system, and enjoying luxury goods. As one critic of this tendency complained, "'Welfare cheater' has become the new code word for the poor, for minorities in general and those temporarily down on their luck." By focusing on single mothers' relationships with men as a strategy for denying them benefits, the government was "peeking under the beds of welfare recipients."[83] Policy makers blamed the poor for their own poverty, but growing income inequality and wage stagnation accompanied these changes, and many employed Americans qualified for supplemental assistance through Medicaid, food assistance, and the earned income tax credit. According to one 2013 calculation, 44 percent of workers in restaurants and food services and 30 percent of those in retail trades received this sort of government assistance.[84] Through all these changes, the fundamental distinction between those in stable and approved employment and those dependent on assistance remained in the American welfare system.[85]

Beginning with Thatcher's attack on the welfare state in the 1980s, the British commitment to social rights weakened, shifting priority from provision of economic security to containing costs and pushing working-age claimants into the labor market.[86] Alongside policy changes, government rhetoric criticized benefits and recipients. This fostered a shift in popular views of the welfare state. In 1993, 55 percent of the British population viewed out-of-work benefits as too low. In 2011, though, only 19 percent responded this way, despite little change in the value of benefits. Survey results showed declining solidarity with those dependent on out-of-work benefits.[87] While the National Health Service remained, the British welfare state turned away from its broader postwar embrace of social rights.

Starting in the 1970s, prolonged unemployment created a crisis in the French welfare system. Employment-based schemes did not cover those who either never entered the labor market or remained unemployed for long periods. As the numbers of those excluded from the system grew, policy makers developed benefits based on broader taxation and not dependent upon a history of employment. The government introduced a broad tax to support social spending, the CSG (*Contribution Sociale Généralisée*). In the 1990s a new program required unemployed individuals to participate in training or job placement in return for a minimum income.[88] With these shifts, the French moved from a strictly employment-based system of entitlement to a system more like that of the British, based on a limited notion of social rights, attenuated by requirements of work or training to qualify for some benefits. In all three settings, late twentieth-century welfare approaches emphasized employment and training as conditions for social support.

WORK AND CLASS

Since 1990, historians have reconsidered the centrality of work and class consciousness in history and paid more attention to language, culture, and complex identities.[89] The links between manual labor, class consciousness, and political mobilization have always been tenuous, and historians have understood the lack of direct and predictable connections between exploitation in the workplace and radical politics. Identification with others reflects individuals' embrace of narratives of commonality and difference that are multiple and varied, based on any number of criteria, including occupational, regional, racial, ethnic, gender, and other factors. Nonetheless, experiences in the workplace, in neighborhoods and communities, in leisure sites, and in interactions with authorities, have fostered distinct working-class cultures and identities. The patterns of inequality described above form essential building blocks for these experiences. In Britain, working-class culture endured through mass unemployment in the interwar period, economic growth and full employment in the 1950s and 1960s and deindustrialization and renewed unemployment since the 1970s. In the United States, class has often been more fragmented, particularly due to ethnic and racial animosity. At times, American workers overcame these differences and identified with a shared working-class interest. Often, however, working-class cultures in the United States reflected difference and animosity rather than class solidarity.[90]

Across the middle decades of the twentieth century, patterns of "traditional" working-class life in Britain persisted, based on experiences at work in class-distinct neighborhoods and in distinctive working-class leisure pursuits. Poverty and unemployment before the Second World War and consistent waged work after the war bolstered this sense of class identity. Keith Barrett recalled the class-specific opportunities in his East Yorkshire town in the 1960s: "the careers officer ... asked me where I lived, what my family did, and he wrote down, on a piece of paper 'job interview for you at Melrose tanners'."[91] Racial and religious differences did divide workers. For example, in 1919 race riots plagued British port cities, as racist attitudes drove attempts to exclude workers from Africa or Asia from getting places on ships.[92] At other times, though, working-class identity flourished across racial or sectarian lines. Richard Hoggart described this sense as developing, "from the feeling that life is hard, and that 'our sort' will usually get 'the dirty end of the stick'."[93] This notion of difference between "us" and "them" also appears in the recollection of Les White, who grew up on a council estate in the 1940s and 1950s: "They always reckon you live at one side of the lines you're not wanted at the other side of the lines ... [where] all the poshies live."[94] Even as the postwar boom raised the standard of living for many working-class men and women, class identity remained strong, as a late-1960s investigator found: "the working class is undoubtedly far, far better than it was. But in essence it *feels* the same, offers the same kind of *experience*."[95]

In the United States, distinctive living and working conditions and economic insecurity also marked the working class though the language of class was more elastic than in the UK. Aside from a brief period in the 1930s, these conditions seldom gave rise to a cohesive or persistent class identity. Working people clustered in neighborhoods that reflected their economic positions but also often their ethnic and racial identities. In their famous study of "Middletown" (Muncie, Indiana) in the late 1920s, Robert and Helen Lynd described "this division into working class and business class that constitutes the outstanding cleavage."[96] Some workers overcame racial differences, uniting in the Congress of Industrial Organizations (CIO), a union movement far more inclusive of black workers than the more established craft unions, as reflected in its slogan, "Black and White, Unite and Fight." Few, though, transcended racial boundaries in their neighborhoods.[97] Collective resistance to integration in white working-class communities in the middle decades of the twentieth century illustrates the power of identities that failed to cross racial lines. Neighborhood homeowners' groups in Detroit organized to keep their communities segregated, and white working-class parents resisted the integration of Little Rock's Central High School.[98] As the authors of a standard survey of the American working-class movement observe: "members of the American working-class did not commonly *think* of themselves as a class."[99]

In the last quarter of the twentieth century, the decline of manufacturing, persistent unemployment and the rise of service industry jobs with lower pay and less security further undermined the position of many working-class men and women. Deindustrialization destroyed the staple industries and large works that had sustained the identities of many working-class communities. In 1971, nearly 55 percent of British workers held manual laboring jobs; by 1991, fewer than 40 percent worked with their hands, with many others in sales positions or low-level office work.[100] In Britain, though, working-class identity remained important, despite the decline in manual employment. A 2002 poll found that 68 percent of respondents aged fifteen and older agreed with the statement, "I'm working class and proud of it."[101] A few years earlier, Robert Turner, a 51-year-old man from Hull, reflected on class difference. Of the middle class, he said, "I just picture them as earning a decent wage and buying their own house." He acknowledged, "we do that too, some of us, don't we? So maybe we're not so different. But I know I'm working class."[102]

In the United States, less clearly defined class identities developed in the late twentieth century. Many white workers shared a general sense of middle-class status, as reflected in Bill Clinton's accepting his nomination for president "in the name of the hardworking Americans who make up our forgotten middle class."[103] At work, though, manual laborers continued to experience subordination, difficult working conditions, and often boredom on their jobs. This created a sense of themselves as "working men." A New Jersey chemical worker reflected this identity: "The working man is the nub of the whole thing. We do all the work." Workers such as this man, though, lived in housing segregated by race, not by class. In their neighborhoods and in leisure sites they mixed with and participated in consumer society alongside white-collar workers and some professionals. A coworker in the chemical plant reflected this view: "I'm middle class. All these guys are middle class."[104] This complex identity often excluded racial and ethnic minorities and the poor, stigmatized as nonworking. Other sectional identities contributed to fragmentation among American workers. For example, a Southern white working-class identity thrived, cultivated by Republican political leaders and media personalities. Comedian Jeff Foxworthy celebrated this blue-collar Southern subculture with gentle mocking of the "redneck": "We're not offended, 'cause we know what we're all about. We get up and go to work, we get up and go to church, and we get up and go to war when necessary."[105] While spreading beyond its Southern roots, this form of working-class identity is heavily male and predominantly white. Thus, inequalities grounded in the workplace stretched into neighborhoods and communities and developed into geographically and racially fragmented identities in the United States. By contrast, in Britain this inequality has given rise to a persistent working-class identity, despite economic changes that undermined much of the industrial economy.

CONCLUSION

Experiences at work and attitudes toward those without work fundamentally shaped class identities and attitudes about belonging. Similarly, the link between work and rights exemplifies the changing connection between the individual's status as citizen and status as worker. Even as suffrage extended to include all adults and social rights expanded concepts of citizenship, employed men became the standard of such citizenship. Beveridge discussed male citizen-workers' status, "carrying with it the rights of citizenship—civil liberty, political power, fatherhood."[106] Though Beveridge imagined an exclusively male worker-citizen, some women claimed citizen status as workers. In 1932, for example, Marcelle Bravey argued for women's suffrage in France, noting that women "each morning run off to the factory, office, or workshop ... pay taxes."[107] Similarly, in 1934 an activist organization in Pittsburgh trumpeted an employment-based definition of citizenship, claiming that "by citizen we do not mean only those persons who are naturalized but all wage-earners."[108] The principle tying work to citizenship, though, meant those unable or unwilling to work lost such status. Beveridge argued that "unemployable" men, dependent upon the state, would suffer, "the complete and permanent loss of all citizen rights—including not only the franchise but civil freedom and fatherhood."[109] Employment did not, in itself, constitute a clear pathway to citizenship. Racial barriers denied black workers political and social rights through much of the twentieth century. Women gained full political rights in Britain only in 1928 and in France at the end of the Second World War. Many immigrants remained outside the boundaries of full citizenship regardless of employment.

Claimants to citizenship sometimes used other arguments instead of or alongside work in making arguments for citizen status. Some women called for citizenship on the basis of motherhood. Thus, a French women's suffrage organization noted in 1908, "The pregnant woman works physiologically and psychologically for the nation." On the other hand, some French observers argued that fathers should enjoy augmented citizenship rights based on their paternity. A father would, "possess, in addition to his own vote, as many votes as he has living minor legitimate or recognized children in his care."[110] Perhaps the most significant challenge to the connection between employment and citizenship came during the 1930s, when many adult men who would otherwise expect to qualify for full citizenship could not find work. Those without work claimed a right to citizenship. In Chicago, the unemployed "demand relief and become indignant when a worker presumes to question their eligibility."[111] Some of those seeking government help inverted the argument that work qualified people (or at least white men) for citizenship. Instead, according to Works Progress Administration (WPA) official and sociologist Nels Anderson in 1935, the unemployed "say in effect: 'We claim the rights of citizens. We want work instead of relief; and we have a right to work'."[112]

Beginning in the 1980s, however, efforts to curtail the welfare state, developed by conservatives but often advanced by Democrats in the United States and New Labour in Britain, again linked social rights to work. Welfare reform in the United States in the 1990s established a work requirement for recipients of TANF benefits. In Britain, an expanding regime of work-related requirements as conditions of unemployment benefits reflects the turn away from social citizenship independent of employment. Implementing these new requirements in 2014, Conservative minister Iain Duncan Smith rejected what he called the "'something for nothing' culture" of the welfare state.[113] At the same time, the spread

FIGURE 7.4 Hunger marchers in Washington, DC, claim rights to employment and relief, December 1931. Courtesy Getty Images.

of low-wage, contingent, and part-time work at the start of the twenty-first century left many of those who entered the labor force in poverty. Sociologist T. H. Marshall argued that social citizenship required not only "a modicum of economic welfare and security," but also "the right to share to the full in the social heritage and to live the life of a civilized being according to the standards prevailing in the society."[114] State-accepted inequalities and the decline of stable manufacturing jobs in industrialized societies made it impossible for many to share fully in the kind of social citizenship Marshall advocated. Unequal access to employment and inequities based on education and skill, racial or ethnic difference, and gender institutionalized inequality in western societies and culture. From the 1940s to the 1970s, strong unions, civil rights, full employment, and the expansion of welfare states helped mitigate this inequality and the enjoyment of social rights spread. Since then growing wage inequality, the abandonment of full-employment policies, the weakening of unions, and welfare state retrenchment all combined to jeopardize access to full citizenship, decent living standards, and dignity for many in otherwise wealthy western societies.

CHAPTER EIGHT

The Political Culture of Work

STEPHEN MEYER

The automobile industry was a paradigmatic example for the exploration of the political culture of work in the twentieth century.[1] In the words of the business historian Peter Drucker: "The automobile industry stands for modern industry all over the globe." As with the nineteenth-century British cotton industry, it was "the industry of industries."[2] Emphasizing the enormous profits that the industry generated for manufacturers in the mid-twentieth century, for Edward D. Kennedy, an auto-industry analyst, this crucial industry was "capitalism's favourite child."[3] And, as the sociologist of automobile workers Ely Chinoy asserted, the Ford assembly line "has been a dominating symbol of modern industrialism."[4]

From its beginning, the auto industry also established the pattern for work and a culture of resistance through the twentieth century. Describing the political culture that animated work and workers in the modern era through the twentieth century, Charles R. Walker, the director of the Yale Technology Project, understood the social and cultural importance of the shop floor. "Persons unfamiliar with mills and factories," he observed, "often remark on visiting them that they seem like another world." He added: "This is particularly true if ... both tradition and technology have strongly and uniquely moulded the ways men think and act when at work." The traditions of people and the forces of technology blended to refashion the social and cultural world of workplace life. Even the new or "green" worker realized how this other world constituted a special and unique space in terms of its "social classes, folklore, ritual, and traditions."[5]

The leftist writer and occasional autoworker Harvey Swados maintained that "hatred, shame and resignation" compounded the "worker's attitude toward his work."[6] Hatred arose from the mindless, mechanized, and routinized regimen of the mass-production factory; shame from the low status of the person who labored at line production and machines in oil and dirt; and resignation from the limited choices available to resist the horrid work and lowly status. But, over the years, workers developed political means to oppose their social and economic degradation, initially in isolated and hidden forms and later in more collective and overt ones that culminated in massive strikes, such as the auto industry's monumental sit-down strikes in the mid-1930s that brought industrial unionism to the United States.

The political anthropologist James C. Scott's notion of the "weapons of the weak" illuminates the subtle "hidden" power dynamics between dominant and subordinate groups such as between managers and workers. Without overt or visible political or economic power, industrial workers, especially after the dawn of mass production, used their "everyday forms of resistance" to redress the grievances and abuses of those who ruled over them. Scott labelled such activities "infrapolitics," the hidden or nonpublic means of resistance "outside the visible spectrum of what usually passes for political activity." Infrapolitics included "the ordinary weapons of relatively powerless groups: foot-dragging, dissimulation, false compliance, pilfering, feigned ignorance, slander, arson, sabotage, and so forth." Though Scott specifically examined preindustrial or peasant forms of resistance, many of these persisted through to the age of mass production, in both its nonpublic and its public forms.[7]

Two labor scholars would have agreed with Scott. Alf Leudtke, a German historian, and Paul Thompson, a British sociologist and oral historian, have noted the social and cultural responses of workers to their situations of powerlessness and subordination. In his investigation of early twentieth-century German factory workers, Leudtke noted the distinction between the officially sanctioned "legal" breaks, or rest periods for "physical replenishment," and "illegal" breaks, or the workers' expropriation of "bits of time formally designated as working time."[8] In shop floor horseplay, workers made claims against "supervisors' demands [by] maintaining customary rights and of striving for the humanity of the individual and his comrades."[9] Similarly, Thompson discovered that British car workers had three possible responses to disciplined and regimented work—avoiding it, changing it, or accepting it and "putting one's heart elsewhere." The latter strategy redefined and reshaped work culture and transformed the shop floor and workplace into a place more amenable to workers' needs or desires.[10] In both instances, this illicit behavior often involved oppositional and confrontational rituals and displays of power to challenge the newly established routinized Taylorist and Fordist industrial order that existed in auto firms.

The politics of worker resistance, either as "everyday resistance" or "open defiance," involved three phases in the evolution of the political culture of work in the United States specifically, though the shifts would largely reflect changes in modern industrial societies more generally. First, individuals confronted with and reacted to the new regime of mass production and the Great Depression through the 1920s and into the early 1930s; second, there was a growing sense of the need for collective forms of resistance and covert and individual efforts in the union-building and union-consolidation processes from the mid-1930s through the 1950s, a very brief twenty-year period of union power. And third, there was a gradual decline in union power in the era of post-1980 neoliberal globalization with industrial decentralization and deunionization and, later, with runaway plants to the nonunion South and less-skilled expensive labor around the globe. With the diminution of union power that actually began in the late 1960s, autoworkers often returned to the hidden forms of the shop cultures of resistance often incorporated into formal grievance processes.

THE INTERWAR YEARS

When the automobile industry began around 1900, its political culture of work rested on craft skills of metal, foundry, and wood, and other highly skilled workers. David Montgomery described the skilled and autonomous craftsman's openly defiant "disciplined ethical code" of worker and union control. It included the "stint" or the fair output quota that the workers established for a job and a "manly bearing toward the boss" that bore notions of "dignity, respectability, defiant egalitarianism, and patriarchal male supremacy." Moreover, "manliness" toward fellow workers meant not being "hoggish" and damaging the possibility of work for others by "running two machines" or "doing work of two men." Workers in craft unions embedded much of this ethic in union work rules and later industrial unions adopted similar, though a less formal work ethos.[11] These work cultures rested on notions of defiance to management oversight and in support of worker control over production.

From 1910 to 1914, Ford mass production totally transformed the craft political culture of work in America and reshaped the social, economic, and cultural forces of the automobile industry through the entire twentieth century. Globally, industrial and industrializing nations fitfully attempted to adopt Fordism from the 1920s on. The Italian Marxist theoretician Antonio Gramsci highlighted the importance of the new industrial technologies in his early 1930s essay "Americanism and Fordism" emphasizing the impact of mass production and mass consumption on everyday life.[12] For different nations, Fordism arrived at different times and in different ways. Although it represented an ideal form for production, few European industrial nations actually achieved the ideal until after the Second World War. For the most part, they had no mass market and initially produced luxury vehicles where the values of craft production and craft work habits persisted. For Germany, luxury vehicles prevailed until the 1930s concept of Hitler's people's car, or Volkswagen, appeared. Although prototypes appeared in the late 1930s, actual production stalled when the Second World War began. France and Italy also emphasized luxury vehicles, although their communist-dominated unions unsuccessfully pushed for Fordist methods seeking its promises of high wages and mass consumption.

FIGURE 8.1 Ford Assembly line, 1923. Photographer unknown, Library of Congress. Public domain.

The British car industry proved a mixed case for the production of Ford, Morris, and Standard cars. With many luxury producers, solid craft traditions persisted in British car factories. Even in firms with limited efforts at mass production, the British shop culture possessed strong shop steward systems and a practice of shop floor bargaining. These traditions limited management control over workplace practices. Even in the immediate post-Second World War era, British assembly lines operated at much slower line speeds than in America, say twenty to thirty per hour compared to the American forty to fifty per hour—not to mention the one hundred per hour in the Lordstown, Ohio, plant in the 1970s.[13]

Mass-production methods and principles much more thoroughly penetrated almost all American firms where auto work became repetitive, monotonous, and degraded. From the earliest years, unskilled mass-production workers became a huge proportion of the automotive workforce at automatic machines and assembly lines; skilled workers represented a much smaller proportion of the workforce that mainly maintained and repaired the machines and assembly lines.[14] As a "high wage, capital-intensive industry" with "relatively little incentive so substitute female labour for its more expensive male equivalent," the automobile work culture was densely masculine and women worked in sex-typed and stereotyped occupations, often segregated in cut-and-sew or small parts production in separate departments or plants.[15] In those rare instances where they encountered men, they endured harassing hoots and catcalls or the sexual predations of supervisors and foremen.[16]

In addition to a division of labor based upon skill and gender, auto work also involved ethnic or racial divisions of labor that shifted through the century. The least respected or valued ethnic or racial group labored at the most despised work or job assignments. In the United States, the most desired work went to American-born or northern European-born workers. Initially southern and Eastern European workers, mainly Italian, Polish, or Hungarian, occupied the man-killing work assignments in the foundries, paint-shops, or wet-sanding departments. As the industry grew, Mexican and African American migrants began to occupy these positions in the 1920s.[17] Other nations followed a similar pattern with such jobs often occupied by similarly disparaged ethnic groups—Irish migrants in Britain, Turks in Germany, or Algerians in France.

In the United States, the Fordist paradigm of production gradually diffused through other automobile firms in the 1920s and 1930s, and especially after the Second World War. Fordism meant the loss of control over work tasks and productive activities. The drive for greater and greater production at lower costs effectively undermined and destroyed the skilled craftsman's work culture. In automobile towns and cities, "open shop" campaigns targeted trade unions, virtually destroying them in automobile firms. Industrial detective agencies and factory spies rooted out dissident and prounion workers. Company-dominated unions attempted to forestall and prevent the appearance of legitimate labor organizations.

Facing everyday domination, humiliations, and indignities, interwar autoworkers increasingly seethed with anger and discontent, especially as the economy moved into a deep depression. For instance, *Auto Workers News* reports of worker accidents generated much hostility on the shop floor. One correspondent described the notable indifference to the loss of fingers in the huge Ford River Rouge facility in Detroit and how an abusive foreman, cowered a worker. A press operator, he reported, "had just lost the small finger on his left hand." A second man "was immediately put to work on the very same press." After producing about a dozen pieces, "he lost the thumb of his right hand." When workers gathered around the machine discussing the two "accidents," shop supervisors rushed over and yelled "Back to work, back to work." And the workers "sullenly obeyed." Then the foreman "brusquely" assigned a third worker to the malfunctioning machine. The man looked at his ten fingers, the machine, and the foreman. He told the foreman that if he wanted to get out production, he should work the machine himself. He then promptly quit before the foreman could fire him.[18]

But this and similar incidents were only some of the smaller everyday worker accidents that occurred so often in auto factories. Workers lost larger limbs to huge presses. Or the limbs became entangled in the mechanisms of conveyors. They suffered horrid deaths from materials falling from overhead cranes or from vats of molten metal accidentally poured over them. Often foremen or supervisors removed the victim from the shop floor, hurriedly found a replacement, and production rolled on. Such gross managerial indifference to the well-being of workers fostered deep worker anger against management and generated indifference to diligent work.

Autoworkers consistently engaged in what contemporary scholars labelled empty labor or organizational misbehavior through their absenteeism from work, malingering and soldiering on the job, restricting their output, or engaging in play and high jinks on the shop floor. Such misbehavior is captured in a popular saying from former Soviet bloc nations: "They pretend to pay us, and we pretend to work."[19]

Despite the general belief among industrial managers and analysts that only skilled and organized workers managed to soldier or restrict output, other accounts confirm a political culture of resistance to work in a modern and mechanized plant. Through the late 1920s, Stanley B. Mathewson and others engaged in participant observation and conducted interviews of unorganized workers in slightly over one hundred modern industrial settings, including machine shops and automobile factories and parts plants.[20] Contrary to conventional wisdom, the Antioch College industrial sociologist discovered that even unorganized and less-skilled workers widely practiced and engaged in numerous and diverse forms of output restriction. The reasons for output restriction varied—the pressures from workmates not to work too fast; the "boss-ordered" restrictions to avoid layoffs and the breakup of work crews; the attempts to maintain equity of effort and pay under incentive schemes to raise productivit; the efforts to defeat time-study men and obtain favorable job times; the fear that over work would result in unemployment; and the personal grievances against supervisors and management policies. His main conclusion: "Restriction is a widespread institution, deeply entrenched in the working habits of American labouring people." Managers, he believed, paid "only superficial attention" to worker productivity and failed to convince workers that they could "freely give his best efforts" without suffering penalties instead of rewards for his hard work.[21]

In his autobiographical memoir, the leftist autoworker Frank Marquart elaborated on the many ways that autoworker shop culture remained through the 1920s and 1930s and allowed workers to assert and reassert control over work. He described how he and his workmates often bested the intrusive efforts of time-study men. Even at simple tasks, his feigned fumbling at bench work he managed to get a good "price" for the job. After such deception, he "had no difficulty 'making out'," or meeting his new quota. His deception created small bits of time that allowed him to earn a higher wage and avoid serious overexertion. This, Marquart concluded: "was similar with other jobs: those of us who worked on the bench could find all kinds of shortcuts—ways we never revealed to the time-study man."[22]

American autoworkers often "stole a trade" or worked through a series of jobs to accumulate the work experience of a skilled worker and to obtain the more lucrative work of a stolen trade. Stan Coultard, a British immigrant to Detroit, stole a trade at Chrysler and had "no qualms about the "cheating," since the Chrysler firm "got it out of my hide before I'd finished."[23]

Marquart and his workmates also criticized the shop rate busters who exceeded a work group's production norms causing supervisors to retime the operation and to lower the piece rates. In his Continental Motors shop, the workers only allowed cylinder grinders to turn out a dozen six-cylinder blocks for a work shift. He and his shop mates knew that if they exceed this limit, rates would be cut. But some "hungry bastards," he added, "were so greedy for extra pay that they turned in fourteen or fifteen blocks." Universally resented, the collective male shop culture ostracized, refused to talk to, and often punished them. "Every time one of them went for a drink of water or to the washroom," he recalled, "the belts on his machines were cut, the grinding wheel was smashed, his personal tools were damaged, the word 'RAT' was chalked on his machine in block letters." Treated as a "scab" by workmates, two "speed kings" eventually quit Continental Motors.[24]

Though the available evidence is sparser for automobile workers in other parts of the world, British vehicle manufacturing workplaces exhibited comparable behavior in shop initiation rituals for novices, pranks among workers, and in the traditions of ca'canny. At Longbridge in the 1930s, one observer identified the existence of "passive resistance and sabotage" on the part of workers. Also, when the theoretical time limits were excessive, workers "ca'cannied [or slowed down] so as not to earn too much"; when wages were "insufficient" they also "went slow" and "lodged a complaint with the foreman."[25] Many British firms used a gang system of group piecework where they believed that workers would discipline other group members. But this devolved into a system of shop floor control, which enhanced worker authority over production norms.[26]

Such weapons of the weak helped unskilled production workers to cope with and to control their work lives in forms of resistance both hidden and covert. The bitter opposition of employers forced such actions underground. But wage cuts and speed-ups compelled many workers to more overt forms of resistance nonetheless. So, despite managerial opposition, a militant minority of activists continuously and covertly spoke out for and organized for unionism on the shop floors of automobile plants. Their aspirations to an inclusive industrial form of unionism proved another means to deal with and to resist the intrusions of management. Throughout the 1920s, the Auto Workers Union (AWU), a descendant of an earlier carriage and wagon workers' union, attempted to organize on an industrial basis.[27]

The Great Depression changed the game and increased the immediacy of worker needs for control. Auto was not alone in this story, but again its history was typical. One major change was the new and increased role of left political parties in worker political culture. Innumerable socialists, communists, independent leftists, and industrial unionists constantly proselytized for the union cause, always speaking with their workmates and distributing leaflet and pamphlets. The seeds that these shop floor radicals planted eventually bore fruit after American workers and their families suffered from the economic ravages of the Great Depression. Along with other committed industrial unionists, they diligently advocated for the industrial union cause in the automobile plants and factories passing out leaflets, pamphlets, and shop newsletters and newspapers.[28] The AWU newspapers, *The Autoworker* and *Autoworker's News*, related the awful shop conditions, horrid accidents, abusive foremen, and other outrages in the Detroit automobile plants.

The communist shop cadres produced a dozen or so mimeographed shop papers, such as the "Ford Worker," "Dodge Worker," "Briggs Worker," and so forth. In an era of intrusive plant guards and undercover factory spies, these committed unionists smuggled these newspapers into the plants to entice workers into their union or political causes. With detailed information about the abuses and abusers, autoworkers avidly read these newspapers and shop papers. Over time, the seeds of discontent so nurtured exploded into the social revolution of industrial unionism incited by the social and economic depredations of the Great Depression.[29]

Unionism finally came to the American and Canadian automobile industry in the mid-1930s in the social and economic revolution of the Congress of Industrial Organizations (CIO). Socialists, communists, former Industrial Workers of the World members, autoworker industrial unionists, and other militants led a number of often spontaneous autoworker demonstrations and strikes in the early 1930s, such as the Ford Hunger March in 1932, the Briggs Strike in 1933, the Toledo general strike in 1934, and the massive General Motors sit-down strikes at Flint and elsewhere in 1936 and 1937 (Figure 8.2).

The heroic drama of the 1936 and 1937 General Motors sit-down strikers transformed American labor relations and resulted in the consolidation of industrial unionism in the United States. The forceful and aggressive actions of the men who sat in General Motors plants around the nation and the women supporters in the Women's Emergency Brigade fiercely defended the male sit downers on picket lines in the streets. Led by the newly

FIGURE 8.2 On strike, these Flint sit-downers occupy themselves with an activity that normally could not be done under the strict production regime of auto work: reading newspapers. Photo: Sheldon Dick, Library of Congress. Public domain.

formed United Automobile Workers (UAW) union, its success resulted in a sit-down fever among autoworkers and others around the nation. Asserting the collective power of organized workers, CIO unionism rapidly spread through the nation. In 1941, Ford was the only holdout of the big three automobile firms. It only succumbed to militant and organized labor after the huge 1941 strike at the Ford River Rouge plant, where Ford officials attempted to pit white workers against black workers. Owing to successful UAW organization in the African American communities, the Ford effort to forestall Ford unionization failed.[30]

THE WAR AND POSTWAR ERA

During the Second World War years, the UAW gradually consolidated its power in all the major automobile firms. Through strikes, large or small, actual or threatened, organized or unorganized, industrial unionism revolutionized the power relations between workers and managers in the automobile industry. With the war, the federal government allowed contracts to maintain membership and to allow dues check-off, consolidation of union finances, and power for the new union. Negotiated contracts established the new rules of the game for shop floor industrial relations. Often shop stewards or committeemen monitored the workplace to discover abusive foremen or to uncover violations of the contract. They processed worker grievances often up to the level of impartial arbitrators. Unfortunately check-off and maintenance of membership in the Second World War years over time lessened the need for stewards and committeemen to collect dues and insure the payment of dues. The decline of this interaction created distance between union leaders and rank-and-file workers. The grievance process continued with less vigour and lessened the connection between the union and its members.[31]

Immediately after the Second World War ended American workers sought to retrieve wages lost in wartime inflation and initiated the largest strike wave in American history. In a conservative reaction to the widespread postwar strikes, the Republican congress passed the Taft-Hartley Act to contain the aggressive union movement in 1947. Its many provisions attempted to roll back and contain the New Deal's favorable attitudes toward unionism. Many UAW leaders and many UAW local unions labelled this vindictive legislation a slave labor law. In an effort to contain the leftist radicalism of the Depression era and against the backdrop of an emerging Cold War, one notorious provision called for union officers to sign affidavits stating that they were not members of the Communist Party. This anticommunist crusade encouraged right-wing shop floor activism through the 1950s and removed leftist militancy from the automotive workplace. Another provision allowed states to pass "Right-to-Work" laws that outlawed union shops, which required all workers to join a union. Creating antiunion islands in many states of the South and Southwest, this would exacerbate the decline of American unions in later years.[32] The antiunion legislation planted the seeds for the consolidation of future neoliberal labor policies and the globalization of auto manufacture.

From the 1940s into the 1960s Cold War antiunion policies complicated efforts by UAW leaders to maintain control over their huge union. Many workers chose a now familiar alternative—covert and hidden forms of resistance—and used the grievance process to sustain the less visible underside of worker resistance to managerial domination. Sometimes they advanced legitimate worker concerns, at other times they deployed symbolic rituals of power against the overbearing regime of supervisory actions. Often these workplace rituals emphasized the individualized aggressive and swaggering postures

THE POLITICAL CULTURE OF WORK 149

FIGURE 8.3 Two women and a man have lunch in the Ford Willow Run plant. Photo: Anne Rosener, Library of Congress. Public domain.

that men exhibited towards their shop floor supervisors. On the shop floor, workers often loafed in the lavatory, gambled with dice or cards, engaged in serious fights with foremen, drank and especially after the 1960s used drugs, engaged in horseplay, challenged supervisors, or otherwise participated in illicit activities. As union leaders cooperated with management, becoming managers of discontent, rank-and-file workers shifted to direct forms of covert resistance into the grievance process.

Individual cases illustrate how autoworkers incorporated their shop floor misbehavior into the grievance process. When management symbolically attempted to separate foremen from workers and insisted on the wearing of neckties, workers sometimes cut off the ties and grieved the sanctions.[33] Other workers insisted on the right to sing or yodel while working.[34] Workers collectively mocked and challenged a shop supervisor, denying him any claim to respect and authority by booing whenever he appeared in the shop.[35] In still another instance, a hundred and forty-five Chevrolet Transmission Division workers, including union officers and committeemen, marched in a "Shirt-Tail Parade" to protest a work rule that insisted that shirttails must be worn tucked inside their pants. Often worker grievances involved the shop toilet, a worker social space for more individual and collective activities that offered relief from the pressures of work, sometimes gambling and sometimes simply reading in the stalls.[36]

In the postwar era, organizational misbehavior persisted in Britain as well as in the US automobile industries. Coventry car workers, for example, engaged in American-style empty labor and workplace misbehavior. This, historian Paul Thompson contended, illustrated "the creative resilience of British workshop culture."[37] Under the gang bonus

FIGURE 8.4 Postwar British assembly line for small automobile in unidentified factory, 1945. Photographer unknown. Imperial War Museum. Public domain.

system, a machinist noted that upon the completion of work "you could sit down and chat with your friends, read a newspaper, drink tea." Workers also "booked" work, saving the extra work for when needed during their off days.[38] They also pilfered parts such as piston rings in order to "decoke" or remove carbon cylinder heads, for their personal cars. During free time from work, they ate at their lockers, played cards, did crossword puzzles, visited mates in other shops, and even went to the pub or served as bookies' runners, taking bets. Some even read books at their machines or on the assembly lines. At one factory, near a railroad line, they even set snares to capture rabbits and then had them "skinned and drawn" in a shop "circular sink." The workshops had a "long-standing tradition of festivity"—for weddings lathes were decorated and for Christmas they would "stop the tracks and stop the conveyors and have a party." The Christmas celebrations continued into the 1970s. For Thompson, such activities represented "more than an escape from work" and revealed "an attempt to make the work world more fully human."[39] Since employers tolerated this workplace culture and shared suspicions about new technology and machines, this may well have contributed to the gradual decline of the British car industry in the second half of the twentieth century.

American workers also continued their illicit behavior while at work. In the late 1940s, Ely Chinoy asked an Oldsmobile worker about "goldbricking," or working without proper effort or care. He responded: "Almost all of them have the attitude of wanting to goldbrick." And he added: "I've heard of fellows causing breakdowns [of the assembly line], too." The reason for misbehavior was: "the work is monotonous as all hell." Among his fellow workers, he believed: "There's a general feeling, that if you produce or not, you won't get anyplace any way."[40]

The American industrial sociologist Donald F. Roy began his career examining such worker misconduct in a variety of industrial settings in the 1950s. His studies of work satisfaction and informal worker interaction included such topics as "efficiency and the fix," "banana time," and goldbricking. He cited one autoworker who claimed that workers believed: "If it weren't for the talking and fooling, you'd go nuts." Such misbehavior, Roy noted, often allowed workers to cope with "the formidable 'beast of monotony'."[41]

Even in unionized settings, autoworkers continued with both older and newly developed strategies to stop from going nuts. They fought with each other and with supervisors, engaged in heavy drinking and later even drug use on the job, read magazines and books, and found isolated corners for sleeping. They sometimes sabotaged their production or threw their proverbial wrenches to stop the operation of machines or assembly lines. They "doubled up," one worker exerting extreme effort to perform two jobs so a workmate could hide or escape to a tavern for half the shift.[42]

Their gambling activities became more involved and sophisticated. At the Ford Brook Park Plant near Cleveland in the early 1960s, a wide network existed, revealing the widespread opposition to plant work rules and alternative uses of workspaces. The US Bureau of Internal Revenue, Justice Department, and the Ohio State Police discovered an extensive operation involving a "numbers game" called a Bolita, based on a Puerto Rican lottery. The participants were mainly Puerto Rican and African American foundry workers. Most of the bookmaking took place in the plant cafeteria, where an informant made his bets and observed others take $1–$2 bets from Ford workers.[43]

Since the percentage of unionized manufacturing workers peaked in the mid-1950s, the postwar heyday of American unionism was remarkably brief. By the 1960s, workers began to suffer from many challenges as various forces weakened unionism in the United States' largest industry.

THE LATE TWENTIETH-CENTURY CRISIS OF WORK

Flexible computerized forms of automation fundamentally restricted auto work in the late 1970s, but were preceded by other efforts by manufacturers to reorganize the industry. Following the war, auto manufacturers undertook a program of decentralization, intending to alleviate the problems of massing workers in a single huge plant such as the Ford River Rouge complex. New plants were smaller and located in supposedly more conservative and rural locations. Taft-Hartley facilitated some plant relocation to Southern antiunion states that passed "Right-to-Work" legislation, that is, laws that no longer required union membership or the payment of union dues. Finally, the federal government experiments in the automated production of artillery shells during the war led to postwar automated manufacture and assembly of automobile engines, notably at the Ford Brook Park and other plants in the early 1950s. In the late 1950s and early

1960s, automation and subsequent unemployment fears became a central issue of labor's left and eventually of the UAW. Though too inflexible to deal with frequent model changes, this established the precedent for more flexible automation—often in the form of robots—that reappeared in the 1970s. It actually reduced the number of autoworkers in some of the most detested jobs such as spray painting and spot welding. The consequent reduction in union members resulted in the steady erosion of autoworker commitment to unionism.

Social and cultural activism generated by the civil rights movement and the opposition to the Vietnam War in the 1960s informed how various social groups, including African Americans, youth, and women, fought to resist the consolidation and automation that was reshaping the automotive workplace. Forms of resistance involved direct and covert actions by African Americans in the Revolutionary Union movements in Detroit and elsewhere and in the youthful and counter-cultural rebellion in Lordstown. In such instances, the direct confrontations of plant-wide wildcat strikes and departmental walkouts challenged management authority with covert resistance such as absenteeism, turnover, malingering, and even workplace sabotage.

Discontented African American autoworkers complained of continuing job discrimination, their assignment to the worst man-killing jobs, and the relentless management efforts to increase their efforts through higher volumes of production. Inspired by the civil rights and black power movements, these workers acted on their new sense of social equity and justice to challenge the workplace traditions that allocated the meanest and dirtiest jobs to black workers. Often using Marxist and black nationalist

FIGURE 8.5 Robots have greatly reduced the proportion of human production workers in modern automobile plants. Photo: Monty Rakuen. Courtesy Getty Images.

rhetoric, the aggressive activities often pitted black workers against white supervisors and sometimes black and white workers against each other in violent confrontations on the shop floor. African American workers also challenged the national and local UAW leaders, resulting in violent plant gate and union hall confrontations between the radical black militants and more conservative white union supporters.[44]

During this period, issues around the quality of American automobiles presented a major challenge for US manufacturers and, as a consequence, to autoworkers' prospects. In the United States, management culture emphasized the cost and volume of production over the quality of the product. Indifferent to worker needs, management imposed a brutal Fordist production system that angered workers. Production managers never really controlled worker misbehavior that resulted in an inferior product. Moreover, despite successful government wartime efforts in quality control, postwar managerial attitudes reverted to lower prewar norms, which stressed cost and how much imperfection would be acceptable in the final product. The foreign manufacturers took a quite different approach to quality and, as a result, from the 1960s, and especially after the two 1970s oil crises, American consumers turned to the more fuel-efficient Japanese and German imports.

Japanese manufacturers followed another strategy. Toyota, too, thoroughly accepted the Fordist production methods, but it also maintained the strict standards for quality first developed in the United States for wartime production. Ironically, two US proponents for statistical quality control, William E. Deming and Walter Shewhart, introduced the American standards to the Japanese car makers during the American occupation and later. To be sure, a Japanese version of welfare capitalism attempted to connect workers to the firm, and quality circles offered the appearance of worker participation while subscribing to a Taylorist notion of picking the workers' brains on production methods. Fully accepted in Japan, statistical quality control, based upon the principle of *kaizen*, or the continuous improvement of output, emphasized perfection in the final product.[45]

The German approach to quality differed as well. It rested on earlier notions embedded in German traditions of the craft pride of skilled worker suffused into the ethic of production workers in the prewar and war years. For labor organizations, socialists, and communists, the notion of "German quality work," Leudtke observed, was "the only means to improve living conditions" and "a principal line of defense" in the "struggle against increases in the division of labour and assembly-line production." Unlike the United States with its "engineering and rigid control" of production, German management and shop cultures highly ranked "dexterity and experience in handling materials and tools at the very point of production." Moreover, the principles of codetermination placed worker or union representatives on corporate boards, lessening the distance and suspicion of workers. Later in the 1970s and 1980s, German manufacturers introduced concepts or teamwork and job enrichment.[46]

The American response to the Japanese and German challenge was Lordstown. To meet foreign competition from Volkswagen, Toyota, and others, General Motors planned to produce a smaller fuel-efficient car, the Vega, at a new technically sophisticated plant. Given earlier experience with automation, the new Lordstown plant deployed Fordist traditions of production that relied on flexible human labor. Creating the General Motors Assembly Division, however, the company designed an intensified work regime (a speed-up) on the Lordstown factory floor. If the standard assembly lines produced fifty or sixty cars per hour, the Lordstown lines exceeded over one hundred per hour. The rate halved the time allowed for the completion of work tasks, but at human costs not lost on the workforce.

According to journalist Judson Gooding, the Lordstown plant with its "greatly increased degree of automation" came to symbolize in the popular mind the problems associated with work and industrial technology in advanced industrial society. On the shop floor, worker resistance and indiscipline, informed by social and cultural values of activist college students of the late 1960s and early 1970s, gave older covert workplace protest new forms: a drug- and alcohol-laced shop culture undermined the conventional work ethic and resulted in excessive absenteeism and frequent wildcat strikes. Gooding detected that the "new attitudes" also "cut across racial lines," where young workers now had "higher expectations of the jobs they fill and the wages they receive, and for the lives they will lead." Rebellious young black and white Americans were "restless changeable, mobile, demanding."[47]

The "churning labour turmoil" resulted in serious worker discontent as indicated by high rates of absenteeism, especially on Mondays and Fridays, and high rates of labor turnover. Earning relatively high wages, the youthful workforce thus revealed their indifference to the needs of efficient and high production. Lordstown workers also expressed their discontent in subversive and covert job actions. The labor turmoil, Gooding wrote, resulted in "wasted manpower, less efficiency, higher costs, a need for more inspections and repairs, more warranty claims—and grievous damage to company reputations." In some instances, this even led to "overt sabotage." The alienated young workers vented their anger on the automobiles that they built. Gooding detailed the sabotage: "Screws have been left in brake drums, tool handles welded into fender compartments (to cause mysterious, unfindable, and eternal rattles), paint scratched, and upholstery cut."[48] *Time* reported "somebody deliberately set fire to the control-box shed, causing the line to shut down."[49] The General Motors management response was strict discipline. In one instance, management sent a worker home for being one minute late. Another, the critic Barbara Garson noted, "was suspended for farting in a car. Yet another for yodelling."[50]

In March 1972, the high line speeds and worker discontent resulted in a 23-day strike and brought the "blue-collar blues" to the nation's attention. Continuous shorter wildcat strikes and stoppages persisted and bedevilled Lordstown production managers and shop supervisors. In the early 1970s, Lordstown came to symbolize the "blue-collar blues" and the general disaffection of the American workforce with the continued monotonous, repetitious, and degraded automotive work regime.

Women too rebelled against their degraded status in the automobile industry. In their separate shops and departments, they endured the low wages, sexual harassment, and even rape by supervisors. As early as the Second World War, they had moved to all male shops and departments to aid the war production effort. For the most part, male workers tolerated their presence and sometimes even protected them as they would their wives, mothers, or sisters. Though mildly harassed with the shouts, grunts, and catcalls as they passed through more densely male shops and departments, they persisted through the war until almost completely purged from the all-male workspaces on shop floor. Those who remained suffered egregiously.[51]

But in the 1970s the social and cultural revolutions brought more and more women into all-male jobs and departments. Unlike the war years, they were no longer partners in the war effort; they now were competitors with men for fewer jobs. They used union grievance processes to attempt to alleviate their harassment, sexual and otherwise. Male union and company officials and arbitrators often ignored their protests, defending male harassers and abusers and often dismissing the complaints with "boys will be boys" or "she asked for it." Only after a series of 1979 Detroit hearings on the complaints of women workers and costly lawsuits did the union, company, and industrial relations officials finally address women's concerns. Though problems continued in the male-dominated industry, women slowly became incorporated into the automobile workforce.[52] But women entered male work in an insecure era of industrial decline and suffered enormous anger and hostility from the men who feared competition for a declining number of jobs.

The globalization of the automobile industry and neoliberal labor policies continued to transform the industry in the last quarter of the century. From the late 1970s and into the 1980s, American auto manufacturers increasingly focused on labor costs of the high-wage and high-benefit packages of unionized automobile workers. With the growing loss of segments of the American automobile market to foreign competitors, they initiated processes of downsizing and plant relocation, often to regions in the South. States in the region, generally inhospitable to unionized labor enacted right-to-work legislation, weakened unions, and thus lowered labor costs. American, and then Japanese and European, automobile firms soon after moved to build their new plants in the right-to-work states. Without an embedded automobile workers' union in their plants, the foreign firms more successfully avoided the high cost of unionized workers in the northern American plants. In another cost-saving policy, American manufacturers outsourced some small parts production in manufacturing zones in Mexico along the American border—the so-called Maquiladora plants. In sum, global automobile production gradually moved to former third world nations such as Korea and Brazil that were newly industrializing. America's "industry of industries" and its workers suffered through the dislocations of plant closings and relocation, of deunionization and deindustrialization.[53]

RIVETHEAD AND THE CASE OF FLINT, MICHIGAN

Autoworker Ben Hamper, nicknamed Rivethead, worked in Flint and offered a vivid example of labor and worker misbehavior in response to the drastic economic transformations of deindustrialization, downsizing, and industrial relocation. The birthplace of General Motors and the site of the UAW's most notable success, General Motors' Flint factories slowly declined from the 1980s, ultimately shutting down in the 1990s and early 2000s. But, as the Swedish sociologist Roland Paulsen noted, the "gradual weakening of trade unions" as they cooperated with and enforced corporate power made "informal workplace behaviours … more relevant" to worker resistance to management.[54] Hamper, a Flint General Motors plant worker from the late 1970s to the mid-1980s, detailed such behaviors and described how he and his coworkers avoided work in an era of industrial decline.[55] For Rivethead and his workmates, avoiding work was the major objective. His oft-times madcap account of shop floor hijinks was studded with examples of in-plant misbehavior—illicit loafing, shop floor games, and escapes from the plant during working hours.

For Hamper and his workmates, "doubling up" was a means that became part of their work-avoidance plans. To begin, Rivethead and others in the General Motors Flint plant strove ceaselessly to find a work partner. Then the two neighboring workers would learn each other's jobs, but one would perform both tasks, allowing the other to do nothing and escape the pressures of line work.[56] Initially doubling-up, Hamper would sit at the shop floor picnic table, reading paperbacks to his working partner. Later he managed to read "two newspapers, a magazine and a good chunk of a novel every evening." He claimed: "It was like being paid to attend the library." Over time, he and his workmate became more adept and adventurous often leaving the department to explore the plant and even escaping the factory to spend the second half of the evening at his favorite tavern. Near the end of his tenure at General Motors, the efforts of managers and supervisors to force him to actually work full shifts resulted in something of a nervous breakdown forcing him to quit.[57]

In order to make work more tolerable, Hamper and his workmates also created numerous diversions to alleviate the horrible monotony and deadening boredom with their work. They developed shop floor pranks and games as their means of salvation from boredom. Their games included Rivet Hockey where workers attempted to kick rivets into the ankles and shins of fellow workers or Dumpster Ball where an empty box was kicked into a garbage container. Other diversions involved "racing to the water fountain and back, chain-smoking, feeding Cheetos to mice, skeet shooting Milk Duds with rubber bands, punting washers into the rafters high above the train depot, spitting contests."[58] For Hamper and his workmates, such subterranean resistance offered an alternative to weakened unions in the twenty-first century.

CONCLUSION

Global competition, plant relocation, and federal anti-labor policies all contributed to the resentful and oppositional political culture of work and the eventual decline of the American automobile industry and its union. By the early twenty-first century, the US automobile industry had lost its premier position in the global auto market and seemed to have reached the end of the line.[59] The *Detroit Free Press* noted that Ford and General Motors faced serious financial crises from a long-term industrial decline. Toyota was poised to replace General Motors and to become the top global automobile producer. In the heyday of American's auto-industrial age, the UAW had achieved a membership peak of 1.5 million workers. In 2016, UAW membership declined to around 400,000 workers. Even though General Motors recovered from the Great Recession, foreign competition remained a threat. The UAW also remained a large union, but it was no longer the formidable power that it once was. As the short heyday of American unionism ended, American workers lost their pathway to the American dream—a world of relatively high wages, health care, and pension benefits, and the possibilities of home ownership, an automobile, and college for their children. The mounting job losses since the 1980s, jobs especially targeted the last hired—African American men and women, who had just gained a foothold in the industrial economy. Since black and women workers were never really securely embedded in the industrial economy, they never had the heightened expectations of white male autoworkers. Relatively unskilled, without a path to relative prosperity, and with only the weapons of the weak for their resistance, many increasingly angry white male autoworkers throughout the industrial heartland of the upper Midwest directed their frustration toward poor others, typically immigrants who they imagined taking jobs. In fact, companies had often moved these jobs to nonunion southern cities or to the global south. After the Great Recession of 2008, and in the run-up to the 2016 elections many white male workers in the United States and across Europe soured on their industrial prospects and the political environment. Virulent racist and xenophobic fears led many to pine for an all-powerful leader who could bring a return to an idealized past.[60] But, like the globalization of the auto industry, the declining fortune and troubled political culture of industrial workers in the new millennium was not just an American problem; it was a global one.[61]

CHAPTER NINE

Work and Leisure

RANDY D. MCBEE

In 1950 David Riesman published *The Lonely Crowd: A Study of the Changing American Character*. To understand how Americans internalized their behavior Riesman compared the nineteenth century when parents and other adults shaped a child's socialization to the mid-twentieth century when a child's socialization became contingent on peer groups and the media. Riesman's discussion about American character also highlighted the shift from a culture of production and scarcity to one of consumption, the question of middle-class conformity, and the lack of workplace autonomy. In the preface to the 1961 edition of the book he added a gendered critique of work and consumption by arguing that "men need to feel adequate: to hold down a job, and then to be related to life through consumership is not enough." The "burden put on leisure by the disintegration of work," he added, "is too huge to be coped with: leisure itself cannot rescue work, but fails with it, and can only be meaningful for most men if work is meaningful."[1]

Throughout the twentieth century workers in the United States and Western Europe have struggled to achieve the balance Riesman spoke about. Corporations and governments in the 1920s introduced sponsored leisure activities to gain worker loyalty or to build national identity. But those efforts often failed to compete with mass amusements where workers had more autonomy and where they could defy the constraints they faced with wage work. By the Depression, men and women in Western Europe and the United States were working a weekly average of forty hours and up until the 1970s the typical workweek in both regions was similar. But a contracting economy and efforts to challenge the gains workers had made in the previous quarter century were also conspicuous. While workers in Europe and the United States experienced unprecedented prosperity in the post-Second World War era, the US government's economic policies favored private investment over the publicly funded model the Europeans favored. As the economy began to collapse in the 1970s, US workers simply had fewer resources with which to negotiate wage work and to protect their leisure. To be sure, the Europeans faced their own backlash as conservative governments gained ground and pushed to privatize certain government services. But even as the European right to leisure has endured, the struggle to achieve and maintain a balance between work and leisure has grown more complicated as the world has become a global marketplace.

THE INTERWAR YEARS

By the interwar years, Americans and Europeans worked a weekly average of forty-eight to fifty hours, and by the Depression the workweek had shrunk to around forty in many Western European countries. France, for example, introduced the forty-hour workweek in 1936 as part of Popular Front reforms.² US workers also saw the workweek shrink to forty with the passage of the Fair Labor Standards Act of 1938. The act established a minimum wage and a forty-hour workweek by requiring employers to pay time and a half above forty hours, paving the way for an end to the traditional half-day on Saturdays and the beginning of a two-day weekend.³

Government-sponsored leisure programs were also popular. The rise of Mussolini in fascist Italy and Hitler in Nazi Germany eliminated workers' rights. But the Germans organized a "Strength through Joy" program that provided workers with cheap vacations, theater and concert tickets, and weekend outings, and by 1939 an estimated four million Italians were participating in government-sponsored sporting clubs, holiday camps, and other cultural events.⁴

The 1920s were also notable for the rise of welfare capitalism, a term to describe corporate benefits programs like wash rooms, savings plans, on-site nurses, and a variety of leisure activities. Companies had been organizing similar programs in the United States and Europe since the nineteenth century, but they became increasingly popular by the 1920s. The Amoskeag Corporation in Manchester, New Hampshire, which employed around fourteen thousand workers and was the world's largest textile mill, established a textile club in 1922 during a strike at the mill that included a reading room, canteen, billiard and pool tables, and card tables.⁵ American companies in the Southwest organized similar programs, including sports teams on both sides of the US–Mexico border. The California Fruit Growers Exchange (also known by the trademark, Sunkist) worked with local citrus growers in the early 1920s to promote a corporate welfare program that featured Americanization classes, worker housing, recreational facilities, and sports clubs.⁶

In some cases, these programs were quite popular, but workers' use of their leisure to contest the problems they faced at work also reflects the more complicated place of corporate leisure in their lives. In those same agricultural areas of the Southwest where employers began sponsoring sports teams, workers spent their time away from work in pool halls to recoup and repair their bodies from an alienating and physically demanding workspace and to compare wage rates and discuss grievances about their employers. Pool halls were such important spaces that in Corona, California, in 1916, the City Council closed them on Sundays and a year later considered closing them permanently after Mexican agricultural workers engaged in a number of strikes to obtain better wages and working conditions.⁷

Corporate-sponsored programs too were generally short-lived as employers were often suspicious of worker leisure, which provided more opportunities for autonomy and independence. For example, in the early twentieth century employers debunked working women in New York who promenaded throughout the city in the latest style and fashion—brightly colored dresses, oversized hats, and silk stockings.⁸ What could appear frivolous to a boss, though, could be a worker's challenge to otherwise grim workaday lives and limitations. This style would profoundly shape the rise of the New Woman or Modern Girl of the 1920s and 1930s. She sported bobbed hair, lipstick and rouge, a slender and athletic body, and became known among contemporaries for her independent and flirtatious attitude. While women in the United States are routinely linked to the style, it was actually a worldwide phenomenon that was conspicuous throughout the world—France, Germany, Britain, South Africa, India, China, and Japan.⁹ The pressure to reconstruct conventional norms was especially prominent in Europe during the interwar years as fears about declining populations swept the region. These fears led several

FIGURE 9.1 Poolroom constructed in 1940 near the Shasta Dam in Shasta County, California. Photo: Russell Lee, Library of Congress. Public domain.

nations to subsidize motherhood and restrict women's economic and social freedoms.[10] The Modern Girl represented a visible challenge to ideas about women's proper role and allowed women to frustrate efforts to limit or dictate their leisure opportunities and fun.

Corporate- and government-sponsored leisure programs were also competing with the rise of a mass culture.[11] By the mid-1920s there were more than twenty thousand movie theaters in the United States, and they were thriving in big and small towns alike. By the end of the 1920s, for example, Chicago had enough theater seats available for one-half of the city's population to attend at least once a day. A Bureau of Labor Statistics survey from the city showed that half of the budget for leisure among working men's families was spent at the movies, and by the Depression of the 1930s, 100 million movie tickets were sold across the country every week.[12] In his history of America's consumer society, historian Daniel Horowitz notes that even people who faced severe economic constraints also looked for ways to maintain pre-Depression standards of living and would stretch their dollars to make car payments or to attend a movie.[13]

Europeans were facing more difficult economic times than their counterparts in the United States, but mass entertainment also flourished during the interwar years. Historian Martin Pugh notes that besides the pub, dancing and the cinema "formed the basis of mass entertainment between the wars." There were eight thousand nightclubs in London in 1918 and eleven thousand by 1925.[14] By the end of the 1930s, Britain had five thousand cinemas, two thousand more than had been available in 1914. One estimate of cinema attendance in Great Britain stood at 963 million admissions a year in the early 1930s,

FIGURE 9.2 The Rialto Theater in Casper, Wyoming, 2015. Photo: Carol H. Highsmith, Library of Congress. Public domain.

which was equal to twenty-two visits a year per head of household. By 1939 annual admissions had risen to 990 million, about double what they were in 1914 and some twenty-five times as many tickets as were sold to football matches. The working class made up a disproportionate share of the moviegoing audience, but during the 1930s a middle-class audience became more prominent as entrepreneurs began to build cinemas that emulated the metropolitan theater.[15]

As these examples suggest, there were limits to the rise of or growth of government- and corporate-sponsored leisure. As the economy worsened in the late 1920s, these programs would struggle to survive as thousands of businesses went bankrupt. The amusements that had grown popular throughout the interwar years had also become critical to day-to-day life, and workers refused to abandon them despite the economic struggles they faced. Indeed, government- and corporate-sponsored leisure programs were less about making the workplace better and more about making workers and citizens more loyal, and neither addressed the problems workers faced on the shop floor or the need to try and find a balance between work and leisure.

THE POSTWAR ERA, 1945–1970s

During the Depression, the Roosevelt administration's commitment to an emerging belief that economic growth went hand in hand with full time, full employment set the stage for federal policy during the Cold War. War production became perpetual military mobilization on the one hand, and a conversion to mass production of consumer goods on the other. Both, in turn, were accompanied by a renewed emphasis on domesticity, breadwinning, consumption, and national security. In the three decades after the passage of the Fair Labor Standards Act, workers' push for a shorter workweek saw virtually no gains,[16] but bread-and-butter unions would strike a bargain with management abandoning the right to shape the production process in exchange for higher wages, greater benefits, and more leisure time.[17] In the United States consumption was attracting more attention than production, and leisure began to overshadow work.

In contrast to the United States, in the aftermath of the war Europeans' struggles with a decimated infrastructure and an industrial base took precedence over leisure. Nonetheless, the postwar period also ushered in an era of prosperity across Western Europe that saw a culture of consumption take root by the 1960s. The Europeans, more so than the Americans, managed a reformed capitalism. A system of negotiation and consultation between government, employers, and unions promoted unprecedented prosperity and the rise of a social welfare state that provided publicly funded medical care and pensions, education, subsidized public housing, transportation, and vacation time. These services fostered a level of disposable wealth that had never been seen before and a degree of security and comfort for a wide range of working people. The right to leisure had been well established in Europe before the Second World War, but it flourished in the postwar years and became linked to national identity.[18]

In the postwar years, Americans and Europeans saw comparable rates of growth and prosperity. Between the late 1940s and early 1970s real per capita disposable income in the United States increased 84 percent, and real median family income doubled. Un employment also averaged less than 5 percent during this period, and union membership reached an all-time high of 32.5 percent of the labor force in 1953.[19] On average Western European economies were growing by 4 percent a year during the 1950s, unemployment in Germany, Italy, Britain, Sweden, and the Netherlands was 4 percent or less throughout much of the 1945 to 1960s period, and real wages also saw dramatic increases. Between 1950 and 1980 the English saw real wages increase by 80 percent.[20]

In the United States during these years of prosperity, new leisure opportunities emerged and paradigmatic of the change—and critically important to it—was the automobile. The number of cars on the road increased from 26 million in 1940 to 107 million by 1974—nearly two automobiles for every three people.[21] Automobile manufacturing alone employed more than a million members of the United Auto Workers, and dozens of other industries emerged or dramatically expanded: motels, garages, service stations, highway construction, suburbanization, and the leisure industry. The automobile did facilitate white flight to the suburbs that left inner-city amusements like movie palaces and amusement parks without the revenue needed to stay afloat, and the parks that replaced them (like Disneyland) were out of reach for inner-city residents, further restricting these pastimes to a largely suburban, white, middle-class population. Yet automobiles also ushered in the golden age of certain leisure pursuits, including drive-in theaters and drive-in restaurants. By 1958 more than four thousand drive-in theaters across the nation in big and small towns alike entertained legions of Americans.[22] Drive-ins became the iconic setting for 1950s-themed movies about teenagers, but drive-in theater owners appealed to young and old alike with a variety of concessions, live bands, and playgrounds for the children. Millions of Americans spent a great deal of their leisure time in automobiles and spent much of their working lives manufacturing them or working in one of the dozens of other industries that were dependent on them.[23]

Europeans also enthusiastically participated in a new world of consumption that bore striking similarities to the American experience. In the postwar years, Europeans enjoyed a housing boom, and home appliances that once seemed unaffordable became the norm. Automobiles, too, profoundly shaped the rural and urban landscape. British car ownership rose from 2 million in 1939 to 8 million by 1964 and then to 11.5 million by the end of the 1960s.[24] The number of two-wheeled vehicles was also on the rise. In Italy, the number of motorcycles and scooters rose from 700,000 in 1950 to 4.3 million by 1964, and the growing interest in automobiles, motorcycles, and scooters led to the formation of social clubs, mass rallies, long-distance tours, and races across the region.[25]

Car and motorcycle customizing also became popular after the Second World War and offer an interesting case study on the continued link between motor vehicles, leisure, and work in both the United States and Europe. During the Second World War consumers lost access to new-model automobiles and became accustomed to working on their own cars. As the war came to an end, car racers and customizers became their own subculture. In January 1948, the Southern California Timing Association held its first exhibition that attracted around fifty-five thousand people. By 1950, hot rod magazines had two hundred thousand readers, and drag racing clubs proliferated. California was the state best known for car customizers and racers, but the subculture also took root in Indiana, Pennsylvania, and New Mexico.[26]

Lowrider culture among Hispanics in East Los Angeles was also taking shape after the Second World War. Los Angeles attracted thousands of Mexican American veterans in search of well-paying jobs and many of them had skills as welders, ironworks, or as painters that were essential to building low or slow cruiser cars. Before long, clubs with names like the Honey Drippers, the Pan Draggers, and the Renegades were congregating at drive-ins or cruising certain well-known Los Angeles hot spots.[27]

Motorcycles also became increasingly popular in the postwar years. After a 1947 motorcycle rally in Hollister, California, degenerated into what the press labelled a riot,

FIGURE 9.3 A bowling alley in Barnsley, England, located at the Monk Bretton Miners Social Centre, 1965. Photo: National Coal Board. Courtesy the UK National Archives.

working-class men dressed in dungarees and leather jackets began to dominate the public image of riders. In Sweden, the press reported fears of motorcyclists also known as the *Skinnknutte* (loosely translated as the leather men). The Germans and Austrians referred to them as the *Halb-starke* (or "half-strong"), the French used the label *Blousons Noirs* (Black Jackets) and in England the Rockers and Mods attracted the attention of the press after a scuffle broke out between the two groups in the 1950s (although the Mods preferred scooters to motorcycles).[28]

In all of these countries motorcyclists began to customize their bikes for style and for racing. In the immediate postwar US motorcyclists "bobbed" or "chopped" their bikes, a term that essentially describes the process of stripping down a stock model to make the bike leaner and easier to maneuver. By the 1950s riders began to build choppers, and by the 1960s the style was widespread. A chopper was the updated version of a bobbed or chopped motorcycle that became identified with the "outlaw" rider and involves a more thorough manipulation of the bike's frame and design (called raking the frame) to extend the front forks and to lengthen the wheelbase and raise the front end.[29]

In Europe, the best-known motorcycles were the café racers the British working class favored, a term that emerged from the practice of racing their bikes from café to café. Cultural critics Steven Alford and Suzanne Ferris note that the Rockers "were devoted to the mechanical improvement of their bikes" and the emphasis was on "speed and the aerodynamic appearance of speed." The most noteworthy example of British mechanical

FIGURE 9.4 Motorcyclist Jack Troop competing in a hill-climbing competition in the United States, mid-1950s. Photographer unknown. Courtesy Don Troop.

know-how was the Triton, a café racer that combined a Triumph and a Norton motorcycle.[30]

Car and motorcycle customizers and mechanics turned used vehicles into highly stylized creations that challenged the aesthetics that are typical of mass-produced commodities and influenced car and motorcycle manufactures to adopt some of their styles and ideas. The work of customizing coincided with expanding efforts to standardize and automatize the production process and suggests that customizing and consuming cars or motorcycles reflected workers' desire to maintain and accentuate skills that were no longer appreciated at work.[31]

The growth of automobiles also facilitated the increasingly common experience of going on vacation. Historian Cindy S. Aron argues that for the first time "between 1935 and 1940 the privilege of vacations with pay was finally extended to a majority of America's industrial labor force."[32] The Second World War would challenge the growing popularity of vacations, but with the unprecedented prosperity and mobility of the postwar years, Americans from all socioeconomic backgrounds eagerly took to the road for vacation sites and campgrounds. For example, African American vacationers were drawn to places such as Atlantic Beach in South Carolina, one of the few African American owned and governed oceanfront resorts in North America. Black Panther Assata Shakur distinctly recalls the years she spent with her family on another beach in South Carolina called Bop City or Freeman's Beach where black vacationers from all over North Carolina, South Carolina, and Virginia gathered for relaxation and leisure.[33]

Vacations were also becoming part of a distinctive European identity. The right to leisure and tourism was already well established in Europe before the Second World

War, but in the postwar years, holidays became what historian John Urry describes as "almost a marker of citizenship, a right to pleasure." After the war, marketing campaigns promoting foreign holidays became common, nations lifted international travel restrictions, and the hotel industry modernized. By the mid-1950s thirty million travellers each year were crossing European borders, and by 1966 the number exceeded one hundred million. Cheap airline and rail service and the availability of automobiles encouraged the mobility but so, too, did government-sponsored vacations. By the 1960s, most employees in Europe were entitled to two weeks of paid vacations, plus holidays while in Norway, Sweden, Denmark, and France, employees were entitled to three weeks of paid vacation.[34]

In the United States Americans were just as enthusiastic vacationers, but American culture in general and government policies in particular that celebrated individualism, privatized day-to-day services and leisure, including vacations. Thus, instead of establishing universal plans to underwrite pensions, housing, and education like those in European countries, the US government favored highway construction instead of mass transit, loans for single detached family dwellings instead of funds to renovate inner-city neighborhoods or to build public housing, and private pension plans and limited government loans for veterans instead of publicly supported options.[35] While some workers benefited from these programs, the gains did not equally serve women or African Americans and Latinos/as, and these policies undercut the institutions and environments that promoted a collective sense of public welfare and social belonging. Thus, women were required to pass means tests for benefits such as family assistance (unlike Social Security available to all workers, who were more likely to be male). Similarly, racial minorities were largely excluded from the expansion of home ownership after the Second World War, and their exclusion from the growing middle-class and working-class white suburbs also denied them access to the garden playgrounds, barbecues, and parks that became idealized in the 1950s as "the good life."[36]

But to enjoy the "good life," workers in the United States had to be able to afford it. Federal Housing Authority loans helped pay for suburban homes, but workers still remained dependent upon their employers for paid vacations or holidays, which meant individually negotiating time off, working through their unions to negotiate for them, or challenging employers on the shop floor to meet their demands. Autoworkers at the Reo Plant in Michigan after the Second World War, for example, consistently pressured Michigan's Congress of Industrial Organizations (CIO) unions to push for better recreational facilities and the leisure time to enjoy them. Hunting was often the particular focus and when those demands were not met, companies repeatedly faced high rates of absenteeism or unexplained flu epidemics at the start of the hunting season. Hunting was not only a popular pasttime for autoworkers but also profoundly shaped how they negotiated their time at work and their conditions for employment.[37]

Against the backdrop of the Cold War and government policies that pumped billions of dollars into the economy in support of it, the United States and Western European standard of living reached unprecedented heights. Prosperity in both regions had in fact become linked to the average worker's ability to consume and to ideas about citizenship. Leisure was not simply critical to understanding the ways in which men and women negotiated their working lives and identities but was beginning to overshadow work.

THE POST-1970s

Economic expansion would stagnate in the post-1970 era and set the stage for a number of changes to men's and women's day-to-day leisure. In the United States through the 1970s economic growth would continue but only at an annual rate of about 2 percent.[38] The decade after 1973 saw unemployment rise above 7 percent and inflation reached 11 percent in 1974, up from 1.3 percent a year in 1960 to 1965.[39] Real wages stagnated for most Americans between the early 1970s to the 1990s and actually dropped by 25 percent for young males.[40] In the 1970s many European nations also experienced inflation and unemployment rates that were often in the double digits. Between 1974 and 1976 the average annual growth rate among Western European nations dropped to zero, which stood in sharp contrast to the 1960s when the average was 4.8 percent. By 1984, a quarter of Western European workers under the age of twenty-five were unemployed.[41]

American and Western European governments' focus on deregulation and anti-union policies exacerbated the struggle to make ends meet and ultimately refocused workers' leisure possibilities. Chancellor Helmut Kohl in West Germany, Prime Minister Margaret Thatcher in Britain, and President Ronald Reagan in the United States advocated for less state regulation, free markets, and more individual achievement. Thatcher, for example, sold nationalized coal, transport, and utility industries to private ownership, spending on social programs as a share of the GDP dropped, trade union membership declined throughout her tenure as prime minister, and her government reduced tax rates for the wealthiest.[42] In the United States President Reagan focused on significant cuts in taxation, the elimination of hundreds of rules regulating business, and a dramatic reduction in federal social spending. These policies led to regional booms in real estate, finance, retail trade, and high-tech manufacturing, but throughout the Midwest and the mid-Atlantic states American industry witnessed wave after wave of plant closings,[43] and between 1980 and 1983 2.4 million workers disappeared from the union rolls.[44]

To try and maintain profits corporations adopted policies that did little more than reduce wages and benefits for American and European workers and increased the disparity between the rich and the poor. American companies moved production facilities to the Sunbelt South, the stretch of land from Virginia to Florida and then west across Texas to southern California where wage and unionization rates were lower, while Western European companies began looking to central or Eastern Europe. Corporations also moved their operations to Mexico, Taiwan, and Indonesia or simply began to outsource labor to export processing zones across the globe where typically young women worked for low wages for contractors or subcontractors from Korea, Taiwan, or Hong Kong to fill orders for companies based in the United States, Britain, Japan, Germany, or Canada. Corporate flight left behind workers with few alternatives, pensions, or transferable skills.[45]

The jobs that remained were increasingly confined to the service sector. The growing impact of service jobs was already noticeable in the twenty-five years after the Second World War when millions of new jobs opened up in education, health care, and government. Not all of these jobs were white collar. Service-sector jobs also include sales assistants, domestic and janitorial workers, cooks, and security staff. These jobs have been traditionally identified with women and racial minorities, and they were often part-time or temporary and paid low wages. In Britain by the mid-1990s about five million workers were employed in manufacturing, construction, and mining, while retail trade and services employed nearly nine million workers.[46] In the United States in 2016 manufacturing makes up the highest percentage of employment in only seven states. In the remaining forty-three states retail trade, accommodation and food service, and health care and social assistance dominate, and only 9 percent of total US employment was in manufacturing.[47]

The adverse effects of a changing economy led critics to blame leisure. As the battle over the power of unions and production exploded in Britain, the Thatcher government used the stereotype of the "lazy" British worker to promote antiunionism.[48] In the United States where Reagan-era neoconservatives deployed the same argument, critics turned the affluence of the postwar years (while ignoring how those gains left working-class minorities behind) against the new generation of white industrial workers. Social scientists and corporate managers argued that the affluence had spoiled the working poor. This generation of industrial workers, they averred, were unfamiliar with scarcity, and they lacked the character of their fathers who had survived the Depression. Workers' problems, according to these critics, were of their own making: they were to blame for rising rates of absenteeism, shoddy workmanship, and an unwillingness to assume their roles as breadwinner. Probusiness conservatives argued that parental overindulgence and a postwar affluence had undermined a work ethic, and they concluded that the productivity lag was a consequence of leisure gone awry as laziness: a generation of men who were indifferent to work and preferred to spend their time at leisure (i.e. not working).[49]

Even children's leisure attracted increasing scrutiny against the backdrop of economic stagnation. Fears about the country's international competitiveness, budget deficits, and street crime led Americans to shift their focus away from the "protected" child of previous decades to the "prepared" childhood of the post-1970 era. Historian Steven Mintz notes that parents were concerned that their children "lagged far behind their foreign counterparts in their knowledge of science, mathematics and technology and lacked the discipline and drive necessary to meet the challenges of the twenty-first century." To that end, the growth of "educationally oriented preschools" took off during the period as parents sought to enhance their children's cognitive, motor, language, and social skills. Parents also pushed to fill up their children's free time after school with additional lessons, enrichment activities, and organized sports, leading critics to complain about "hyper parenting" or parents who placed too much stress on their children to achieve while eliminating opportunities for free play. Surveys of children's unstructured play and other outdoor activities for children three to eleven years old actually declined by close to 40 percent between the early 1980s and late 1990s.[50]

The other major theme surrounding the economic polarization of the era focused on the privatization of leisure. Simply put, growing numbers of men and women who were struggling to make ends meet were spending more of their leisure time at home when compared to their counterparts from previous generations. In Britain by the 1980s the main growth areas in leisure spending was on "sound and vision reproducing equipment, telecommunications and computer technology," and by the 2000s, mass media and related communication technologies consumed more time than other forms of leisure. By this time, the typical British man or woman spent an average of twenty-six hours each week watching television, nineteen hours each week listening to the radio, and four out of ten households had a home computer. Other home-based leisure activities included do-it-yourself home projects and repairs, decorating, car maintenance, and gardening, which were the most popular hobbies in Great Britain by the 1990s when two-thirds of Britain's dwellings were owner-occupied.[51]

Most forms of out-of-home recreation also saw a decline if they could be replicated or closely substituted by in-home entertainment. While cinema admissions doubled in the

FIGURE 9.5 An abandoned drive-in theatre in Chester, West Virginia. Photo: Carol H. Highsmith. Library of Congress. Public domain.

thirty years since the early 1980s, sociologist Kenneth Roberts describes the audiences for the theater and spectator sporting events as "in long-term and continuing decline." The British, too, consumed more alcohol per capita in the 1980s than any previous decade in the twentieth century but more of that alcohol was consumed at home—less at public houses. As a consequence, the success of sports had become increasingly dependent on primetime television coverage, and drink, sports and film producers have put more resources into home-based markets and into made-for-television movies and video distribution.[52]

By the end of the century, out-of-home recreation showed signs of growth in participant sports and tourism. Concerns about health and fitness in the 1970s led to a decline in smoking, increased popularity of health foods and diets, and a rise in jogging and mass participation in marathons. More of the British also went on vacations or took day trips to coastal and countryside destinations, and the growing interest in travel led to the rise of theme parks. A quarter of the population now take two or more holidays a year and a third at least one.[53]

Yet economic polarization has also shaped the trend toward out-of-home recreation. While growing numbers of men and women participated in regular exercise, a third of men and half of women engaged in no regular exercise, and health concerns were most evident among the middle and upper classes.[54] By the mid-twentieth century, four out of five British men fifteen years of age or older smoked.[55] As health concerns mounted, the numbers of smokers would decrease and by 2014 just under one in five adults smoked. But smoking rates remain significantly higher among poorer people. Only 13 percent of adults in managerial and professional occupations smoked in 2014 compared with 30 percent of adults in routine and manual occupations.[56] Holiday excursions were no different. By the postwar years, holiday travel and vacations had emerged as a sign of British identity but by the early twenty-first century about four-tenths of the population have no holiday trips at all, and that proportion has not changed since the mid-1970s when the standard of living began to decline across Western Europe.[57]

"Connoisseur leisure" has also grown in popularity. Connoisseur leisure consists of small groups of enthusiasts with finely tuned skills and exceptional knowledge about any number of activities—spectator sports, the arts, the countryside, wines, and home improvement. These enthusiasts demand a different standard of service and commit considerable cash, time, and energy to their pastimes. The economic polarization of the era facilitated the growth of these wealthier subcultures of leisure enthusiasts who stood in sharp contrast to the overwhelming majority of the working and middle classes whose leisure was increasingly homebound or consisted of mass-marketed goods and packaged experiences.[58]

The unequal distribution of wealth in Western Europe also exacerbated the alienation of poor and working-class youth, whose leisure opportunities dissipated with the economic downturn of the 1970s and 1980s. With unemployment for those under twenty-five at 25 percent many of them had no jobs and no disposable wealth. Yet unlike their elders, they were not homebound, generally spending their leisure time hanging out with friends or wandering the streets. The growing numbers of unemployed in fact gave rise to fears about hooliganism, a particularly conspicuous problem linked to football matches across Europe in the 1970s and 1980s. They were the children of parents who came of age during the prosperity of the immediate postwar years but lacked the resources needed to take part in the culture of consumption that had taken root in British culture. As their presence became more conspicuous, they became linked to crime and lawlessness.[59]

The privatization of out-of-home leisure distinguished US recreation during this same period. As early as 1982, one survey by Scripps-Howard found that eight out of the ten most popular American leisure activities were home-based. In his study of community engagement sociologist Robert Putnam explores the reasons for the withdrawal from civic involvement and the problems he points to are the same ones shaping Western Europe. Putnam notes, "people with lower incomes and those who feel financially strapped are much less engaged in all forms of social and community life, than those who are better off." Financial anxiety, he adds, means "less time spent with friends, less card playing, less home entertaining, less frequent attendance at church, less volunteering and less interest in politics." The withdrawal from these activities has affected women who work full time the most, and Putnam highlights the future potential impact of the electronic mass media and especially the internet on civic engagement. Like Western Europe, this problem, according to Putnam, began with the growing popularity of the television, which absorbed almost 40 percent of the average American's free time in 1995, "an increase of roughly one-third since 1965." By 2000, the average American spends four hours a day watching television and at least half of all of them usually watch alone. A major effect of television's arrival, he concludes, "was the reduction in participation in social, recreational and community activities among people of all ages."[60]

The economic polarization that became most conspicuous by the 1980s also translated into a public discourse that celebrated both wealth and leisure. The most prominent symbol was the yuppie, a term for those young upwardly mobile professionals in the United States who also had counterparts in Western Europe (Sloane Rangers in Great Britain and the *bon chic bon* genre in France).[61] All three attracted increasing attention in the 1980s, an era in which professional-managerial "workers" in finance, trade, the legal profession, and banking lauded the ostentatious display of wealth.[62] The wealthiest have long been associated with conspicuous consumption, but ostentatious displays of wealth and leisure defined the modern era and shaped popular culture. American television dramas such as *Dynasty* and *Dallas*, which also aired throughout Eastern and Western Europe, further promoted wealth and gave ordinary working Americans and Europeans a glimpse of the luxury homes and yachts that dominated discussions about leisure and the high life in the 1980s.[63] While American and European workers struggled to maintain the prosperity that they had helped produce in the postwar era, media barraged them with images of a "good life" denied to them, according to neoliberal policymakers, by their simply being too lazy.

To be sure, differences remained between Western Europe and the United States. What gains working- and middle-class Americans saw in their family incomes during the post-1970 era came from growing numbers of family members entering the labor market. In the quarter century after 1970 women's labor force participation in the United States increased from about 40 percent to 60 percent and virtually all the income gains among white two-parent families in the years after 1967 can be accounted for by the wages of wives and daughters.[64] According to historian Juliet Schor, the average employed person in 1989 was working 163 hours more a year than what that person was working in 1969, an extra two and a half weeks for men and seven additional weeks for women.[65]

In Western Europe by the 1960s, most employees were entitled to two weeks' paid vacation plus holidays, and in Norway, Sweden, Denmark, and France workers were entitled to three weeks' paid vacation. In fact, employees have the most time off in countries where a collective bargaining agreement covers the largest number of them. While collective bargaining agreements only covered about 18 percent of American workers in 2004, collective bargaining agreements covered about 90 percent or more of workers in Sweden, France, Germany, Austria, Belgium, and Finland. By this year, Germany and Italy had the highest number of paid holidays and vacation days (thirty-nine days), and Europeans worked 20 percent less than their American counterparts or forty weeks each year compared to forty-six weeks a year for the average American working full time.[66]

The average number of hours worked in the United States was comparable to the average in Europe until the 1970s. By this time and as the economy began to contract, union strength in Europe was reaching a peak in many countries and reducing the workweek become a strategy that Europeans adopted to keep everyone employed.[67] More recently, the European Union's Working Time Directive of 1998 set a limit of forty-eight hours per week, and in 2000 France adopted a thirty-five-hour work. The average across Europe by this time was thirty-seven to thirty-nine hours a week[68] while full-time workers in the United States worked about forty-seven hours each week.[69]

With paid vacations but limited means, Europeans consistently struggle to strike a balance between work and leisure. While the EU set a limit of forty-eight hours per week in 1998, workers may opt out of the requirement if they wish to and about a fifth of Britain's workforce has. In 2003, 11 percent of the British workforce was working more than forty-eight hours a week and 13.1 percent by 2007. More than a third of men with children in their households worked more than fifty hours per week, and two-thirds of the women who hold managerial and professional positions work more than forty-eight hours each week. The country also witnessed a sharp increase in the number of men and women working overtime between 1988 and 1998, and 22 percent of men who are fully employed work more than forty-eight hours each week. Less than half of all workers also fail to take their full holidays, and in 2012 more than a third of senior civil servants took no annual leave.[70]

The burden has been particularly hard on women. Feminists in the 1970s began using the phrase "work–life balance" to characterize their fight for policies that would make it easier for mothers to engage in paid work. What became clear from the ensuing discussion is that the amount of paid work for women has increased since the mid-1970s, and women perform substantially more unpaid work than men despite the decades-old push for more balanced gender roles. European women's leisure time since the 1970s has decreased by about forty minutes each day.[71]

In addition, current corporate trends in the twenty-first century suggest that even the best attempts to find an effective balance between work and leisure have had limited results. Google prides itself on its overarching philosophy: to "create the happiest, most productive workplace in the world" and thus foster the kind of creativity needed to remain successful. Google offers its employees 100 percent health-care coverage and onsite childcare facilities, paid maternity leave for both parents, numerous cafés and cafeterias that provide free food, and various play and conversation areas that allow employees to destress or meditate, and Google does not require employees to work in the office. The company celebrates work as a part of a community in which workers are surrounded by friends and other coworkers who are there to help and thus relieve any stress.[72]

Like Google, the high-tech industry generally prides itself on its worker-friendly environment, yet it remains unclear how long this trend will last or if it is likely to spread to other companies. At Yahoo the company's CEO, Marissa Mayer, ended its policy of allowing employees to work at home in 2015 because it was adversely affecting collaboration and innovation.[73] Critics and employees have complained that the culture of the high-tech industry only values younger employees, who typically do not have children and have fewer responsibilities. In a 2007 interview Facebook's cofounder Mark Zuckerberg summed up this point when he said: "Young people just have simpler lives. We may not own a car. We may not have family. Simplicity in life allows you to focus on what's important." Indeed, critics note that the high-profile examples of the company's executives balancing family and work tell us little about average workers because these privileges are not always available to them. Marissa Mayer, for example, had a nursery built next to her office after she returned to work two weeks after having her baby. And even some of the benefits that are available to your typical worker reinforce the idea that workers need to be committed to the workplace. Free food in the cafeterias and on-site laundry facilities make things easier in a pinch, but they also discourage employees from leaving work.[74]

High-tech corporate efforts to strike a balance between work and leisure to promote happiness and productivity also bear remarkable similarity to the welfare capitalism of the 1920s. Play areas, conversation spaces, and the other leisure facilities are merely momentary distractions workers can make use of to help them cope with stress and then quickly resume the work they have been paid to perform. While workers appear empowered and have a range of options to choose from, the corporation makes all the decisions about what constitutes leisure. The other amenities they offer are provided to make it easier to stay at work longer, but ironically these "amenities" limit the amount of time for leisure and autonomy. Leisure appears, thus, as an afterthought, sandwiched between moments of restlessness in the workplace. These programs give little thought to structured leisure, which is inconspicuous at best.

CONCLUSION

While workers have often achieved a rich and fulfilling life of leisure, there has been no constant progress toward achieving the balance between work and leisure that Riesman imagined in his mid-century study of American character. Workers' successes and failures have often been the consequence of unstable or expanding economies and government- or corporate-sponsored leisure programs that generally failed to recognize that a fulfilling leisure life was also dependent upon a rewarding work experience.

Multinational corporations and contemporary business practices have only added to the problems workers face. The constant push to maximize profits has come at the expense of workers' rights and effectively compromised their time for leisure. Indeed, outsourcing to the lowest bidder and temporary employment undercuts the social relations necessary for meaningful work and the networks critical to organizing and sustaining leisure. Ironically, nowhere are these changes more obvious than within the tourism and leisure industry. Worldwide tourism alone accounts for 8 percent of all exports, or, in terms of employment, one out of every twelve jobs. Its growth rate has in fact shown a high and almost constant upward trend since 1950.[75] The leisure industry has shown similar gains. In Great Britain, it provides 9 percent of UK employment, which is roughly 2.6 million jobs, or more workers than manufacturing, transport, construction, or jobs in the financial services sector, and its revenue is growing by over 7 percent a year. Most leisure employment, like other service work, is also temporary, low-wage, and insecure, hence 21 percent of the workforce is made up of sixteen to twenty-five year olds, and women constitute a majority of workers.[76]

National boundaries also increasingly make less sense in a global world. While workers in some Western European countries have secured more vacation time and a shorter workweek, they still face enormous pressure to maintain a certain level of productivity and hence legitimize their commitment to the corporation. The high-tech industry has attracted the most attention for those efforts, and the list of amenities they offer employees is impressive. Yet these efforts have proceeded without keeping in mind the broader relationship between work and leisure, and their efforts remain focused on finding ways to make workers more productive and loyal—like welfare capitalism during the interwar years. These corporations only affect a small percentage of the American or European labor force, and the demands of the job have attracted young people with few responsibilities and no children—a conspicuous cohort but one that does not reflect the typical worker. Leisure, as David Riesman reminds us, cannot rescue the disintegration of work, and leisure can only be meaningful if work is.

NOTES

Introduction

1. Paul A. Baron and Paul M. Sweezy, *Monopoly Capital: An Essay on the American Economic and Social Order* (New York, NY: Monthly Review Press, 1966).
2. C. Wright Mills, *White Collar: The American Middle Classes* (New York, NY: Oxford University Press, 1951).
3. David Halle, *America's Working Man: Work, Home and Politics Among Blue Collar Property Owners* (Chicago, IL: University of Chicago Press, 1984); Daniel J. Walkowitz, *Working with Class: Social Workers and the Politics of Middle-Class Identity* (Chapel Hill: University of North Carolina Press, 1999).
4. Seth Koven and Sonya Michel, "Womanly Duties: Maternalist Politics and the Origins of Welfare States in France, Germany, Great Britain, and the United States, 1880–1920," *American Historical Review* 95, no. 4 (October 1990): 1076–108.
5. Ibid., 1101.
6. Stephen Meyer, III, *The Five Dollar Day: Labor Management and Social Control in the Ford Motor Company, 1908–1921* (Albany: State University of New York Press, 1981).
7. Loren Baritz, *Servants of Power: A History of the Use of Social Science in American Industry* (Middletown, CT: Wesleyan University Press, 1960).
8. For a good historiographic essay published in 1975–6 to commemorate the fiftieth anniversary of the General Strike, see Alastair Reid and Steven Tolliday, "The General Strike," *The Historical Journal* 20, no. 4 (1977): 1001–12. On the Passaic Textile Strike, see, David J. Goldberg, "Passaic Textile Strike of 1926," in *Encyclopedia of Radicalism*, eds. Mari Jo Buhle, Paul Buhle, and Dan Georgakas (New York, NY: Garland Publishing Co., 1990), 560; J. A. Zumoff, "Hell in New Jersey: The Passaic Textile Strike, Albert Weisbord, and the Communist Party," *Journal for the Study of Radicalism*, 9, no. 1 (2015): 125–69.
9. Koven and Michel, "Womanly Duties"; Susan Pedersen, *Family, Dependence, and the Origins of the Welfare State: Britain and France, 1919–1946* (New York, NY: Cambridge University Press, 1993).
10. Jonathan D. Bloom, "Brookwood Labor College, 1921–33: Training Ground for Union Organizers" (M.A. thesis, Rutgers University, Department of History, 1978); Jonathan D. Bloom, "Brookwood Labor College and the Progressive Network of Interwar United States, 1921–1937" (Ph.D. dissertation, Department of History, New York University, 1992).
11. Walkowitz, *Working with Class*, 92.
12. Miss Levy and the chairman, in *Proceedings, Annual Session* (1923), 195–97, National Conference of Jewish Social Service, YIVO archive.
13. Barbara Melosh, *The Physician's Hand: Nurses and Nursing in the Twentieth Century* (Philadelphia, PA: Temple University Press, 1982); Marjorie Murphy, *Blackboard Unions: The AFT and the NEA, 1900–1980* (Ithaca, NY: Cornell University Press, 1991); Daniel J. Opler, *For All White Collar Workers: The Possibilities of Radicalism in New York City's Department Store Unions, 1934–1953* (Columbus: Ohio State University Press, 2003);

Jürgen Kocka, *White Collar Workers in America, 1890–1940*, (London: Sage Publications, 1980). See also, Lorraine Gray, producer, "With Babies and Banners: The Story of the Women's Emergency Brigade" (1979), a 45-minute documentary of the United Auto Workers' strike in 1936 to 1937.

14 Mark Naison, "The Battle of the Bronx," in *The Tenant Movement in New York City, 1904–1984*, chap. 3. http://tenant.net/Community/history/hist03d.html (accessed November 14, 2016).
15 Ibid.
16 See, Walkowitz, *Working with Class*, chaps. 3 and 4.
17 Lizabeth Cohen, *Making a New Deal: Industrial Workers in Chicago, 1919–1939* (New York, NY: Cambridge University Press, 1990).
18 Ibid., and Lizabeth Cohen, *A Consumers' Republic: The Politics of Mass Consumption in Postwar America* (New York, NY: Random House, 2008); Walkowitz, *Working with Class*, chap. 5.
19 Walkowitz, *Working with Class*, chaps. 6–7.
20 David M. Gordon, Richard Edwards, and Michael Reich, *Segmented Work, Segmented Workers: The Historical Transformation of Labor in the United States* (New York, NY: Cambridge University Press, 1982).
21 Judith Stein, *Running Steel, Running America: Race, Economic Policy and the Decline of Liberalism* (Chapel Hill: University of North Carolina Press, 2000); Paul D. Standohar and Holly E. Brown, eds., *Deindustrialization and Plant Closure* (Lexington, MA: D.C. Heath, 1987).
22 Ivan Moskelenko, in "Perestroika from Below," 58-minute video, Barbara Abrash and Daniel J. Walkowitz, producers, Past Time Productions, 1990.
23 Herrick Chapman, "Pittsburgh's and Europe's Metallurgical Cities: A Comparison," in *City at the Point: Essays on the Social History of Pittsburgh*, ed. Samuel P. Hays (Pittsburgh, PA: University of Pittsburgh Press, 1981), 407–35.
24 "Coal and Jobs in the United States." http://Sourcewatch.org/index.php/coal (accessed November 15, 2016).
25 "Closure of Kellingley pit brings deep coal mining to an end." http://BBCNews.com/news/uk/England_york_north_yorkshire_3524077 (accessed November 22, 2016).
26 "The rise and fall of German's coal mining industry." www.dw.com/en/the_rise_and_fall_of_germanys_ coal_mining_industry/a-2331545 (accessed November 22, 2016).
27 See, Daniel J. Walkowitz, "'Normal Life' The Crisis of Identity Among Donetsk's Miners," in *Workers of the Donbass Speak: Survival and Identity in the New Ukraine, 1989–1992*, eds. Lewis Siegelbaum and Daniel J. Walkowitz (Albany: State University of New York Press, 1995), 159–84, and Richard Boyer and David Savagean, eds., *Place Rated Almanac*, 2nd ed. (New York: Prentice Hall, 1985), quoted in Walkowitz, "Normal Life."
28 "In desperate 1983, there was no place for Pittsburgh's economy to go but up," *Pittsburgh Gazette*, December 23, 2012. http://www.post-gazette.com/business/businessnews/2012/12/23/In-desperate-1983-there-was-nowhere-for-Pittsburgh-s-economy-to-go-but-up/stories/201212230258 (accessed November 24, 2016).
29 Ibid.
30 Walkowitz, "Normal Life."
31 "Men-and Women-In-the-Street," interviews with Lewis Siegelbaum and Daniel J. Walkowitz, Donestk, May 26, 1991, quoted in *Workers of the Donbass*, 165.
32 Sarah Zelermyer, realtor, interview with the author, November 24, 2016.
33 Quentin Hardy, "To Innovate, Workplaces Think Like Programmers," *New York Times*, November 25, 2016, B1, B3.

34 "New Oxfam report says half of global wealth held by the 1%," *The Guardian*, January 19, 2015. https://www.theguardian.com/business/2015/jan/19/global-wealth-oxfam-inequality-davos-economic-summit-switzerland (accessed December 14, 2016).

Chapter One

1 John Schmitt and Kris Warner, *The Changing Face of Labor, 1983–2008* (Washington, DC: Center for Economic and Policy Research, 2009), 1.
2 Susan Porter-Benson, *Household Accounts: Working-class Household Economies in the Interwar United States* (Ithaca, NY: Cornell University Press, 2007), 18.
3 Ibid., 18.
4 Karen Orren, *Belated Feudalism: Labor, the Law, and Liberal Development in the United States* (New York, NY: Cambridge University Press, 1991), 176–7.
5 Victoria DeGrazia, *Irresistible Empire: America's Advance Through 20th Century Europe* (Cambridge, MA: Harvard University Press, 2005), chap. 2.
6 Vanessa H. May, *Unprotected Labor: Household Workers, Politics, and Middle-Class Reform in New York, 1870–1940* (Chapel Hill: University of North Carolina Press, 2011).
7 Bruce Nelson, *Workers on the Waterfront: Seamen, Longshoremen, and Unionism in the 1930s* (Urbana: University of Illinois Press, 1988), 106; Ella Baker and Marvel Cooke, "The Bronx Slave Market," *Crisis* 42, no. 11 (November 1935): 330–1, 340.
8 Sanford M. Jacoby, *Modern Manors: Welfare Capitalism Since the New Deal* (Princeton, NJ: Princeton University Press, 1997), 11.
9 Steven Fraser, *Labor Will Rule: Sidney Hillman and the Rise of American Labor* (New York, NY: The Free Press, 1991), 29, 35.
10 Florence Kelley, "The Sweating System," in *Hull House Maps and Papers: A Presentation of Nationalities and Wages in a Congested District of Chicago, Together with Comments and Essays on Problems Growing Out of the Social Conditions* (New York, NY: Thomas V. Crowell, 1895).
11 Nelson Lichtenstein, *State of the Union: A Century of American Labor* (Princeton, NJ: Princeton University Press, 2002), 23.
12 Jennifer Klein, *For All These Rights: Business, Labor, and the Shaping of America's Public-Private Welfare State* (Princeton, NJ: Princeton University Press, 2003); Jacoby, *Modern Manors*, 20–1.
13 Jacoby, *Modern Manors*, 56–73.
14 Fraser, *Labor Will Rule*, 75–6, 81–3.
15 Ibid., 127–8; Joseph A. McCartin, *Labor's Great War: The Struggle for Industrial Democracy and the Origins of Modern American Labor Relations, 1912–1921* (Chapel Hill: University of North Carolina Press, 1997).
16 Jacoby, *Modern Manors*, 73.
17 Mary Nolan, *The Transatlantic Century: Europe and America, 1890–2010* (New York, NY: Cambridge University Press, 2012), 105, 108, 117.
18 Nolan, *The Transatlantic Century*, 120.
19 Ibid., 123–8; Marie Rodet, "Forced Labor, Resistance, and Masculinities in Kayes, French Sudan, 1919–1946," *International Labor and Working Class History*, 86 (Fall 2014): 107–23.
20 Fraser, *Labor Will Rule*, 272, 274; Nelson Lichtenstein, "Tribunes of the Shareholder Class," in *A Contest of Ideas: Capital, Politics, and Labor* (Urbana: University of Illinois Press, 2013), 48–51.

21 Lichtenstein, *State of the Union*.
22 Jean-Christian Vinel, *The Employee: A Political History* (Philadelphia: University of Pennsylvania Press 2013), 56–57; Fraser, *Labor Will Rule*, 270.
23 Vinel, *The Employee*, 3.
24 Ibid., 79, 84, 167.
25 Ibid., 61, 161–3.
26 Lichtenstein, *State of the Union*, 49; 52–5.
27 Katherine Van Wezel Stone, "The Post-War Paradigm in American Labor Law," *Yale Law Journal*, 90, no. 7 (June 1981): 1514; Nelson Lichtenstein, *The Most Dangerous Man in Detroit: Walter Reuther and the Fate of American Labor* (NewYork, NY: Basic Books, 1995), 181–2.
28 Lichtenstein, *State of the Union*, 61.
29 Jack Metzgar, *Striking Steel: Solidarity Remembered* (Philadelphia, PA: Temple University Press, 2011), 6.
30 Klein, *For All These Rights*, chap. 6.
31 John S. Bugas, "Labor Relations and Productivity," Delivered to American Management Association, New York, October 2, 1947, reprinted in *Vital Speeches of the Day* (New York, NY: City News Publishing Co., 1947), 56.
32 Jill Quadagno, *One Nation Uninsured: Why the US Has No National Health Insurance* (Oxford: Oxford University Press, 2005), 3; Deborah Stone, "The Struggle For the Soul of Health Insurance," in *The Politics of Health Care Reform: Lessons From the Past, Prospects for the Future*, eds. James A. Morone and Gary S. Belkin (Durham, NC: Duke University Press, 1994), 33.
33 Klein, *For All These Rights*.
34 Ibid.
35 Bruce Western, *Between Class and Market: Post-War Unionization in the Capitalist Democracies* (Princeton, NJ: Princeton University Press, 1997), 11, 30–41; Peter Swenson, *Capitalists Against Markets: The Making of Labor Markets and Welfare States in the United States and Sweden* (New York, NY: Oxford University Press, 2002), 15–16, 43, 123.
36 Gosta Esping-Andersen, *The Three Worlds of Welfare Capitalism* (Princeton, NJ: Princeton University Press, 1990), 115, chaps. 5–6.
37 Swenson, *Capitalists Against Markets*, 268–75.
38 Ibid., pt. I and pt. III.
39 Ines Perez and Santiago Canevaro, "Languages of Affection and Rationality: Household Workers' Strategies Before the Tribunal of Domestic Work, Buenos Aires, 1956–2013", *International Labor and Working Class History* 88 (Fall 2015): 109–29; Henrique Espada Lima, "Wages of Intimacy: Domestic Workers Wages in the Higher Courts of Nineteenth Century Bracial," *International Labor and Working Class History* 88 (Fall 2015): 30–48.
40 Dorothy Sue Cobble, *The Other Women's Movement: Workplace Justice and Social Rights in Modern America* (Princeton, NJ: Princeton University Press, 2004), 156–7.
41 Quadagno, *One Nation Uninsured*, 52.
42 Harry I. Greenfield, *Allied Health Manpower: Trends and Prospects*, foreword by Eli Ginzberg (New York, NY: Columbia University Press, 1969).
43 Greenfield, 29–30, 34–5, 97.
44 Ibid., viii, 28.
45 Colin Gordon, *Dead on Arrival: The Politics of Health Care in Twentieth Century America* (Princeton, NJ: Princeton University Press, 2003), 96.

46 Leon Fink and Brian Greenberg, *Upheaval in the Quiet Zone: A History of Hospital Workers Union, Local 1199* (Urbana: University of Illinois Press, 1989), 8.
47 Ariel Ducey, *Never Good Enough: Health Care Workers and the False Promise of Job Training* (Ithaca, NY: ILR Press, 2009), 12.
48 Karen Brodkin Sacks, *Caring By the Hour: Women, Work, and Organizing at Duke University Medical Center* (Urbana: University of Illinois Press, 1988), 3, 18–19.
49 Fink and Greenberg, *Upheaval in the Quiet Zone*, 6.
50 Cindy Hahamovitch, *No Man's Land: Jamaican Guestworkers in America and the Global History of Deportable Labor* (Princeton, NJ: Princeton University Press, 2011), 2, 24, 27–8; Mae Ngai, *Impossible Subjects: Illegal Aliens and the Making of Modern America* (Princeton, NJ: Princeton University Press 2004), 135.
51 Hahamovitch, *No Man's Land*, 2, 9.
52 Ngai, *Impossible Subjects*, 138–40.
53 Ibid., 146–8.
54 Ibid., 143.
55 Hahamovitch, *No Man's Land*, 44–5.
56 Ibid., 2, 9–11, 25.
57 Ngai, *Impossible Subjects*, 129; Hahamovitch, *No Man's Land*, 11.
58 Hahamovitch, *No Man's Land*, 6–7, 18; Ngai, *Impossible Subjects*, 128.
59 Fink and Greenberg, *Upheaval in the Quiet Zone*, 6–13; Joseph Slater, *Public Workers: Government Employee Unions, the Law, and the State, 1900–1962* (Ithaca, NY: ILR Press, 2004).
60 Joseph A. McCartin, "A Wagner Act for Public Employees: Labor's Deferred Dream and the Rise of Conservatism, 1970–1976," *Journal of American History* 95, no. 1 (June 2008): 123–4.
61 Eileen Boris and Jennifer Klein, *Caring for America: Home Health Workers in the Shadow of the Welfare State* (New York, NY: Oxford University Press, 2012).
62 Boris and Klein, *Caring for America*.
63 Ibid., 7.
64 John Logan, "The Union Avoidance Industry in the United States," *British Journal of Industrial Relations* 44, no. 4 (December 2006): 652–6, 660, 663, 667.
65 Lisa Furchtgott, "Tents Amid the Fragments: The Law at Greenham Common," *Journal of Social History* 48, no. 4 (Summer 2015): 794.
66 Vinel, *The Employee*, chap. 7 and Epilogue.
67 Erin Hatton, *The Temp Economy: From Kelly Girls to Permatemps in Postwar America* (Philadelphia, PA: Temple University Press, 2012), 7–9, 11, chap. 1, 74–6, 84–5.
68 Ibid., 107.
69 Ibid., 12–16, 74–6.
70 Ibid., 84–108, 115.
71 David Weil, *The Fissured Workplace: Why Work Became So Bad for So Many and What Can Be Done to Improve It* (Cambridge, MA: Harvard University Press, 2014) 7.
72 Ibid., 8–9.
73 Sarah Mosoetsa, Joel Stillerman, and Chris Tilly, "Precarious Labor, South and North," *International Labor and Working Class History* 89 (Spring 2016): 6, 11, 15.
74 Ibid., 12–13; Rina Agarwala, "Redefining Exploitation: Self-Employed Workers' Movements in India's Garments and Trash Collection Industries," *International Labor and Working Class History* 89 (Spring 2016): 107–30.
75 Weil, *The Fissured Workplace*, 3, 10.

76 Annette Bernhardt et al., *Confronting the Gloves Off Economy: America's Broken Labor Standards and How to Fix Them* (Champaign, IL: National Employment Law Project, Labor and Employment Relations Association, July 2009).
77 UCLA Labor Center, "What is Wage Theft?" www.labor.ucla.edu (accessed July 20, 2016).
78 Steven Greenhouse, "More Workers Are Claiming Wage Theft," *New York Times*, August 31, 2014, A1.
79 Tom Juravich, *At the Altar of the Bottom Line: The Degradation of Work in the 21st Century* (Amherst: University of Massachusetts Press, 2009), 3, 5–8.
80 Jodi Kantor, "Work Anything But 9 to 5," *New York Times*, August 13, 2014.
81 Ibid.; Bryant Simon, "Consuming Lattes and Labor, or Working at Starbucks," *International Labor and Working-Class History* 74, no. 1 (September 2008): 195–6.
82 Natasha Singer, "In the Sharing Economy, Workers Find Both Freedom and Uncertainty," *New York Times*, August 16, 2014, BU1.
83 Josh Bevins, "The Decline in Labor's Share of Corporate Income Since 2000." http://www.epi.org/publication/the-decline-in-labors-share-of-corporate-income-since-2000-means-535-,billion-less-for-workers/ (accessed October 6, 2016); Isaac Shapiro and Aviva Aron-Dine, "Share of Income Going to Wages and Salaries at Record Low in 2006." http://www.cbpp.org/research/share-of-national-income-going-to-wages-and-salaries-at-record-low-in-2006 (accessed October 6, 2016); Colin Gordon, *Growing Apart: A Political History of American Inequality* (Institute for Policy Studies, 2013). http://www.scalar.usc.edu (accessed July 21, 2016).
84 Gordon, *Growing Apart*.
85 Jake Rosenfeld, *What Unions No Longer Do* (Cambridge, MA: Harvard University Press, 2014), 2.

Chapter Two

1 For more on this movement, see Christine Lodder, *Russian Constructivism* (New Haven, CT: Yale University Press, 1983).
2 Dorothea Lange, "The Assignment I'll Never Forget: Migrant Mother," *Popular Photography*, 46, no. 2 (February 1960): 42.
3 See Leah Ollman, *Camera as Weapon: Worker Photography Between the Wars* (San Diego, CA: Museum of Photographic Arts, 1991).
4 The interwar worker-photography movement and the postwar evaluation of its legacy have been the subject of two important recent exhibitions curated by Jorge Ribalta for the Museo Nacional Centro de Arte Reina Sofia, Madrid: *A Hard, Merciless Light: The Worker-Photography Movement, 1926–1939* (2011) and *Not Yet: On the Reinvention of Documentary and the Critique of Modernism* (2015). See Jorge Ribalta, ed. *The Worker-Photography Movement (1926–1939): Essays and Documents* (Madrid: Museo Nacional Centro de Arte Reina Sofia, 2011) and *Not Yet: On the Reinvention of Documentary and the Critique of Modernism: Essays and Documents, 1972–1991* (Madrid: Museo Nacional Centro de Arte Reina Sofia, 2015).
5 Edwin Hoernle, "Das Auge des Arbeiters," *Der Arbeiter-Fotograf* 4, no. 7 (1930): 49.
6 Published in *AIZ*, no. 38, September 1931 and *Proletarskoe foto*, no. 4 (December 1931). The German replica of the reportage, "Die deutschen Filipows," produced by a group of Berlin worker-photographers led by Erich Rinka, was published in *AIZ*, no. 48 (December 1931) and in a different version in *Der Arbeiter-Fotograf* (January 1932).
7 See Edward Steichen, ed., *Family of Man* (New York: Museum of Modern Art, 1955).

8 Fred Turner, "The Family of Man and the Politics of Attention in Cold War America," *Public Culture* 24, no. 1 (2012): 55. For an analysis of critical responses to the exhibition, see Monique Berlier, "The Family of Man: Readings of an Exhibition," in *Picturing the Past: Media, History, and Photography*, eds. Bonnie Brennan and Hanno Hardt (Urbana: University of Illinois Press, 1999), 206–41.
9 Susan Sontag, *On Photography* (Harmondsworth: Penguin, 1977).
10 Dave Isay, "Foreword," in Dave Isay, David Miller, and Harvey Wang, *Milton Rogovin: The Forgotten Ones* (New York, NY: Quantuck Lane Press, 2003), 11.
11 The most comprehensive biography is Melanie Anne Herzog, *Milton Rogovin: The Making of a Social Documentary Photographer*, Tucson: Center for Creative Photography (Seattle: University of Washington Press, 2006).
12 Bertolt Brecht, "A Worker Reads History," in Bertolt Brecht, *Selected Poems*, trans. H. R. Hayes (New York, NY: Harcourt Brace Jovanovich, 1947), 109. Melanie Herzog reports this to have been Rogovin's favorite translation, the one he always recited, Herzog, *Rogovin*, 167, n. 68.
13 Herzog, *Rogovin*, 18.
14 Milton Rogovin, *The Mining Photographs* (Los Angeles, CA: J. Paul Getty Museum, 2005).
15 Milton Rogovin and Michael Frisch, *Portraits in Steel* (Ithaca, NY: Cornell University Press, 1993).
16 Milton Rogovin, *The Forgotten Ones*, The Albright-Knox Art Gallery, Buffalo (Seattle: University of Washington Press, 1985), and *Triptychs: Buffalo's Lower West Side Revisited* (New York, NY: W. W. Norton, 1994); and Isay, Miller, and Wang, *Milton Rogovin*.
17 Rogovin and Frisch, *Portraits in Steel*, 181.
18 Ibid.
19 Ibid., 186–7.
20 Ibid., 190–1.
21 See Mierle Laderman Ukeles, *Manifesto for Maintenance Art 1969!* Reprinted in Patricia Phillips, *Mierle Laderman Ukeles: Maintenance Art* (New York, NY: Prestel, 2016).
22 Allan Sekula, *Aerospace Folktales*, 1972. Transcription provided: http://foundation.generali.at/en/collection/artist/sekula-allan/artwork/aerospace-folktales.html (accessed December 31, 2016).
23 Manfred Herms, "Allan Sekula," *Frieze*, no. 78, October 10, 2003. https://frieze.com/article/allan-sekula (accessed December 31, 2016).
24 Allan Sekula, "Dismantling Modernism, Reinventing *Documentary* (Notes on the Politics of Representation)," *The Massachusetts Review* 19, no. 4 (December 1978): 859–83.
25 David Coggins, "Steve McQueen," *Interview Magazine*, February 17, 2009. http://www.interviewmagazine.com/art/steve-mcqueen/ (accessed December 31, 2016).
26 T. J. Demos, "The Art of Darkness: On Steve McQueen," *October*, no. 114, Fall 2005, 88.
27 Harun Farocki, "Workers Leaving the Factory," in *Harun Farocki: Working on the Sightlines*, ed. Thomas Elsaesser and trans. Laurent Faasch-Ibrahim (Amsterdam: Amsterdam University Press, 2004), 237–43. Originally published as "Arbeiter verlassen die Fabrik," *Meteor* no. 1 (December 1995): 49–55.
28 Harun Farocki, "Workers Leaving the Factory in 11 Decades," http://www.harunfarocki.de/installations/2000s/2006/workers-leaving-the-factory-in-eleven-decades.html (accessed December 15, 2016).
29 The work of contemporary artists interested in representing labor has been the subject of numerous recent exhibitions, including *Manifesta 9* (Genk, Belgium, 2011); *The Workers* (Mass MoCA, Northampton, MA, 2012); *Overtime: The Art of Work* (Albright-Knox Art Gallery, Buffalo, NY, 2014) among many others.

Chapter Three

1 Richard A. Greenwald, *The Triangle Fire, the Protocols of Peace, and Industrial Democracy in Progressive Era New York, Labor in Crisis* (Philadelphia, PA: Temple University Press, 2005).
2 Sidney and Beatrice Webb, *Industrial Democracy* (New York, NY: Augustus M. Kelley, 1965).
3 Nancy L. Green, *Read-to-Wear and Ready-to-Work: A Century of Industry and Immigrants in Paris and New York* (Durham, NC: Duke University Press, 1997).
4 Stanley Nadel, "Reds Versus Pinks: A Civil War in the International; Ladies Garment Workers Union," *New York History* 66, no. 1 (1985): 38–47; Daniel E. Bender and Richard A. Greenwald, *Sweatshop USA: The American Sweatshop in Historical and Global Perspective* (New York, NY: Routledge, 2003).
5 Kenneth C. Wolensky, Nicole H. Wolensky, and Robert P. Wolensky, *Fighting for the Union Label: The Women's Garment Industry and the ILGWU in Pennsylvania* (University Park, PA: Pennsylvania State University Press, 2002).
6 Landon R. Y. Storrs, *Civilizing Capitalism: The National Consumers' League, Women's Activism, and Labor Standards in the New Deal Era* (Chapel Hill: University of North Carolina Press, 2000).
7 Ellen Israel Rosen, *Making Sweatshops: The Globalization of the US Apparel Industry* (Berkeley: University of California Press, 2002).
8 Bender and Greenwald, *Sweatshop USA*; Andrew Ross, *No Sweat Fashion, Free Trade, and the Rights of Garment Workers* (New York, NY: Verso, 1997).
9 Andrew Herod, "Labor's Spatial Praxis and the Geography of Contract Bargaining in the Us East Coast Longshore Industry, 1953–1989," *Political Geography* 16, no. 2 (1997): 145–69.
10 "On the Waterfront, It's Union vs. Tech; Jobs at Stake as Shippers Seek Productivity," *Washington Post*, January 5, 2002, E:1; "A Union Wins the Global Game," *New York Times*, October 6, 2002, 4:1.
11 Author interviews conducted in 2011 at various locations, in author's possession.
12 The following section relies on: Andrew Gibson and Arthur Donovan, *The Abandoned Ocean: A History of United States Maritime Policy*, Studies in Maritime History (Columbia: University of South Carolina Press, 2000); William J. Mello, *New York Longshoremen: Class and Power on the Docks, Working in the Americas* (Gainesville: University Press of Florida, 2010); Bruce Nelson, *Workers on the Waterfront: Seamen, Longshoremen, and Unionism in the 1930s, The Working Class in American History* (Urbana: University of Illinois Press, 1988); Howard Kimeldorf, *Reds or Rackets?: The Making of Radical and Conservative Unions on the Waterfront* (Berkeley: University of California Press, 1988); Colin J. Davis, *Waterfront Revolts: New York and London Dockworkers, 1946–61*, The Working Class in American History (Urbana: University of Illinois Press, 2003).
13 The following section relies on: Dalton Conley, *Elsewhere, USA*, 1st ed. (New York, NY: Pantheon Books, 2009); Daniel H. Pink, *Free Agent Nation: How America's New Independent Workers Are Transforming the Way We Live* (New York, NY: Warner Books, 2001); Steven Hill, *Raw Deal: How the Sharing Economy and Naked Capitalism Are Screwing American Workers* (New York, NY: Palgrave Macmillan Trade, 2015); Sara Horowitz and Toni Sciarra Poynter, *The Freelancer's Bible: Everything You Need to Know to Have the Career of Your Dreams on Your Terms* (New York, NY: Workman Publishing Co., 2012); Richard Greenwald, "To Boost the Economy, Help the Self-Employed," *Bloomsberg BusinessWeek*, August 4, 2011; "How to Succeed in the Age of Going Solo;

Anybody Can Become a Consultant. But Not Everybody Does It Well. Here's What You Need to Know to Thrive," *Wall Street Journal*, February 8, 2010. https://www.wsj.com/articles/SB10001424052748704825504574581900293220092 (accessed June 26, 2017); "Freelancers Find It Pays to Team up," *Wall Street Journal*, February 3, 2014. https://www.wsj.com/articles/freelancers-find-it-pays-to-team-up-1389267711 (accessed June 26, 2017); Richard A. Greenwald and Daniel Katz, *Labor Rising: The Past and Future of Working People in America* (New York, NY: The New Press, 2012). Elaine Pofeldt, "Shocker: 40% of Workers Now Have 'Contingent' Jobs, Says US Government," *Forbes*, May 25, 2015. https://www.forbes.com/sites/elainepofeldt/2015/05/25/shocker-40-of-workers-now-have-contingent-jobs-says-u-s-government/2/#30eb52ac6fcb (accessed February 21, 2018). As well as author interviews.

14 Author interview conducted in a Williamsburg coffee shop, October 2011. In author's possession.
15 Author interviews with freelancers in author's possession. Interviews recorded February 2011.
16 William Hollingsworth Whyte, *The Organization Man* (Philadelphia: University of Pennsylvania Press, 2002), 7. Author interviews with freelancers, in author's possession. Interviews recorded February 2011.
17 Joanne J. Meyerowitz, *Not June Cleaver: Women and Gender in Postwar America, 1945–1960*, Critical Perspectives on the Past (Philadelphia, PA: Temple University Press, 1994).
18 Barbara Ehrenreich, *Bait and Switch: The (Futile) Pursuit of the American Dream*, 1st ed. (New York, NY: Metropolitan Books, 2005); Robert B. Reich, *Aftershock: The Next Economy and America's Future* (New York, NY: Vintage Books, 2013).
19 Conley, *Elsewhere, USA*.
20 Bryant Simon, *Everything but the Coffee: Learning About America from Starbucks* (Berkeley: University of California Press, 2009).
21 Horowitz interview conducted by author in her FU Office in Dumbo on September 15, 2011, in author's possession.
22 From www.freelancersunion.org (accessed January 4, 2010).

Chapter Four

1 Barry Bluestone and Bennett Harrison, *The Deindustrialization of America* (New York, NY: Basic Books, 1982), 7; Steven High, *Industrial Sunset: The Making of North America's Rust Belt, 1969–1984* (Toronto: University of Toronto Press, 2003), 93.
2 Jonathan D. Cohen, "This is Your Hometown: Collective Memory, Industrial Flight, and the Fate of Freehold, New Jersey," *New Jersey Studies* 2, no. 1 (2016): 185–212.
3 Sherry Lee Linkon and John Russo, *Steeltown U.S.A.: Work and Memory in Youngstown* (Lawrence: University of Kansas Press, 2005), 145.
4 Daniel Wolff, *4th of July, Asbury Park: A History of the Promised Land* (New York, NY: Bloomsbury, 2006); Daniel Weeks, "From Riot to Revolt: Asbury Park in July 1970," *New Jersey Studies* 2, no. 2 (2016): 80–111.
5 Jefferson Cowie and Lauren Boehm, "Dead Man's Town: 'Born in the U.S.A.,' Social History, and Working-Class Identity," *American Quarterly* 58, no. 2 (2006): 353–78.
6 Brian Hiatt, "Bruce Springsteen Calls Donald Trump a 'Moron'," *Rolling Stone*, September 23, 2016. http://www.rollingstone.com/music/news/bruce-springsteen-calls-donald-trump-a-moron-w441761 (accessed September 23, 2016).

7   Andrew Perchard, "'A Dying Mutual Friend': Industrial Closures, Working Lives and National Culture in Post-War Scotland," Paper to the European Social Science History conference, Glasgow, 2012; Ian Watson, *Song and Democratic Culture in Britain: An Approach to Popular Culture in Social Movements* (London: Croom Helm, 1983); Jackie Clarke, "Closing Moulinex: Thoughts on the Visibility and Invisibility of Industrial Labour in Contemporary France," *Modern & Contemporary France* 19, no. 4 (2011): 443–58.
8   Andrew Newell, "Structural Change," in *Work and Pay in 20th Century Britain*, eds. Nicholas Crafts, Ian Gazeley, and Andrew Newell (Oxford: Oxford University Press, 2007), 35–54.
9   Tatyana B. Soubbotina and Katherine A. Sheram, *Beyond Economic Growth: Meeting the Challenges of Global Development* (Washington, DC: World Bank, 2000).
10 Tracy E. K'Meyer and Joy L. Hart, *I Saw It Coming: Worker Narratives Of Plant Closings And Job Loss* (Basingstoke: Palgrave Macmillan, 2010), 1.
11 Jefferson Cowie and Joseph Heathcott, "The Meanings of Deindustrialization," in *Beyond the Ruins: The Meanings of Deindustrialization*, eds. Jefferson Cowie and Joseph Heathcott (Ithaca, NY: ILR Press, 2003), 1.
12 Steven S. Saeger, "Globalization and Deindustrialization: Myth and Reality in the OECD," *Review of World Economics* 133, no. 4 (1997): 579–608; David Brady and Ryan Denniston, "Economic Globalization, Industrialization and Deindustrialization in Affluent Democracies," *Social Forces* 85, no.1 (2006): 297–329.
13 Christopher H. Johnson, *The Life and Death of Industrial Languedoc, 1700–1920* (Oxford: Oxford University Press, 1995); Jefferson Cowie, *Capital Moves: RCA's Seventy-year Quest for Cheap Labor* (Ithaca, NY: Cornell University Press, 1998); Bert Altena and Marcel van der Linden, eds., *De-industrialization: Social, Cultural, and Political Aspects* (Cambridge: Cambridge University Press, 2002); Cowie and Heathcott, *Beyond the Ruins*; Steven High and David L. Lewis, *Corporate Wasteland: The Landscape and Memory of Deindustrialization* (Ithaca, NY: Cornell University Press, 2007); Tim Strangleman, "Deindustrialisation and the Historical Sociological Imagination: Making Sense of Work and Industrial Change," *Sociology* 51, no. 2 (2017): 466–82; Steven High, Lachlan MacKinnon, and Andrew Perchard, eds., *The Deindustrialized World: Confronting Ruination in Post-Industrial Places* (Vancouver: University of British Columbia Press, 2017).
14 Marie Jahoda, Paul Felix Lazarsfeld, and Hans Ziesel, *Marienthal: The Sociography of an Unemployed Community* (New York, NY: Transaction, 2002), 358.
15 Altena and van der Linden, *De-industrialization*, 5–6.
16 Carlo Morelli, *The Decline of Jute: Managing Industrial Change* (Abingdon: Pickering and Chatto, 2011).
17 David Koistinen, "Business and Regional Economic Decline: The Political Economy of Deindustrialization in Twentieth-Century New England," *Business and Economic History On-Line* 12 (2014), Table 2. http://www.thebhc.org/publications/BEHonline/2014/koistinen2.pdf.
18 Cowie, *Capital Moves*.
19 Christian Shepherd, "China Faces Trouble to Recast Steel Workers for Service Sector," *Financial Times*, March 28, 2016. http://www.ft.com/cms/s/0/e5eb8716-f0c7-11e5-aff5-19b4e253664a.html#axzz4Kc7lOMwe (accessed September 20, 2016).
20 Jane L. Collins, "Deterritorialization and Workplace Culture," *American Ethnologist* 29, no. 1 (2002): 167.
21 Christopher H. Johnson, "Introduction: De-industrialization and Globalization," *International Review of Social History* 47, no. S10 (2002): 29.

22 High and Lewis, *Corporate Wasteland*; Mike Savage, *Social Class in the 21st Century* (London: Penguin, 2015).
23 Barbara Garson, "How to Become a Part-Time Worker Without Really Trying" *The Nation*, August 20, 2013. https://www.thenation.com/article/how-become-part-time-worker-without-really-trying/ (accessed September 20, 2016).
24 Guy Standing, *Work After Globalization: Building Occupational Citizenship* (Cheltenham: Edward Elgar, 2009); Strangleman, "Deindustrialisation."
25 Tim Strangleman, "The Remembrance to a Lost Work: Nostalgia, Labour and the Visual," in *Ming Jue: Photographs of Longbridge and Nanjing*, ed. Stuart Whipps (Walsall: New Art Gallery, 2009).
26 C. Wright Mills, *The Sociological Imagination* (New York, NY: Oxford University Press, 1959), 3, 5.
27 Raymond Williams, *Culture and Society 1780–1950* (New York, NY: Anchor Books, 1960), 285, and *Marxism and Literature* (Oxford: Oxford University Press, 1977).
28 Alistair Thomson, *Anzac Memories* (Oxford: Oxford University Press, 1995).
29 Linkon and Russo, *Steeltown U.S.A.*
30 Andrew Perchard, "'Broken Men' and 'Thatcher's Children': Memory and Legacy in Scotland's Coalfields," *International Labor and Working Class History* 84, no. 1 (2013): 78–98; and "'A Dying Mutual Friend'."
31 Neal Acheson, *Stone Voices: The Search for Scotland* (London: Granta, 2002), 115–16.
32 H. Paul Chalfant and Emily LaBeff, *Understanding People and Social Life* (Berkeley: University of California Press, 1988), 28.
33 Charles Perrow, *Organizing America: Wealth, Power, and the Origins of Corporate Capitalism* (Princeton, NJ: Princeton University Press, 2002).
34 E. P. Thompson, *The Making of the English Working Class* (London: Penguin, 1963), 12.
35 Bryan D. Palmer, *E. P. Thompson: Objections and Oppositions* (London: Verso, 1994), 65.
36 Strangleman, "Deindustrialisation,"13.
37 Victoria De Grazia, *The Culture of Consent: Mass Organization of Leisure in Fascist Italy* (New York, NY: Cambridge University Press, 1981).
38 Catherine Epstein, *Nazi Germany: Confronting the Myths* (Oxford: John Wiley & Sons, 2015), 102.
39 Tim Strangleman, "Networks, Place and Post-Industrial Mining Communities," *International Journal of Urban and Regional Research* 25 (2001), 27.
40 Keith Gildart, "Mining Memories: Reading Coalfield Autobiographies," *Labor History* 50, no. 2 (2009): 144.
41 Interview, Tam Coulter quoted in Perchard, "Broken Men," 87.
42 Ibid.
43 Strangleman, "Networks."
44 Gerald Feldman and Klaus Tenfelde, eds., *Workers, Owners and Politics in Coal Mining: An International Comparison of Industrial Relations* (Oxford: Berg, 1990).
45 Joy L. Parr, *Sensing Changes: Technologies, Environments, and the Everyday, 1953–2003* (Vancouver: UBC Press, 2009), 1.
46 Interview, Michael McGahey quoted in Suzanne Najam, "A Radical Past: The Legacy of the Fife Miners" (Ph.D. thesis, University of Edinburgh, 1988), 101.
47 Jim Phillips, *Collieries, Communities and the Miners' Strike in Scotland, 1984–1985* (Manchester: Manchester University Press, 2012).
48 Interview, Bill Marshall, Kirkcaldy, Fife, August 24, 2003.
49 Ibid.

50 Andrew Perchard, *The Mine Management Professions in the Twentieth-Century Scottish Coal Mining Industry* (Lampeter: Edwin Mellen Press, 2007); Andrew Perchard and Jim Phillips, "Transgressing the Moral Economy: Wheelerism and Management of the Nationalised Coal Industry in Scotland," *Contemporary British History* 25, no. 3 (2011): 387–405.
51 Interview, Tom Coulter quoted in Perchard, "Broken Men," 90.
52 Interview, Alec Mills quoted in ibid., 88; Arthur McIvor and Ronald Johnston, *Miners' Lung: A History of Dust Disease in British Coal Mining* (Abingdon: Ashgate, 2007).
53 Interview, Bill Marshall, Kirkcaldy, Fife, August 24, 2003.
54 Michael Roper, *Masculinity and the British Organization Man since 1945* (Oxford: Oxford University Press, 2003).
55 Sue Bruley, *The Women and Men of 1926: A Gender and Social History of the General Strike and Miners' Lockout in South Wales* (Cardiff: University of Wales Press, 2010).
56 Gill Burke, "Women Miners: Here and There, Now and Then," in *Women Miners in Developing Countries: Pit Women and Others*, eds. Kuntala Lahiri-Dutt and Martha Macintyre (Aldershot: Ashgate, 2006), 31–2; Camille Guerin-Gonzalez, "From Ludlow to Camp Solidarity: Women, Men, and Cultures of Solidarity in U.S. Coal Communities, 1912–1990," in *Mining Women: Gender in the Development of a Global Industry, 1670–2005*, eds. Jaclyn J. Gier and Laurie Mercier (London: Palgrave Macmillan, 2006), 303; Eva Blomberg, "Gender Relations in Iron Mining Communities in Sweden, 1900–1940," in ibid., 121.
57 Susan M. Pierce, "Women in the Southern West Virginia Coalfields," in *Restoring Women's History through Historic Preservation*, eds. Gail Lee Dubrow and Jennifer B. Goodman (Baltimore, MD: Johns Hopkins University Press, 2002), 161–76.
58 Burke, "Women Miners," 34.
59 Quoted in Guerin-Gonzalez, "From Ludlow," 305.
60 Quoted in ibid.
61 Interview, Coulter.
62 Interview, Carl Martin quoted in Perchard, "Broken Men," 88.
63 Ibid.
64 Alan Campbell, *The Scottish Miners, 1874–1939, Vol.1: Work, Industry and Community* (Aldershot: Ashgate, 2000); Phillips, *Collieries, Communities*.
65 Richard Ralston, "On the Mines (1850–1950): Work, Leisure, and Resistance in the Folklore of South African and Appalachian Mine Workers," in *Comparative Perspectives on South Africa*, ed. Ran Greenstein (Basingstoke: Macmillan Press, 1998), 134–84.
66 Ian Roberts, *Craft, Class and Control: Sociology of a Shipbuilding Community* (Edinburgh: Edinburgh University Press, 1993); Alan McKinlay, *Making Men, Making Ships: Working for John Brown's Between the Wars* (Clydebank: Clydebank District Libraries, 1991).
67 Tom Gallagher, *Glasgow: The Uneasy Peace* (Manchester: Manchester University Press, 1987).
68 William Kenefick, *"Rebellious and Contrary": The Glasgow Dockers, 1853–1932* (East Linton: Tuckwell Press, 2000).
69 Milton Rogovin and Michael Frisch, *Portraits in Steel* (Ithaca, NY: Cornell University Press, 1993); Robert Duncan, *Sons of Vulcan: Ironworkers and Steelmen of Scotland* (Edinburgh: Birlinn, 2009); Pascal Raggi, "Deindustrialization and the Recomposition of Labour Solidarity in the Iron Mines and Steel Mills of Lorraine, France, 1963–2013," in High et al., *The Deindustrialized World*, 312–27.
70 Christine J. Walley, *Exit 0: Family and Class in Postindustrial Chicago* (Chicago, IL: University of Chicago Press, 2013), 1.
71 Interview T089, National Museum of Scotland.

72 Elizabeth Roberts, *A Woman's Place: An Oral History of Working-Class Women 1890–1940* (Oxford: Wiley-Blackwell, 1995), 17.
73 Tim Strangleman, *Work Identity at the End of the Line? Privatisation and Culture Change in the UK Rail Industry* (Basingstoke: Palgrave Macmillan, 2004).
74 Perchard and Phillips, "Transgressing the Moral Economy."
75 Linda Carlson, *Company Towns of the Pacific Northwest* (Seattle: Washington University Press, 2004); L. J. Butler, *Copper Empire: Mining and the Colonial State in Northern Rhodesia, c.1930–64* (Basingstoke: Palgrave Macmillan, 2007).
76 Greg Grandin, *Fordlandia: The Rise and Fall of Henry Ford's Forgotten Jungle City* (New York, NY: Icon, 2010); José Igartua, *Arvida ou Saguenay: Naissance d'une ville industrielle* (Montréal: McGill-Queen's University Press, 1996).
77 Brad Cross, "Bound Together yet Worlds Apart: Comparing Alcan's Industrial Town of Guyana and Canada in the mid-20th century," in *Aluminium: du métal de luxe au métal de masse (XIXe–XXIe siècle)*, eds. Dominique Barjot and Marco Bertilorenzi (Paris: Presses de l'université Paris-Sorbonne, 2014), 289–309.
78 Andrew Perchard, *Aluminiumville: Government, Global Business and the Scottish Highlands* (Lancaster: Crucible Books, 2012).
79 Igartua, *Arvida*.
80 Ibid; Cross, "Bound together"; Perchard, *Aluminiumville*; Gérard Vindt, *Les hommes de l'aluminium. Histoire sociale de Pechiney, 1921–1973* (Paris: Éditions de l'Atelier, 2006).
81 Interview, Sandy Walker quoted in Perchard, *Aluminiumville*,
82 Quoted in K'Meyer and Hart, *I Saw It Coming*, 21.
83 Tim Strangleman, "Rethinking Industrial Citizenship: The Role and Meaning of Work in an Age of Austerity," *British Journal of Sociology* 66, no. 4 (2015): 673–90; Steven High, "Placing the Displaced Worker: Narrating Place in Deindustrializing Sturgeon Falls, Ontario," in *Placing Memory and Remembering Place in Canada*, eds. James Opp and John C. Walsh (Vancouver: UBC Press, 2010), 289–309; Clarke, "Closing Moulinex."
84 James C. Scott, *Weapons of the Weak: Everyday Forms of Peasant Resistance* (New Haven, CT: Yale University Press, 1985).
85 Perchard, *Aluminiumville*.
86 Kyle Bruce and Chris Nyland, "Elton Mayo and the Deification of Human Relations," *Organization Studies* 32, no. 3 (2011): 391.
87 Howard Gitelman, *Legacy of the Ludlow Massacre: A Chapter in American Industrial Relations* (Philadelphia: University of Pennsylvania Press, 1988), 337.
88 Bruce and Nyland, "Elton Mayo," 383.
89 E. P. Thompson, "Time, Work-Discipline, and Industrial Capitalism," *Past and Present* 38 (1967): 56–97; Jonathan Zeitlin and Steven Tolliday, eds., *Between Fordism and Flexibility: The Automobile Industry and Its Workers* (London: Bloomsbury Academic, 1992); Jonathan Zeitlin and Garry Herrigel, eds., *Americanization and Its Limits: Reworking US Technology and Management in Post-war Europe and Japan* (Oxford: Oxford University Press, 2000).
90 Glasgow Labour History Workshop, *The Singer Strike Clydebank, 1911* (Clydebank: Clydebank District Library, 1989); Laura Lee Downs, "Industrial Decline, Rationalization and Equal Pay: The Bedaux Strike at Rover Automobile Company," *Social History* 15, no. 1 (1990): 45–73.
91 Barbara Weinstein, *For Social Peace in Brazil: Industrialists and the Remaking of the Working Class in São Paulo, 1920–1964* (Durham: University of North Carolina Press, 1996); Rajnarayan Chandavarkar, "Workers' Resistance and the Rationalization of Work in Bombay between the Wars," in *Contesting Power: Resistance and Everyday Social Relations in South Asia*, eds. Douglas E. Haynes and Gyan Prakash (Berkeley: University of California Press, 1991), 109–44.

92   Huw Beynon, *Working for Ford* (London: Penguin, 1973); Alison Gilmour, "The Trouble with Linwood: Compliance and Coercion in the Car Plant, 1963–1981," *Journal of Scottish Historical Studies* 27, no. 1 (2008): 75–93.
93   Andrew G. Lawrence, *Employer and Worker Collective Action: A Comparative Study of Germany, South Africa, and the United States* (Cambridge: Cambridge University Press, 2014); Ralston "On the Mines."
94   Stanford Jacoby, *Modern Manors: Welfare Capitalism since the New Deal* (Princeton, NJ: Princeton University Press, 1997), 5.
95   Lizabeth Cohen, *Making a New Deal: Industrial Workers in Chicago, 1919–1939* (Chicago, IL: Chicago University Press, 1990).
96   Tim Strangleman and Tracey Warren, *Work and Society: Sociological Approaches, Themes and Methods* (London: Routledge, 2008), 278–82.
97   David Marsh, *The New Politics of British Trade Unionism: Union Power and the Thatcher Legacy* (London: Palgrave Macmillan, 1992); Ben Jackson and Roberts Saunders, eds., *Making Thatcher's Britain* (Cambridge: Cambridge University Press, 2012); Judith Stein, *Pivotal Decade: How the United States Traded Factories for Finance in the Seventies* (New Haven, CT: Yale University Press, 2011).
98   Paul Almeida and Allen Cordero Ulate, eds., *Handbook of Social Movements across Latin America* (Dordrecht: Springer, 2015).
99   High and Lewis, *Corporate Wasteland*, 24.
100 High, *Industrial Sunset*.
101 Ibid; Linkon and Russo, *Steeltown U.S.A*; Walley, *Exit 0*.
102 Quoted in High et al., *The Deindustrialized World*, 415.
103 Ibid.
104 Andy Clark, "'And the Next Thing the Chairs Barricaded the Door': The Lee Jeans Factory Occupation, Trade Unionism and Gender in Scotland in the 1980s," *Scottish Labour History* 48 (2013): 116–35; Charles Woolfson and John Foster, *Track Record: The Story of the Caterpillar Occupation* (London: Verso, 1988).
105 Quoted in Clarke, "Closing Moulinex," 456.
106 Peter Bain and Phil Taylor, "Entrapped by the 'Electronic Panoptican'? Worker Resistance in the Call Centre," *New Technology, Work and Employment* 15, no. 1 (2002): 2–18.
107 Arne L. Kalleberg, "2008 Presidential Address: Precarious Work, Insecure Workers: Employment Relations in Transition," *American Sociological Review* 74 (2009): 1.
108 Mills, *The Sociological Imagination*, 6.
109 E. P. Thompson, *Customs in Common* (London: Penguin, 1993), 188

Chapter Five

1   Simon Head, *The New Ruthless Economy* (Oxford: Oxford University Press, 2003).
2   Stanley Aronowitz and William DiFazio, *The Jobless Future*, 2nd ed. (Minneapolis: University of Minnesota Press, 2010).
3   E. P. Thompson, *The Making of the English Working Class* (London: Victor Gollancz, 1963); Harry Braverman, *Labor and Monopoly Capital* (New York: New York University Press, 1974); Aronowitz and DiFazio, *Jobless Future*.
4   Sven Beckert, *Empire of Cotton: A Global History* (New York, NY: Knopf, 2014).
5   David Noble, *Forces of Production: A Social History of Industrial Automation* (New York, NY: Knopf, 1984).
6   Braverman, *Labor and Monopoly Capital*.

7   Head, *New Ruthless Economy*.
8   Barbara Townley, *Reframing Human Resource Management* (London: Sage, 1994); Braverman, *Labor and Monopoly Capital*; Park Doing, "'Lab Hands' and the 'Scarlet O': Epistemic Politics and (Scientific) Labor," *Social Studies of Science* 34, no.3 (2004): 313.
9   Karl Marx, *Capital, Volume 1* (1867; New York, NY: Penguin Books, 1976), 492.
10 Eileen Boris, *Home to Work: Motherhood and the Politics of Industrial Homework in the United States* (Cambridge: Cambridge University Press, 1994), 2.
11 Douglas Harper, *Working Knowledge* (Berkeley: University of California Press, 1987); Mike Rose, *The Mind at Work* (New York, NY: Penguin, 2004).
12 Edward E. Baptist, *The Half Has Never Been Told: Slavery and the Making of American Capitalism* (New York, NY: Basic Books, 2014); Siddharth Kara, *Bonded Labor: Tackling the System of Slavery in South Asia* (New York, NY: Columbia University Press, 2012); Charles Dew, *Bond of Iron* (New York, NY: W. W. Norton, 1994).
13 Judith Carney, *Black Rice: The African Origins of Rice Cultivation in the Americas* (Cambridge, MA; Harvard University Press, 2002); Dew, *Bond of Iron*; Warwick Anderson, *Colonial Pathologies* (Durham, NC: Duke University Press, 2006); Rudolf Mrazek, *Engineers of Happy Land* (Princeton, NJ: Princeton University Press, 2002).
14 Noble, *Forces of Production*; Head, *New Ruthless Economy*; Tamara Kneese, "Airport Ipads are a New Way to Alienate Labor," Aljazeera American, January 31, 2016. http://america.aljazeera.com/opinions/2016/1/airport-ipads-are-a-new-way-to-alienate-labor.html (accessed January 31, 2016).
15 Noble, *Force of Production*.
16 Frederick Winslow Taylor, *Principles of Scientific Management* (1911; New York, NY: W. W. Norton, 1967); Jennifer Karns Alexander, *The Mantra of Efficiency* (Baltimore, MD: Johns Hopkins University Press, 2008).
17 Ibid.; Stephen Meyer III, *The Five Dollar Day* (Albany: State University of New York Press, 1981); Richard Gillespie, *Manufacturing Knowledge* (Cambridge: Cambridge University Press, 1991).
18 Lundy Braun, *Breathing Race into the Machine: The Surprising History of Spirometry from Plantation to Genetics* (Minneapolis: University of Minnesota Press, 2014); Baptist, *The Half Has Never Been Told*.
19 Alexander, *Mantra of Efficiency*.
20 Nelson Lichtenstein, *The Retail Revolution* (New York, NY: Picador, 2009), 121–2.
21 Loren Baritz, *Servants of Power* (Middletown, CT: Wesleyan University Press, 1960).
22 Ibid.; Gillespie, *Manufacturing Knowledge*.
23 Baritz, *Servants of Power*, 105.
24 Gillespie, *Manufacturing Knowledge*, 5, 175.
25 Townley, *Reframing Human Resource Management*; Marta B. Calas and Linda Smircich, "Past Postmodernism? Reflections and Tentative Directions," *Academy of Management Review* 24, no. 4 (1999): 649–71.
26 David Hounshell, *From the American System to Mass Production, 1800–1932* (Baltimore, MD: Johns Hopkins University Press, 1984); Rose, *Mind at Work*, 14–19.
27 Amy E. Slaton, *Reinforced Concrete and the Modernization of American Building, 1900–1930* (Baltimore, MD: Johns Hopkins University Press, 2001).
28 Ibid.; David R. Roediger, *Working Towards Whiteness* (New York, NY: Basic Books, 2006).
29 Jennifer Light, "When Computers Were Women," *Technology and Culture* 40, no. 3 (1999): 455–83, 461.
30 Amy E. Slaton, *Race, Rigor and Selectivity: The History of an Occupational Color Line* (Cambridge, MA: Harvard University Press, 2010); William Harris, *The Harder*

We Run: Black Workers Since the Civil War (New York, NY: Oxford University Press, 1982).

31 Ruth Milkman, "Rosie the Riveter Revisited: Management's Postwar Purge of Women Automobile Workers," in *On the Line: Essays in the History of Auto Work*, eds. Nelson Lichtenstein and Stephen Meyer (Urbana: University of Illinois Press, 1989).
32 Light, "When Computers were Women," 457.
33 Slaton, *Race, Rigor and Selectivity*, 48–54.
34 David Serlin, *Replaceable You: Engineering the Body in Postwar America* (Chicago, IL: University of Chicago Press, 2004).
35 Milkman, "Rosie the Riveter."
36 Seonghee Lim, "Automation and San Francisco Class 'B' Longshoremen: Power, Race, and Workplace Democracy, 1958–1981" (Ph.D. diss., University of California–Santa Barbara, 2015).
37 Marc Levinson, *The Box: How the Shipping Container Made the World Smaller and the World Economy Bigger* (Princeton, NJ: Princeton University Press, 2006), 101–26; Lim, "Automation," 93–120.
38 Aronowitz and DiFazio, *Jobless Future*, xxvi.
39 Lim, "Automation," 364.
40 Ibid.; Robert Caro, *The Power Broker: Robert Moses and the Fall of New York* (New York, NY: Vintage Books, 1974); Benjamin Chesluk, *Money Jungle: Imagining the New Times Square* (New Brunswick, NJ: Rutgers University Press, 2008), 18–22.
41 David Harvey, *A Brief History of Neoliberalism* (Oxford: Oxford University Press, 2007), 19, 15.
42 Kristin Mitchell, "From Whitehall to Brussels: Thatcher, Delors and the Europeanization of the TUC," *Labor History* 53, no. 1 (2012): 26.
43 Bart Cole and Christine Cooper, "Deskilling in the 21st Century: The Case of Rail Privatization," *Critical Perspectives on Accounting* 15, no. 5 (2006): 601.
44 Andrew Perchard, "'Broken Men' and 'Thatcher's Children': Memory and Legacy in Scotland's Coalfields," *International Labor and Working-Class History* 84, no. 1 (2013): 78–98.
45 Cole and Cooper, "Deskilling in the 21st Century."
46 Aronowitz and DiFazio, *Jobless Future*, 48–50.
47 Edna Bonacich and Jake B. Wilson, *Getting the Goods: Ports, Labor and the Logistics Revolution* (Ithaca, NY: Cornell University Press, 2008).
48 Guy Standing, *The Rise of the Precariat: The New Dangerous Class* (London: Bloomsbury Academic, 2011).
49 Deborah Kaminski and Cheryl Geisler, "Survival Analysis of Faculty Retention in Science and Engineering by Gender," *Science* 335, no. 6070 (February 2012): 864–6.
50 Aronowitz and DiFazio, *Jobless Future*, 4.
51 Ruth Schwartz Cowan, *More Work for Mother* (New York, NY: Basic Books, 1983); Boris, *Home to Work*.
52 Cowan, *More Work for Mother*.
53 Boris, *Home to Work*, 4.
54 Jefferson Cowie, *Capital Moves: RCA's Seventy-Year Quest for Cheap Labor* (New York, NY: New Press, 1999), 85–7, 182.
55 Judith Light Feather and Miguel F. Aznar, *Nanoscience Education, Workforce Training and K-12 Resources* (Boca Raton, FL: CRC Press, 2011).
56 "Summary Report for: 17-3029.12, Nanotechnology Engineering Technicians." http://www.onetonline.org/link/summary/17-3029.12 (accessed January 27, 2016).

57 "Find a Nano Program." www.nano4me.org (accessed July 16, 2016).
58 Mihail C. Roco, Chad A. Mirkin, and Mark. C. Hersam, *Nanotechnology Research Direction for Societal Needs in 2020: Retrospective and Outlook Summary* (Dordrecht: Springer Netherlands, 2011).
59 National Nanotechnology Infrastructure Network, "Education & Training." http://www.nnin.org/news-events/spotlights/nanotechnology-careers (accessed December 4, 2015).
60 Ibid.
61 Mary F. Ebeling and Amy E. Slaton, "Promise Her Anything: Education for Work in the US 'Nanoeconomy'," MS in preparation.
62 Ibid.; Carl Van Horn and Aaron Fichtner, "The Workforce Needs of Companies Engaged in Nanotechnology Research in Arizona," Report produced by Heldrich Center/Center for Nanotechnology in Society, Arizona State University, 2008.
63 National Academy of Science, National Academy of Engineering, and Institute of Medicine, *Expanding Underrepresented Minority Inclusion: America's Science and Technology Talent at the Crossroads* (Washington, DC: National Academies Press, 2011); White House Press Release: "Building American Skills Through Community Colleges." https://www.whitehouse.gov/issues/education/higher-education/building-american-skills-through-community-colleges (accessed February 3, 2016).
64 Harvard Graduate School of Education, "Pathways to Prosperity: Meeting the Challenge of Preparing Young Americans for the 21st Century," 2011.
65 Samuel Bowles and Herbert Gintis, *Schooling in Capitalist America* (New York, NY: Basic Books, 1976).
66 Steven Brint and Jerome Karabel, *The Diverted Dream* (Oxford: Oxford University Press, 1989); Steven Brint, "Few Remaining Dreams: Community Colleges Since 1985", *Annals of the American Academy of Political and Social Science* 586, no. 1 (2003): 25.
67 Townley, *Reframing Human Resource Management*, 14, 25.
68 Ibid., 11.
69 Interviews conducted by Amy E. Slaton at Southwest Center for Microelectronics Education, Albuquerque, New Mexico, 2015.
70 Judith A. McGaw, *Most Wonderful Machine: Mechanization and Social Change in Berkshire Paper Making, 1801–1885* (Princeton, NJ: Princeton University Press, 1987). Mackenzie, in *Knowing Machines*, finds this dual causality in Marx's own description of capital, 30–1.
71 Amy E. Slaton, *All Good People: Difference, Diversity and Opportunity in High-Tech America* (MS in preparation).
72 Slaton, *Race, Rigor and Selectivity*.

Chapter Six

1 Leslie Page Moch, "Mobilité des hommes, mobilité des femmes. Perspective historique de la migration européenne," *Cahiers de l'Institut Universitaire d'Études Du Développement* 23 (1993): 106–17; Leslie Page Moch, *Moving Europeans: Migration in Western Europe Since 1650*, 2nd ed., Interdisciplinary Studies in History (Bloomington: Indiana University Press, 2003), chap. 4.
2 Moch, *Moving Europeans*, 149; Robin Cohen, ed., *The Cambridge Survey of World Migration* (Cambridge: Cambridge University Press, 1995).
3 Southern and Eastern Europeans went from 45 percent of admissions under the 1921 law to 15 percent under the 1924 law. Mae Ngai, *Impossible Subjects: Illegal Aliens and the Making*

of Modern America (Princeton, NJ: Princeton University Press, 2004), intro. and chap. 1, passim.
4 Elisa Camiscioli, *Reproducing the French Race: Immigration, Intimacy, and Embodiment in the Early Twentieth Century* (Durham, NC: Duke University Press, 2009).
5 Gary S. Cross, *Immigrant Workers in Industrial France: The Making of a New Laboring Class* (Philadelphia, PA: Temple University Press, 1983).
6 Ibid., 53.
7 Bertrand Nogaro and Lucien Weil, *La main-d'œuvre étrangère et coloniale pendant la guerre* (Paris: Presses universitaires de France, 1926), 18, 25.
8 Mary Dewhurst Lewis, *The Boundaries of the Republic: Migrant Rights and the Limits of Universalism in France, 1918–1940* (Stanford, CA: Stanford University Press, 2007).
9 "L'Emploi de la main-d'oeuvre féminine pendant la guerre," *Bulletin du Ministère du Travail* 25, no. 1–2, (January–February 1918): 15–17.
10 Louise Tilly and Joan Wallach Scott, *Women, Work, and Family* (New York, NY: Holt, Rinehart and Winston, 1978); Nancy Green, *Ready-to-Wear and Ready-to-Work: A Century of Industry and Immigrants in Paris and New York* (Durham, NC: Duke University Press, 1997); Linda Guerry, *Le genre de l'immigration et de la naturalisation: L'exemple de Marseille (1918–1940)* (France: ENS Éditions, 2013).
11 Nimisha Barton, *Reproductive Citizens: Gender, Immigration and the State in France, 1880–1940* (MS in progress).
12 Mae Ngai, "The Strange Career of the Illegal Alien: Immigration Restriction and Deportation Policy in the United States, 1921–1965," *Law and History Review* 21, no. 1 (Spring 2003): 84–95.
13 Ibid., 82.
14 Camille Guerin-Gonzales, *Mexican Workers and American Dreams: Immigration, Repatriation, and California Farm Labor, 1900–1939* (New Brunswick, NJ: Rutgers University Press, 1994); John Weber, *From South Texas to the Nation: The Exploitation of Mexican Labor in the Twentieth Century* (Chapel Hill: University of North Carolina Press, 2015), chap. 4.
15 George I. Sanchez, *Becoming Mexican American: Ethnicity, Culture, and Identity in Chicano Los Angeles, 1900–1945* (New York, NY: Oxford University Press, 1993), chap. 10.
16 Michael B. Katz, *The Price of Citizenship: Redefining the American Welfare State* (Philadelphia, PA: University of Pennsylvania Press, 2008), chap. 1.
17 Gary Gerstle, *American Crucible: Race and Nation in the Twentieth Century* (Princeton, NJ: Princeton University Press, 2001), 162–3; Devra Weber, Dark Sweat, *White Gold: California Farm Workers, Cotton, and the New Deal* (Los Angeles: University of California Press, 1994), 113–14, 123–6.
18 Jefferson Cowie, *The Great Exception: The New Deal and the Limits of American Politics* (Princeton, NJ: Princeton University Press, 2016), 129–32.
19 Ibid., 131.
20 Ana Elizabeth Rosas, *Abrazando el Espiritu: Bracero Families Confront the US-Mexico Border* (Oakland: University of California Press, 2014), 6–7, chap. 1.
21 Lizabeth Cohen, *A Consumer's Republic: The Politics of Mass Consumption in Postwar America* (New York, NY: Vintage Books, 2003), 152–64.
22 Ngai, *Impossible Subjects*, 238–9.
23 Cindy Hahmovitch, *No Man's Land: Jamaican Guestworkers in America and the Global History of Deportable labor* (Princeton, NJ: Princeton University Press, 2011), 117–19; Hahamovitch, phone conversation with the author, September 11, 2012.

24 Andrew Hazelton, "Open-Shop Fields: The Bracero Program and Farmworker Unionism, 1942–1964" (Ph.D. diss., Georgetown University, 2012), 7.
25 Ibid., 180.
26 See table 2 in Jacob Clayman, "Testimony before Subcommittee on Equipment, Supplies, and Manpower of the House Committee on Agriculture," April 7, 1960, file 47, box 35, RG28-001, George Meany Memorial Archives, Silver Spring, Maryland.
27 Linda Majka and Theo Majka, *Farm Workers, Agribusiness, and the State* (Philadelphia, PA: Temple University Press, 1982), 153.
28 Rosas, *Abrazando el Espiritu*, chap. 3.
29 Hazelton, "Open-Shop Fields," chap. 4.
30 Kitty Calavita, *Inside the State: The Bracero Program, Immigration and the I.N.S.* (New York, NY: Routledge, Chapman & Hall, 1992), appendix A.
31 Swing, as quoted in ibid., 53–60.
32 Juan Ramon García, *Operation Wetback: The Mass Deportation of Mexican Undocumented Workers in 1954* (Westport, CT: Greenwood Press, 1980).
33 Maria Cecilia Hwang and Rhacel Solazar Parreñas, "Not Every Family: Selective Reunification in Contemporary US Immigration Laws," *International Labor and Working-Class History* 78, no. 1 (Fall 2010): 100–9; Ngai, *Impossible Subjects*, 258–65.
34 Cohen, *Cambridge Survey*, pt. 9.
35 Nermin Abadan-Unat, "Turkish Migration to Europe" in ibid; Moch, *Moving Europeans*, 186–9.
36 Cohen, *Cambridge Survey*, pts. 9–10.
37 Cowie, *The Great Exception*, chap. 6; Judith Stein, *Pivotal Decade: How the United States Traded Factories for Finance in the Seventies* (New Haven, CT: Yale University Press, 2010).
38 Joseph A. McCartin, *Collision Course: Ronald Reagan, the Air Traffic Controllers, and the Strike that Changed America* (New York, NY: Oxford University Press, 2011), 359–64.
39 Jefferson Cowie, *Capital Moves: RCA's Seventy-Year Quest for Cheap Labor* (Ithaca, NY: Cornell University Press, 1999), intro.
40 Ibid., 110–14; Kevin J. Middlebrook, *The Paradox of Revolution: Labor, the State, and Authoritarianism in Mexico* (Baltimore, MD: Johns Hopkins University Press, 1995), chap. 7.
41 Kathleen C. Schwartzman, *The Chicken Trail: Following Workers, Migrants, and Corporations across the Americas* (Ithaca, NY: Cornell University Press, 2013), 100–19.
42 Hahamovitch, *No Man's Land*, 202–07; Mae Ngai, "The Civil Rights Origins of Illegal Immigration," *International Labor and Working-Class History* 78, no. 1 (Fall 2010): 93–9, 98.
43 For the full case study, see Schwartzman, *The Chicken Trail*, preface, chaps. 1 and 5.
44 Pat Buchanan, "Buchanan Campaign Speech," C-SPAN video, 01:08:06, January 10, 2000. http://www.c-span.org/video/?154783-1/buchanan-campaign-speech (accessed July 25, 2016).
45 Alexander Burns, "Donald Trump, Pushing Someone Rich, Offers Himself," *New York Times*, June 16, 2015. http://www.nytimes.com/2015/06/17/us/politics/donald-trump-runs-for-president-this-time-for-real-he-says.html (accessed July 25, 2016).
46 Nicholas Confessore, "For Whites Sensing Decline, Donald Trump Unleashes Words of Resistance," *New York Times*, July 13, 2016. http://www.nytimes.com/2016/07/14/us/politics/donald-trump-white-identity.html (accessed July 25, 2016).
47 Philip Ogden, "Labour Migration to France" in Cohen, *Cambridge Survey*, 289–96; Moch, *Moving Europeans*, 189.
48 Eleonore Kofman, *Gender and International Migration in Europe: Employment, Welfare, and Politics* (London: Routledge, 2000).

49 Andrew Higgins, "Norway Offers Migrants a Lesson in How to Treat Women," *New York Times*, December 19, 2015. http://www.nytimes.com/2015/12/20/world/europe/norway-offers-migrants-a-lesson-in-how-to-treat-women.html (accessed July, 25 2016); Alison Smale, "As Germany Welcomes Migrants, Sexual Attacks in Cologne Point to a New Reality," *New York Times*, January 14, 2016. http://www.nytimes.com/2016/01/15/world/europe/as-germany-welcomes-migrantssexual-attacks-in-cologne-point-to-a-new-reality.html (accessed July, 25 2016).

Chapter Seven

1   William Beveridge, *Social Insurance and Allied Services* (London: His Majesty's Stationery Office, 1942), 6, 8.
2   William Beveridge, *Full Employment in a Free Society* (New York, NY: W. W. Norton, 1945), 244, 248–9.
3   Mark Thomas, "Labour Market Structure and the Nature of Unemployment in Interwar Britain," in *Interwar Unemployment in International Perspective*, eds. Barry Eichengreen and T. J. Hatton (Dordrecht: Kluver Academic, 1988), 99; US Department of Commerce, *Historical Statistics of the United States: Colonial Times to 1970*, (Washington, DC: US Department of Commerce, 1975), pt. I, 135.
4   Barry Eichengreen, "Unemployment in Interwar Britain: New Evidence from London," *Journal of Interdisciplinary* History 17, no. 2 (Autumn 1986): 354.
5   Andrew August, *The British Working Class, 1832–1940* (Harlow: Pearson Longman, 2007), 193; John J. Wallis, "Employment in the Great Depression: New Data and Hypotheses," *Explorations in Economic History* 26, no. 1 (1989): 57.
6   Richard J. Jensen, "The Causes and Cures of Unemployment in the Great Depression," *Journal of Interdisciplinary History* 19, no. 4 (Spring, 1989): 570.
7   Peter Pagnamenta and Richard Overy, *All Our Working Lives* (London: British Broadcasting Company, 1984), 36.
8   Thomas Piketty and Emmanuel Saez, "Income Inequality in the United States, 1913–1998," *Quarterly Journal of Economics* 118, no. 1 (February 2003): 8–9.
9   Peter H. Lindert, "Three Centuries of Inequality in Britain and America," in *Handbook of Income Distribution*, vol. I, eds. Anthony B. Atkinson and François Bourguignon (Amsterdam: Elsevier, 2000), 194.
10 James Denman and Paul McDonald, "Unemployment Statistics from 1881 to the Present Day," *Labour Market Trends* 104, nos. 15–18 (January 1996): 6–7.
11 US Department of Commerce, *Historical Statistics of the United States*, 135.
12 Jonathan Zeitlin, "Flexibility and Mass Production at War: Aircraft Manufacture in Britain, the United States, and Germany, 1939–1945," *Technology and Culture* 36, no. 1 (January, 1995): 49.
13 Robert Mackay, *The Test of War: Inside Britain 1939–1945* (London: University College London Press, 1999), 77.
14 Selina Todd, *The People: The Rise and Fall of the Working Class* (London: John Murray, 2014), 140; Mark H. Leff, "The Politics of Sacrifice on the American Home Front in World War II," *Journal of American History* 77, no. 4 (March 1991): 1314.
15 Chris Tilly and Charles Tilly, *Work Under Capitalism* (Boulder, CO: Westview, 1998), 213–14.
16 Daniel Béland and Randall Hansen, "Reforming the French Welfare State: Solidarity, Social Exclusion and the Three Crises of Citizenship," *West European Politics* 23, no. 1 (2000): 53.
17 Organisation for Economic Co-operation and Development, "Labour Force Statistics: Summary Tables," *OECD Employment and Labour Market Statistics* (Database). http://dx.doi.org/10.1787/data-00286-en (accessed November 6, 2015).

18 Jefferson Cowie, *Stayin' Alive: The 1970s and the Last Days of the Working Class* (New York, NY: The New Press, 2010), 28.
19 Jack Metzgar, *Striking Steel: Solidarity Remembered* (Philadelphia: Temple University Press, 2000), 4; Cowie, *Stayin' Alive*, 28.
20 James Cronin, *Labour and Society in Britain, 1918–1979* (London: Batsford, 1984), 157–8.
21 Judith Stein, *Pivotal Decade: How the United States Traded Factories for Finance in the Seventies* (New Haven, CT: Yale University Press, 2010), 2.
22 David Schwartzman, "Black Unemployment," *Review of Black Political Economy* 25, no. 3 (Winter, 1997): 84; Stein, *Pivotal Decade*, 17.
23 Stein, *Pivotal Decade*, 14–15.
24 Todd, *The People*, 259.
25 OECD, "Labour Force Statistics." 2013 figures are the most recent available.
26 Michael B. Katz, *In the Shadow of the Poorhouse: A Social History of Welfare in America* (New York, NY: Basic Books, 1986), 275–6.
27 Todd, *The People*, 336.
28 Tony Gore and Emma Hollywood, "The Role of Social Networks and Geographical Location in Labour Market Participation in the UK Coalfields," *Environment and Planning C: Government and Policy* 27, no. 6 (2009): 1010.
29 Tim Strangleman, "Networks, Place and Identities in Post-Industrial Mining Communities," *International Journal of Urban and Regional Research* 25, no. 2 (June 2001): 258. In the east Durham coal district, 47 percent of the workforce depended on the coal sector in 1981.
30 Ibid., 241, 273.
31 Tali Kristal, "Good Times, Bad Times: Postwar Labor's Share of National Income in Capitalist Democracies," *American Sociological Review* 75, no. 5 (October 2010): 733.
32 Lawrence Mishel et al., *The State of Working America*, 12th ed. (Ithaca, NY: Cornell University Press, 2012), 186.
33 Ray Hudson, "Thatcherism and its Geographical Legacies: The New Map of Socio-Spatial Inequality in the Divided Kingdom," *Geographical Journal* 179, no. 4 (December 2013): 379.
34 Alice Kessler-Harris, *Out to Work: A History of Wage-Earning Women in the United States*, rev. edn. (Oxford: Oxford University Press, 2003), 258, 301.
35 US Bureau of Labor Statistics, "BLS Spotlight on Statistics: Women at Work," March, 2011. http://www.bls.gov/spotlight/2011/women/data.htm#ilc_labor_force (accessed November 23, 2015). These figures include those actually earning wages and those seeking work but unemployed.
36 Patricia Cooper, "The Faces of Gender: Sex Segregation and Work Relations at Philco, 1928–1938," in *Work Engendered: Toward a New History of American Labor*, ed. Ava Baron (Ithaca, NY: Cornell University Press, 1991): 326–7, 330.
37 Kessler-Harris, *Out to Work*, 332–3.
38 Anne Phillips and Barbara Taylor, "Sex and Skill: Notes Towards a Feminist Economics," *Feminist Review*, no. 6 (1980): 79–88.
39 Sheila Rowbotham, *A Century of Women: A History of Women in Britain and the United States* (New York, NY: Viking, 1997), 349.
40 R. M. Blackburn, *Union Character and Social Class: A Study of White-Collar Unionism* (London: Batsford, 1967), 71.
41 On struggles by female professionals to claim a professional identity and earn adequate incomes, see Daniel J. Walkowitz, *Working with Class: Social Workers and the Politics of Middle-Class Identity* (Chapel Hill: University of North Carolina Press, 1999).

42 Laura L. Downs, *Manufacturing Inequality: Gender Division in the French and British Metalworking Industries, 1914–1939* (Ithaca, NY: Cornell University Press, 1995), 117.
43 Kessler-Harris, *Out to Work*, 230, 289–90, 311, 326.
44 Organisation for Economic Co-operation and Development, "Employment: Gender Gap." http://stats.oecd.org/index.aspx?queryid=54751# (accessed November 24, 2015).
45 Suzanne M. Bianchi et al., "Housework: Who Did, Does or Will Do It, and How Much Does It Matter?," *Social Forces* 91, no. 1 (September, 2012): 56.
46 Lizabeth Cohen, *Making a New Deal: Industrial Workers in Chicago, 1919–1939* (Cambridge: Cambridge University Press, 1990), 205.
47 Thomas J. Sugrue, "The Structure of Urban Poverty: The Reorganization of Space and Work in Three Periods of American History," in *The "Underclass" Debate: Views from History*, ed. Michael B. Katz (Princeton, NJ: Princeton University Press, 1993), 106.
48 Steven A. Reich, *A Working People: A History of African American Workers since Emancipation* (Lanham, MD: Rowman and Littlefield, 2013), 108.
49 Sugrue, "The Structure of Urban Poverty," 106–7.
50 Harley L. Browning, Sally C. Lopreato, and Dudley L. Poston, Jr., "Income and Veteran Status: Variations among Mexican Americans, Blacks and Anglos," *American Sociological Review* 38, no. 1 (February 1973): 81.
51 Mishel et al., *State of Working America*, 233.
52 Emilio Reyneri and Giovanna Fullin, "Labour Market Penalties of New Immigrants in New and Old Receiving West European Countries," *International Migration* 49, no. 1 (2011): 32.
53 Laura Frader, *Breadwinners and Citizens: Gender in the Making of the French Social Model* (Durham, NC: Duke University Press, 2008), 15, 89.
54 Todd, *The People*, 290.
55 Reich, *A Working People*, 87.
56 Cohen, *Making a New Deal*, 242.
57 Mishel et al., *State of Working America*, 339.
58 Tilly and Tilly, *Work under Capitalism*, 217–19.
59 August, *British Working Class*, 193.
60 Lydia Morris, *Dangerous Class: The Underclass and Social Citizenship* (London: Routledge, 1994), 101.
61 Mishel et al., *State of Working America*, 341.
62 Thomas Sugrue, *The Origins of the Urban Crisis: Race and Inequality in Postwar Detroit* (Princeton, NJ: Princeton University Press, 1996), 269–70.
63 William J. Wilson, *The Truly Disadvantaged: The Inner City, the Underclass, and Public Policy* (Chicago, IL: University of Chicago Press, 1987), 57.
64 Michael K. Dorsey, "Race, Poverty, and Environment," *Legal Studies Forum* 22, nos. 1–3 (1998): 507.
65 Béland and Hansen, "Reforming the French Welfare State," 54–5.
66 Katharyne Mitchell, "Marseille's Not for Burning: Comparative Networks of Integration and Exclusion in Two French Cities," *Annals of the Association of American Geographers* 101, no. 2 (2011): 707.
67 Hudson, "Thatcherism and its Geographical Legacies," 379.
68 Cohen, *Making a New Deal*, 181–2.
69 Rick Halpern, "The Iron Fist and the Velvet Glove: Welfare Capitalism in Chicago's Packinghouses, 1921–1933," *Journal of American Studies* 26, no. 2 (August 1992): 181.
70 Morris, *Dangerous Class*, 64; Katz, *In the Shadow of the Poorhouse*, 238.

71 Chad Goldberg, *Citizens and Paupers: Relief, Rights, and Race, from the Freedmen's Bureau to Workfare* (Chicago, IL: University of Chicago Press, 2007), 161.
72 Reich, *A Working People*, 91.
73 Jennifer Klein, *For All These Rights: Business, Labor, and the Shaping of America's Public-Private Welfare State* (Princeton, NJ: Princeton University Press, 2003), 258.
74 Katz, *In the Shadow of the Poorhouse*, 264.
75 Premilla Nadasen, *Welfare Warriors: The Welfare Rights Movement in the United States* (New York, NY: Routledge, 2005), 22.
76 August, *British Working Class*, 184.
77 Marjorie Levine-Clark, *Unemployment, Welfare, and Masculine Citizenship: "So Much Honest Poverty" in Britain, 1870–1930* (Basingstoke: Palgrave Macmillan, 2015), 89–91.
78 In 1975, the sources for social spending in Britain were: employers 46.5 percent, employees 30.4 percent, and the state 20.6 percent. Susan Pedersen, *Family, Dependence and the Origins of the Welfare State: Britain and France, 1914–1945* (Cambridge: Cambridge University Press, 1993), 417.
79 Joan C. Brown, "Poverty in Post-War Britain," in *Understanding Post-War British Society*, eds. James Obelkevich and Peter Catterall (London: Routledge, 1994), 118.
80 Frader, *Breadwinners and Citizens*, 178; Pedersen, *Family, Dependence*, 423.
81 Giuliano Bonoli and Bruno Palier, "From Work to Citizenship? Current Transformations in the French Welfare State," in *Citizenship and Welfare State Reform in Europe*, ed. Jet Bussemaker (London: Routledge, 1999), 45, 52.
82 Goldberg, *Citizens and Paupers*, 193–5, 231–2.
83 Julilly Kohler-Hausmann, "'The Crime of Survival': Fraud Prosecutions, Community Surveillance, and the Original 'Welfare Queen'," *Journal of Social History* 41, no. 2 (Winter, 2007): 334–5, 337.
84 Fred Magdoff and John B. Foster, "The Plight of the US Working Class," *Monthly Review* 65, no. 8 (January 2014): 16.
85 Klein, *For All These Rights*, 275.
86 Jochen Clasen, "Towards a New Welfare State or Reverting to Type? Some Major Trends in British Social Policy since the Early 1980s," *The European Legacy* 8, no. 5 (2003): 580, 583.
87 Christopher Deeming, "Foundations of the Workfare State—Reflections on the Political Transformation of the Welfare State in Britain," *Social Policy and Administration* 49, no. 7 (December 2015): 864, 867, 871, 879–80.
88 Béland and Hansen, "Reforming the French Welfare State," 53, 57–8; Bruno Palier, "'Defrosting' the French Welfare State," *West European Politics* 23, no. 2 (2000): 130.
89 Andrew August, "Narrative, Experience and Class: Nineteenth-Century Social History in Light of the Linguistic Turn," *History Compass* 9, no. 5 (2011): 384–96.
90 Cohen, *Making a New Deal*, 286–7, 364–5; Robert H. Zieger, Timothy J. Minchin, and Gilbert J. Gall, *American Workers, American Unions: The Twentieth and Early Twenty-First Centuries* 4th ed. (Baltimore, MD: Johns Hopkins University Press, 2014), 49.
91 Stefan Ramsden, "Remaking Working-Class Community: Sociability, Belonging and 'Affluence' in a Small Town, 1930–1980," *Contemporary British History* 29, no. 1 (2015): 9.
92 August, *British Working Class*, 231; Race rioting occurred elsewhere in 1919 as well. In Chicago, for example, thirty-eight people died in such a riot in July of that year. See Cohen, *Making a New Deal*, 36–7.

93 Richard Hoggart, *The Uses of Literacy: Aspects of Working Class Life with Special Reference to Publication and Entertainments* (Harmondsworth: Penguin, 1957), 61.
94 Ramsden, "Remaking Working-Class Community," 12.
95 Brian Jackson, *Working Class Community: Some General Notions Raised by a Series of Studies in Northern England* (London: Routledge and Kegan Paul, 1968), 166, emphasis in original.
96 Robert S. Lynd and Helen M. Lynd, *Middletown: A Study in Modern American Culture* (New York, NY: Harcourt Brace Jovanovich, 1929), 23–4.
97 Shelton Stromquist, "Building a New Working-Class Politics from Below," in *Labor Rising: The Past and Future of Working People in America*, ed. Daniel Katz and Richard A. Greenwald (New York: New Press, 2012), 15.
98 Jennifer Klein, "A New Deal Restoration: Individuals, Communities, and the Long Struggle for the Collective Good," *International Labor and Working-Class History* 74, no.1 (Fall, 2008): 43–4.
99 Zieger, Minchin, and Gall, *American Workers*, 49.
100 A. H. Halsey and Josephine Webb, *Twentieth-Century British Social Trends* (Basingstoke: Macmillan, 2000), 288; Todd, *The People*, 346.
101 "Most Britons are Working Class and Proud of It," *Guardian*, August 20, 2002. http://www.theguardian.com/uk/2002/aug/21/britishidentity (accessed December 21, 2015).
102 Decca Aitkenhead, "How a Lad from Hull Got Above Himself," *Independent*, April 13, 1996. http://www.independent.co.uk/news/uk/home-news/how-a-lad-from-hull-got-above-himself-1304746.html (accessed December 21, 2015).
103 Walkowitz, *Working with Class*, xvi.
104 David Halle, *America's Working Man: Work, Home, and Politics among Blue-Collar Property Owners* (Chicago, IL: University of Chicago Press, 1984), 206, 221; see Walkowitz, *Working with Class*, 264.
105 Catherine E. Davies, "Joking as Boundary Negotiation among 'Good Old Boys': 'White Trash' as a Social Category at the Bottom of the Southern Working Class in Alabama," *Humor* 23, no. 2 (2010): 184.
106 William Beveridge, "The Problem of the Unemployed," *Sociological Papers* 3 (1907): 327.
107 Frader, *Breadwinners and Citizens*, 187.
108 Miriam Cohen and Michael Hanagan, "Politics, Industrialization and Citizenship: Unemployment Policy in England, France and the United States, 1890–1950," *International Review of Social History* 40, Supp. 3 (1995): 121.
109 Beveridge, "Problem of the Unemployed," 327.
110 Frader, *Breadwinners and* Citizens, 186, 34. See also, K. S. Childers, "Paternity and the Politics of Citizenship in Interwar France," *Journal of Family History* 26, no. 1 (January 2001): 99.
111 Cohen, *Making a New Deal*, 271.
112 Goldberg, *Citizens and Paupers*, 116.
113 Levine-Clark, *Unemployment, Welfare, and Masculine Citizenship*, 232.
114 T. H. Marshall, *Citizenship and Social Class and Other Essays* (Cambridge: Cambridge University Press, 1950), 11.

Chapter Eight

1 This industry that I know well exemplifies many of the developments, tensions, and contradictions in the twentieth-century culture of the workplace. A rich labor press, union

records, and especially grievance cases offer rare windows into how workers lived and acted on the shop floor.
2   Peter F. Drucker, *The Concept of the Corporation* (New York, NY: Transaction Publishers 1983), 149.
3   Edward D. Kennedy, *The Automobile Industry: The Coming of Age of Capitalism's Favorite Child* (New York, NY: Reynal and Hitchcock, 1941), 314.
4   Ely Chinoy, "Manning the Machines—The Assembly-Line Worker," in *The Human Shape of Work: Studies in the Sociology of Occupations*, ed. Peter Berger (New York, NY: Macmillan, 1964), 51.
5   Charles R. Walker, *Steeltown: An Industrial Case History of the Conflict between Progress and Security* (New York, NY: Harper, 1950), 51. Walker's Technology and Society Project conducted in-plant surveys of workers the General Motors Framingham and Linden factories that produced two books on workers and foremen on the assembly line.
6   "The Myth of the Happy Worker," in Harvey Swados, *On the Line* (Urbana: University of Illinois Press, 1990), 237. Essay originally published in *The Nation*, August 17, 1957.
7   James C. Scott, *Two Cheers for Anarchism: Six Easy Pieces on Autonomy, Dignity, and Meaningful Work and Play* (Princeton, NJ: Princeton University Press, 2012); James C. Scott, *Weapons of the Weak: Everyday Forms of Peasant Resistance* (New Haven, CT: Yale University Press, 1989), 29.
8   Alf Leudtke, "Cash, Coffee Breaks, Horseplay: Eigensinn and Politics among Factory Workers circa 1900," in *Confrontation, Class Consciousness, and the Labour Process*, eds. Michael Hanagan and Charles Stephenson (Westport, CT: Greenwood Press, 1986), 80.
9   Ibid., 82.
10 Paul Thompson, "Playing at Being Skilled: Factory Culture and Pride in Work Skills among Coventry Car Workers," *Social History*, 13, no. 1 (1988): 58.
11 David Montgomery, *Workers' Control in America* (Cambridge: Cambridge University Press 1979), 11–19 and Stephen Meyer, *Five Dollar Day: Labour Management and Social Control in the Ford Motor Company, 1908–1921* (Albany: State University of New York Press, 1981), 9–36.
12 Antonio Gramsci, "Americanism and Fordism," in *The Gramsci Reader: Selected 1916–1935* ed. David Forgacs (New York, NY: Lawrence and Wishart, 1968), 275–99.
13 Wayne Lewchuk, *American Technology and the British Vehicle Industry* (New York, NY: Cambridge University Press, 1987); Stephen Tolliday, "High Tide and After: Coventry Engineering and Shopfloor Bargaining, 1945–1980," in *Life and Labour in a 20th Century City: The Experience of Coventry*, eds. Bill Lancaster and Tony Mason (Coventry: Cryfield Press, 1986), 204–39; Jonathan Zeitlin, "The Emergence of Shop Steward Organization and Job Control in the British Car Industry," *History Workshop* 10, no.1 (Autumn 1980): 119–37.
14 Meyer, *The Five Dollar Day*, 46–51; Stephen Meyer, "The Persistence of Fordism: Workers and Technology in the American Automobile Industry," in *On the Line: Essays in the History of Auto Work*, eds. Nelson Lichtenstein and Stephen Meyer (Urbana: University of Illinois Press, 1989), passim.
15 Ruth Milkman, *Gender at Work: The Dynamics of Job Segregation by Sex During World War II* (Urbana: University of Illinois Press, 1987), 12.
16 Stephen Meyer, *Manhood on the Line: Working-Class Masculinities in the American Heartland* (Urbana: University of Illinois Press, 2016), 141–3.
17 Ibid., 24–5.
18 *Auto Workers News*, March 1928.

19 Daniel Rosenblum, "'They Pretend to Pay Us … ': The Wage Arrears Crises in the Post-Soviet States," *Demokratizatsiya* 5, no. 2 (Spring 1997): 298.
20 Stanley B. Mathewson, *Restriction of Output among Unorganized Workers* (1931; Carbondale: Southern Illinois Press, 1969).
21 Ibid., 146–7.
22 Frank Marquart, *An Auto Worker's Journal: The UAW from Crusade to One-Party Union* (University Park, PA: Penn State University Press, 1975), 11.
23 Tony Lane, "A Merseysider in Detroit," *History Workshop Journal* 11, no. 1 (Spring 1981): 145.
24 Marquart, *An Auto Worker's Journal*, 24.
25 Lewchuk, *American Technology*, 91.
26 Thompson, "Playing at Being Skilled," 63, and Tolliday, "High Tide and After," 298.
27 Jack W. Skeels, "Early Carriage and Auto Unions," *Industrial and Labour Relations Review* 17, no. 4 (July 1964): 568–83; Roger Keeran, "Communist Influence in the Automobile Industry," *Labour History* 20, no. 2 (Spring 1979): 189–225.
28 On the activities of early autoworker organizers, see Wyndham Mortimer, *Organize: My Life as a Union Man* (Boston, MA: Beacon Press, 1971) and Clayton W. Fountain, *Union Guy* (New York, NY: Viking Press, 1949).
29 Skeels, "Early Carriage and Auto Unions" and Keeran, "Communist Influence in the Automobile Industry," passim.
30 Sydney Fine, *Sit-down: The General Motors Strike of 1936–1937* (Anne Arbor: University of Michigan Press, 1969); August Meier and Elliott Rudwick, *Black Detroit and the Rise of the UAW* (New York, NY: Oxford University Press, 1979), 136–62.
31 On the operation of grievance processes, see Stephen Meyer, *"Stalin Over Wisconsin:" The Making and Unmaking of Militant Unionism, 1900–1950* (New Brunswick, NJ: Rutgers University Press, 1991), 105–46.
32 Nelson Lichtenstein, *Most Dangerous Man in Detroit: Walter Reuther and the Fate of American Labor* (New York, NY: Basic Books, 1995), 261–6; and Robert H. Zieger, *CIO, 1935–1955* (Chapel Hill: University of North Carolina Press, 1995), 246–8.
33 Ralph T. Steward, "Umpire Decision C–329: Discharge for Assaulting a Supervisor," March 6, 1945, F. 7, B. 72, General Motors Department Collection, ALHUA.
34 "Complaint No. I–647," March 14, 1940, F. Grievances, Mack Ave, 1940, Box 10, UAW Local 212 Papers, ALHUA.
35 Early Reynolds to R. W. Conder, March 16, 1944, and "Grievance #279: Management Statement," 1–2, F. 6, Box 101, Chrysler Department Collection, ALHUA.
36 G. Allan Dash, "Umpire Decision No. C–150: Disciplinary Layoff of 145 Employees," December 14, 1943, 501–02, Box 3, UAW Local 174 Collection, and "Board of Review on Umpire Appeals," Case E–65, December 18, 1947, and Case F–197, September 25, 1950, F. GM Board of Review Decisions, V. 1, B. 1, UAW General Motors Papers, both ALHUA.
37 Thompson, "Playing at Being Skilled," 67.
38 Ibid., 63.
39 Ibid., 64–6.
40 Interview No. 20a, 6/10/47, 7–8, F. Thesis Drafts, 1946, B. 2, Eli Chinoy Papers, ALHUA.
41 Donald F. Roy, "'Banana Time': Job Satisfaction and Informal Interaction," *Human Organization* 18, no. 4 (1958): 158. See also Roy, "Efficiency and 'the Fix': Informal Intergroup Relations in a Piecework Shop," *American Journal of Sociology* 60, no. 3 (1954):

255–66, and "Quota Restriction and Gold Bricking in a Machine Shop," *American Journal of Sociology* 57, no. 5 (1952): 427–42.

42 Frank Marquart, "The Auto Worker," in *Voices of Dissent*, eds. Stanley Diamond et al. (New York, NY: Grove Press, 1969), 144.

43 "'Brief for the Ford Motor Company, Umpire Case 23448" and "Meeting in the Offices of Umpire Harry Platt," May 23, 1963, F. UAW Local 1250 Correspondence, B. 5, UAW Region 2 Papers, ALHUA.

44 Heather Ann Thompson, *Whose Detroit? Political, Labour, and Race in a Modern American City* (Ithaca, NY: Cornell University Press, 2001), 103–27; Dan Georgakas and Marvin Surkin, *Detroit: I Do Mind Dying: A Study in Urban Revolution* (Cambridge, MA: South End Press, 1998); and David M. Lewis-Coleman, *Race Against Liberalism: Black Workers and the UAW in Detroit* (Urbana: University of Illinois Press, 2008), 97–105.

45 Satoshi Kamata, *Japan in the Passing Lane: An Insider's Account of Life in a Japanese Auto Factory* (New York, NY: Pantheon Books, 1982).

46 Alf Leudtke, "'German Quality Work'—Did it Shape the Production of Automobiles in (West-) Germany after 1945," in *Towards Mobility: Varieties of Automobilism in East and West*, eds. Manfred Grieger, Ulrike Gutzman, and Dirk Schlinkert (Wolfsburg: Volkswagen AG, 2009), 178–86.

47 Judson Gooding, "Blue-Collar Blues on the Assembly Line," *Fortune*, July 1970, 69. See also, Barbara Garson, "Luddites in Lordstown: It's Not the Money, It's the Job," *Harpers Magazine*, June 1972, 68–72; and Michel Basquet, "The Prison Factory," *New Left Review* (May–June 1972): 23–34.

48 Gooding, "Blue-Collar Blues," 70.

49 Ken Weller, *The Lordstown Struggle and the Real Crisis in Production* Solidarity Pamphlet, n.d.. https://ratical.org/corporations/linkscopy/weller.html (accessed July 14, 2016).

50 *Time* and Garson cited in Ibid., n.p.

51 Meyer, *Manhood on the Line*, 140–64, and Milkman, "Rosie the Riveter Revisited," 132–46.

52 Meyer, *Manhood on the Line*, 201–4.

53 On deindustrialization and deunionization, Ruth Milkman, *Farewell to the Factory: Auto Workers in the Late 20th Century* (Berkeley: University of California Press, 1997), 79–136; Kathryn Dudley, *The End of the Line: Lost Jobs, New Lives in Post Industrial America* (Chicago, IL: University of Chicago Press, 1994); and Jefferson R. Cowie, *Capital Moves: RCA's Seventy-year Quest for Cheap Labour* (Ithaca, NY: Cornell University Press, 1999).

54 Paulsen, *Empty Labour*, 59–60.

55 Ben Hamper, *Rivethead: Tales from the Assembly Line* (New York, NY: Warner Books, 1972).

56 Marquart, "The Auto Worker," 144.

57 Hamper, *Rivethead*, 35 and 39–40.

58 Ibid., 95.

59 Brian Phillips, *Global Production and Domestic Decay: Plant Closings in the U.S.* (New York, NY: Routledge, 1998).

60 *Detroit Free Press*, December 7, 2006.

61 Nicholas Confessore, "Trump Mines Grievances of Whites Who Feel Lost," *New York Times* (July 14, 2016): 1 and 14–15, and Chris Matthews, "The Death of the Middle Class Is Worse Than You Think," *Fortune On-line Edition*, July 13, 2016. http://fortune.com/2016/07/13/middle-class-death/ (accessed July 14, 2016).

Chapter Nine

1. David Riesman, *The Lonely Crowd: A Study of the Changing American Character* (New Haven, CT: Yale University Press, 1961), lvi–lvii.
2. Dan Stone, ed., *The Oxford Handbook of Postwar European History* (Oxford: Oxford University Press, 2015), 432–3.
3. Roy Rosenzweig et al., *Who Built America? Working People and the Nation's Economy, Politics, Culture, and Society, Volume Two Since 1877* (New York, NY: Worth Publishers, 2000), 429.
4. Brian Levack et al., *The West: Encounters & Transformations* (New York, NY: Pearson, 2004), 842, 845.
5. Tamara Hareven, *Amoskeag: Life and Work in an American Factory-City* (Lebanon: UNPE, 1995), 21–2.
6. Jose M. Alamillo, *Making Lemonade out of Lemons: Mexican American Labor and Leisure in a California Town, 1880–1960* (Urbana: University of Illinois Press, 2006), 101–2.
7. Ibid., 66.
8. Kathy Peiss, *Cheap Amusements: Working Women and Leisure in Turn-of-the-Century New York* (Philadelphia, PA: Temple University Press, 1986), 56–87.
9. Kathy Peiss, "Girls Lean Back Everywhere," in *The Modern Girl Around the World: Consumption, Modernity, and Globalization*, eds. Alys Eve Weinbaum et al. (Durham, NC: Duke University Press, 2008), 347–53.
10. Levack et al., *The West*, 838–9.
11. Ibid., 146.
12. Rosenzweig et al., *Who Built America*, 336; Lizabeth Cohen, *Making a New Deal: Industrial Workers in Chicago, 1919–1939* (Cambridge: Cambridge University Press, 1990), 120.
13. Daniel Horowitz, *The Morality of Spending: Attitudes Toward the Consumer Society in America, 1875–1940* (Baltimore, MD: Johns Hopkins University Press, 1985), 153–61.
14. Martin Pugh, *"We Danced All Night": A Social History of Britain Between the Wars* (London: The Bodley Head, 2008), 218.
15. Stuart Hanson, *From Silent Screen to Multi-Screen: A History of Cinema Exhibition in Britain since 1896* (Manchester: Manchester University Press, 2007), 26–7, 66.
16. Philip S. Foner and David R. Roediger, *Our Own Time: A History of American Labor and the Working Day* (New York, NY: Greenwood Press, 1989), 258.
17. George Lipsitz, *Rainbow at Midnight: Labor and Culture in the 1940* (Urbana: University of Illinois Press, 1994), 256–62.
18. Stone, *The Oxford Handbook of Postwar European History*, 423–6.
19. Kim Moody, *An Injury to All: The Decline of American Unionism* (New York, NY: Verso, 1988), 99. Thomas Ferguson and Joel Rogers, *Right Turn: The Decline of the Democrats and the Future of American Politics* (New York, NY: Hill and Wang, 1987), 48–9.
20. Levack, *The West*, 948–9.
21. Randy D. McBee, *Born to Be Wild: The Rise of the American Motorcyclist* (Chapel Hill: University of North Carolina Press, 2015), 72; Kenneth T. Jackson, *Crabgrass Frontier: The Suburbanization of the United States* (New York, NY: Columbia University Press, 1987), 247.
22. Ibid., 255.
23. Elizabeth McKeon, *Cinema Under the Stars: America's Love Affair with the Drive-In Movie Theater* (Nashville, TN: Cumberland House Publishing, 1998), 4.

24 Francesca Carnevali and Julie Marie Strange, eds., *Twentieth Century Britain: Economic, Cultural and Social Change* (New York, NY: Routledge, 2007), 113.
25 Stone, *The Oxford Handbook of Postwar European History*, 426–7.
26 Lipsitz, *Rainbow at Midnight*, 266–7.
27 Charles M. Tatum, *Lowriders in Chicano Culture: From Low, to Slow, to Show* (New York, NY: Greenwood Press, 2011), 7–10.
28 McBee, *Born to Be Wild*, 19–33; Steven Alford and Suzanne Ferriss, *Motorcycle* (London: Reaktion Books, 2007), 78–80.
29 McBee, *Born to Be Wild*, 35–7, 103–4.
30 Alford and Ferriss, *Motorcycle*, 81–2.
31 Lipsitz, *Rainbow at* Midnight, 266–7.
32 Cindy S. Aron, *Working at Play: A History of Vacations in the United States* (Oxford; Oxford University Press, 2001), 238.
33 Assata Shakur, *An Autobiography* (New York, NY: Lawrence Hill Books, 2001), 22–5.
34 Ibid., 433, 437.
35 Lipsitz, *Rainbow at Midnight*, 256.
36 Ibid.
37 Lisa M. Fine, "Rights of Men, Rights of Passage: Hunting and Masculinity at Reo Motors of Lansing, Michigan, 1945–1975," *Journal of Social History* 33, no. 4 (Summer 2000): 805–23.
38 Moody, *An Injury to All*, 95.
39 Ibid., 94–6.
40 Rosenzweig et al., *Who Built America?*, 684.
41 Levack et al., *The West*, 966–7.
42 Tejvan Pettinger, "Economic Impact of Margaret Thatcher," November 2010, 2017. http://www.economicshelp.org/blog/274/uk-economy/economic-impact-of-margaret-thatcher/ (accessed February 22, 2018); "Economic Policies of Thatcher," March 23, 2015. https://www.ukessays.com/essays/politics/economic-policies-of-thatcher.php (accessed May 21, 2015).
43 William C. Berman, *America's Right Turn: From Nixon to Clinton* (Baltimore, MD: Johns Hopkins University Press, 1994), 85–119.
44 Kim Moody, *US Labor in Trouble and Transition: The Failure of Reform from Above, the Promise of Revival from Below* (New York, NY: Verso, 2007), 100–1.
45 Rosenzweig et al., *Who Built America*, 688–90; Naomi Klein, *No Logo* (New York, NY: Picador, 1999), 204–6.
46 Klein, *No Logo*, 235.
47 "Largest Industries by State," Bureau of Labor Statistics, July 28, 2014. http://www.bls.gov/opub/ted/2014/ted_20140728.htme (accessed May 6, 2016); Robert E. Scott, Economic Policy Institute, "The Manufacturing Footprint and the Importance of U.S. Manufacturing Jobs," January 22, 2015. http://www.epi.org/publication/the-manufacturing-footprint-and-the-importance-of-u-s-manufacturing-jobs/ (accessed May 7, 2016).
48 Alan Booth, *The British Economy in the Twentieth Century* (London: Palgrave Macmillan, 2001), 148.
49 Natasha Zaretsky, *No Direction Home: The American Family and the Fear of National Decline, 1968–1980* (Chapel Hill: North Carolina University Press, 2007), 111–14.
50 Steven Mintz, *Huck's Raft: A History of American Childhood* (Cambridge, MA: Harvard University Press, 2004), 340–1, 47.

51 C. Critcher, Peter Bramham, and Alan Tomlinson, eds., *Sociology of Leisure: A Reader* (New York, NY: Taylor & Francis, 1994), 11–15.
52 Ibid.
53 Ibid.
54 BBC News, "The Way the British Smoke," June 29, 2007. http://news.bbc.co.uk/2/hi/4709394.stm (accessed June 21, 2016).
55 Matthew Hilton, *Smoking in British Popular Culture, 1800–2000* (Manchester: Manchester University Press, 2000), 2.
56 "ASH: Facts at a Glance." http:// www.ash.org.uk/files/documents/ASH_93.pdf (accessed June 21, 2016).
57 Ibid.
58 Ibid.
59 Ibid.
60 Robert D. Putnam, *Bowling Alone: The Collapse and Revival of American Community* (New York, NY: Simon & Schuster, 2000), 193, 200, 222–37.
61 Russell W. Belk, "Yuppies as Arbiters of the Emerging Consumption Style," *Advances in Consumer Research* 13 (1986): 514–59. http://www.acrwebsite.org/volumes/6543/volumes/v13/NA-13 (accessed May 21, 2016).
62 McBee, *Born to Be Wild*, 188–9.
63 Rosenzweig et al., *Who Built America?*, 712–73; Jan Wieten, Graham Murdock, and Peter Dahlgren, eds., *Television Across Europe: A Comparative Introduction* (New York, NY: Sage Publications, 2012), 91–2; Aniko Imre, *TV Socialism* (Durham, NC: Duke University Press, 2016), 176.
64 Rosenzweig et al., *Who Built America?*, 714.
65 Juliet Schor, *The Overworked American: The Unexpected Decline of Leisure* (Repr., New York, NY: Basic Books, 1993), 29–30.
66 Alberto Alesina, Edward Glaeser, and Bruce Sacerdote, "Work and Leisure in the United States and Europe: Why So Different," Harvard Institute of Economic Research, Discussion Paper Number 2068, April 2005, 16, 61. http://post.economics.harvard.edu/hier/2005papers/2005list.html (accessed January 24, 2016).
67 Moody, *U.S. Labor in Trouble and Transition*, 100; Alesina, Glaeser, and Sacerdote, "Work and Leisure in the United States and Europe," 46.
68 Stone, *The Oxford Handbook of Postwar European History*, 432–3.
69 Lydia Saad, "The Forty Hour Work Week Is Actually Longer—By Seven Hours," Gallup. http://www.gallup.com/poll/175286/hour-workweek-actually-longer-seven-hours.aspx (accessed May 23, 2016).
70 Hugh Cunningham, *Time, Work and Leisure: Life Changes in England since 1700* (Manchester: Manchester University Press, 2014), 185–9.
71 Ibid., 189–95.
72 James B. Stewart, "Looking for a Lesson in Google's Perks," *New York times*, March 15, 2003. http://www.nytimes.com/2013/03/16/business/at-google-a-place-to-work-and-play.html (accessed January 24, 2016).
73 Christopher Tkaczyk, "Marissa Mayer Breaks Her Silence on Yahoo's Telecommuting Policy," *Fortune*, April 19, 2013. http://fortune.com/2013/04/19/marissa-mayer-breaks-her-silence-on-yahoos-telecommuting-policy/ (accessed January 24, 2016).
74 Claire Cain Miller, "Silicon Valley: Perks for Some Workers, Struggles for Parents," *New York Times*. http://www.nytimes.com/2015/04/08/upshot/silicon-valley-perks-for-some-workers-struggles-for-parents.html (accessed January 24, 2016).

75 Klaus Weiemair and Christine Mathies, *The Tourism and Leisure Industry: Shaping the Future* (New York, NY: Routledge, 2012), 93.
76 "UK Leisure Industry Worth Over £200 Billion: Report," Leisure Tourism. http://www.cabi.org/leisuretourism/news/22327 (accessed May 27, 2016).

FURTHER READINGS

Ackroyd, Stephen, and Paul Thompson. *Organizational Misbehaviour*. London: Sage Publications, 1999.
Alamillo, Jose M. *Making Lemonade out of Lemons: Mexican American Labour and Leisure in a California Town, 1880–1960*. Urbana: University of Illinois Press, 2006.
Alford, Steven, and Suzanne Ferriss. *Motorcycle*. London: Reaktion Books, 2007.
Altena, Bert, and Marcel van der Linden, eds. *De-industrialization: Social, Cultural, and Political Aspects*. Cambridge: Cambridge University Press, 2002.
Aronowitz, Stanley, and William DiFazio. *The Jobless Future*. 2nd ed. Minneapolis: University of Minnesota Press, 2010.
August, Andrew. *The British Working Class, 1832–1940*. Harlow: Pearson Longman, 2007.
Baritz, Loren. *Servants of Power*. Middletown, CT: Wesleyan University Press, 1960.
Berlier, Monique. "The Family of Man: Readings of an Exhibition." In *Picturing the Past: Media, History, and Photography*, edited by Brennan, Bonnie and Hanno Hardt, 206–41. Urbana: University of Illinois Press, 1999.
Bender, Daniel E. *Sweated Work, Weak Bodies: Anti-Sweatshop Campaigns and Languages of Labor*. New Brunswick, NJ: Rutgers University Press, 2003.
Bender, Daniel E., and Richard A. Greenwald. *Sweatshop USA: The American Sweatshop in Historical and Global Perspective*. New York, NY: Routledge, 2003.
Bluestone, Barry, and Bennett Harrison. *The Deindustrialization of America*. New York, NY: Basic Books, 1982.
Bonacich, Edna, and Jake B. Wilson. *Getting the Goods: Ports, Labor, and the Logistics Revolution*. Ithaca, NY: Cornell University Press, 2008.
Boris, Eileen. *Home to Work: Motherhood and the Politics of Industrial Homework in the United States*. Cambridge: Cambridge University Press, 1994.
Boris, Eileen, and Jennifer Klein. *Caring for America: Home Health Workers in the Shadow of the Welfare State*. New York, NY: Oxford University Press, 2012.
Brint, Steven, and Jerome Karabel. *The Diverted Dream*. Oxford: Oxford University Press, 1989.
Camiscioli, Elisa. *Reproducing the French Race: Immigration, Intimacy, and Embodiment in the Early Twentieth Century*. Durham, NC: Duke University Press, 2009.
Chaffee, Cathleen. *Overtime: The Art of Work*. Buffalo, NY: Albright-Knox Art Gallery, 2014.
Cohen, Lizabeth. *Making a New Deal: Industrial Workers in Chicago, 1919–1939*. Cambridge: Cambridge University Press, 1990.
Cohen, Robin, ed. *The Cambridge Survey of World Migration*. Cambridge: Cambridge University Press, 1995.
Conley, Dalton. *Elsewhere, U.S.A.* 1st ed. New York, NY: Pantheon Books, 2009.
Cowie, Jefferson. *Capital Moves: RCA's Seventy-year Quest for Cheap Labor*. Ithaca, NY: Cornell University Press, 1999.
Cowie, Jefferson. *Stayin' Alive: The 1970s and the Last Days of the Working Class*. New York, NY: New Press, 2010.

Cowie, Jefferson, and Joseph Heathcott, eds. *Beyond the Ruins: The Meanings of Deindustrialization*. Ithaca, NY: ILR Press, 2003.

Coy, Peter. "The Disposable Worker." *Bloomberg BusinessWeek*, January 7, 2010. https://www.bloomberg.com/news/articles/2010-01-07/the-disposable-worker (accessed February 20, 2018).

Critcher, C., Peter Bramham, and Alan Tomlinson, eds. *Sociology of Leisure: A Reader*. New York, NY: Taylor & Francis, 1994.

Cronin, James. *Labour and Society in Britain, 1918–1979*. London: Batsford, 1984.

Cunningham, Hugh. *Time, Work and Leisure: Life Changes in England since 1700*. Manchester: Manchester University Press, 2014.

Davis, Colin J. *Waterfront Revolts: New York and London Dockworkers, 1946–61*. Urbana: University of Illinois Press, 2003.

Farocki, Harun. "Workers Leaving the Factory." In *Harun Farocki: Working on the Sightlines*, edited by Thomas Elsaesser, translated by Laurent Faasch-Ibrahim, 237–43. Amsterdam: Amsterdam University Press, 2004.

Fassman, Heinz, and Rainer Munz, eds. *European Migration in the Late Twentieth Century*. London: Edward Elgar Publishing Limited, 1994.

Frader, Laura. *Breadwinners and Citizens: Gender in the Making of the French Social Model*. Durham, NC: Duke University Press, 2008.

Fraser, Steven. *Labor Will Rule: Sidney Hillman and the Rise of American Labor*. New York, NY: The Free Press, 1991.

Galarza, Ernesto. *Merchants of Labor: The Mexican Bracero Story: An Account of the Managed Migration of Mexican Farm Workers in California, 1942–1960*. Charlotte, NC: McNally & Loftin, Publishers, 1964.

García, Juan Ramon. *Operation Wetback: The Mass Deportation of Mexican Undocumented Workers in 1954*. Westport, CT: Greenwood Press, 1980.

Gartman, David. *Auto Slavery: The Labor Process in the American Automobile Industry*. New Brunswick, NJ: Rutgers University Press, 1986.

Gibson, Andrew, and Arthur Donovan. *The Abandoned Ocean a History of United States Maritime Policy*, Studies in Maritime History. Columbia: University of South Carolina Press, 2000.

Gillespie, Richard. *Manufacturing Knowledge*. Cambridge: Cambridge University Press, 1991.

Goldberg, Chad. *Citizens and Paupers: Relief, Rights, and Race, from the Freedmen's Bureau to Workfare*. Chicago, IL: University of Chicago Press, 2007.

Green, Nancy. *Ready-to-Wear and Ready-to-Work: A Century of Industry and Immigrants in Paris and New York*. Durham, NC: Duke University Press, 1997.

Greenwald, Richard A. "How to Succeed in the Age of Going Solo; Anybody Can Become a Consultant. But Not Everybody Does It Well. Here's What You Need to Know to Thrive." *Wall Street Journal (Online)*, February 10, 2010. https://www.wsj.com/articles/SB10001424052748704825504574581900293220092 (accessed June 26, 2017).

Greenwald, Richard A. "To Boost the Economy, Help the Self-Employed." *BusinessWeek*, August 4, 2011.

Hahamovitch, Cindy. *No Man's Land: Jamaican Guestworkers in America and the Global History of Deportable Labor*. Princeton, NJ: Princeton University Press, 2011.

Halle, David. *America's Working Man: Work, Home, and Politics among Blue-Collar Property Owners*. Chicago, IL: University of Chicago Press, 1984.

Hanson, Stuart. *From Silent Screen to Multi-Screen: A History of Cinema Exhibition in Britain since 1896*. Manchester: Manchester University Press, 2007.

Hatton, Erin. *The Temp Economy: From Kelly Girls to Permatemps in Postwar America.* Philadelphia, PA: Temple University Press, 2012.

Head, Simon. *The New Ruthless Economy.* Oxford: Oxford University Press, 2003.

Herod, Andrew. "Labor's Spacial Praxis and the Geography of Contract Bargaining in the US East Coast Longshore Industry, 1953–1989." *Political Geography* 16 (1997): 145–69.

Herzog, Melanie Anne. *Milton Rogovin: The Making of a Social Documentary Photographer.* Tucson, AZ: Center for Creative Photography. Seattle: University of Washington Press, 2006.

High, Steven. *Industrial Sunset: The Making of North America's Rust Belt, 1969–1984.* Toronto: University of Toronto Press, 2003.

High, Steven, and David L. Lewis. *Corporate Wasteland: The Landscape and Memory of Deindustrialization.* Ithaca, NY: Cornell University Press, 2007.

High, Steven, Lachlan MacKinnon, and Andrew Perchard, eds. *The Deindustrialized World: Confronting Ruination in Post-Industrial Places.* Vancouver: University of British Columbia Press, 2017.

Hill, Steven. *Raw Deal: How the Sharing Economy and Naked Capitalism Are Screwing American Workers.* New York, NY: Palgrave Macmillan Trade, 2015.

Hollifield, James. *Immigrants, Markets, and States: The Political Economy of Postwar Europe.* Cambridge, MA: Harvard University Press, 1992.

Horowitz, Sara, and Toni Sciarra Poynter. *The Freelancer's Bible: Everything You Need to Know to Have the Career of Your Dreams–on Your Terms.* New York, NY: Workman Publishing, 2012.

Isay, Dave, David Miller, and Harvey Wang. *Milton Rogovin: The Forgotten Ones.* New York, NY: Quantuck Lane Press, 2003.

Juravich, Tom. *At the Altar of the Bottom Line: The Degradation of Work in the 21st Century.* Amherst: University of Massachusetts Press, 2009.

Katz, Michael. *In the Shadow of the Poorhouse: A Social History of Welfare in America.* New York, NY: Basic Books, 1986.

Kaya, Bulent. *The Changing Face of Europe—Population Flows in the 20th Century.* Strasbourg: Council of Europe Publishing, 2002.

Kessler-Harris, Alice. *Out to Work: A History of Wage-Earning Women in the United States.* Revised ed. Oxford: Oxford University Press, 2003.

Kimeldorf, Howard. *Reds or Rackets?: The Making of Radical and Conservative Unions on the Waterfront.* Berkeley: University of California Press, 1988.

Klein, Jennifer. *For All These Rights: Business, Labor, and the Shaping of America's Public-Private Welfare State.* Princeton, NJ: Princeton University Press, 2003.

Kofman, Eleonore. *Gender and International Migration in Europe: Employment, Welfare, and Politics.* London: Routledge, 2000.

Koistinen, David. *Confronting Decline: The Political Economy of Deindustrialization in Twentieth-Century New England.* Gainesville: University Press of Florida, 2013.

Levinson, Marc. *The Box: How the Shipping Container Made the World Smaller and the World Economy Bigger.* Princeton, NJ: Princeton University Press, 2006.

Lewchuk, Wayne. *American Technology and the British Vehicle Industry.* New York, NY: Cambridge University Press, 1987.

Lichtenstein, Nelson. *State of the Union: A Century of American Labor.* Princeton, NJ: Princeton University Press, 2002.

Lichtenstein, Nelson, and Stephen Meyer, eds. *On the Line: Essays in the History of Auto Work.* Urbana: University of Illinois Press, 1989.

Linkon, Sherry Lee, and John Russo. *Steeltown U.S.A.: Work and Memory in Youngstown*. Lawrence: University of Kansas Press, 2005.

Lodder, Christine. *Russian Constructivism*. New Haven, CT: Yale University Press, 1983.

McBee, Randy D. *Born to Be Wild: The Rise of the American Motorcyclist*. Chapel Hill: University of North Carolina Press, 2015.

Meier, August, and Elliot Rudwick. *Black Detroit and the Rise of the UAW*. Oxford: Oxford University Press, 1979.

Mello, William J. *New York Longshoremen: Class and Power on the Docks*. Gainesville: University Press of Florida, 2010.

Meyer, Stephen. *Manhood on the Line: Working-Class Masculinities in the American Heartland*. Urbana: University of Illinois Press, 2016.

Milkman, Ruth. *Gender at Work: The Dynamics of Job Segregation by Sex during World War II*. Urbana: University of Illinois Press, 1987.

Milkman, Ruth. *Farewell to the Factory: Auto Workers in the Late Twentieth Century*. Berkeley: University of California Press, 1997.

Miller, Mark J., and Stephen Castles, eds. *The Age of Migration: International Population Movements in the Modern World*. 4th ed. New York, NY: Guilford Press, 2009.

Mills, C. Wright. *The Sociological Imagination*. New York, NY: Oxford University Press, 1959.

Mills, C. Wright. *White Collar: The American Middle Classes*. 50th anniversary ed. New York, NY: Oxford University Press, 2002.

Mink, Gwendolyn. *Old Labor and New Immigrants in American Political Development: Union, Party, and State, 1875–1920*. Ithaca, NY: Cornell University Press, 1990.

Mishel, Lawrence, Josh Bivens, Elise Gould, and Heidi Shierholz. *The State of Working America*. 12th ed. Ithaca, NY: Cornell University Press, 2012.

Mitchell, Don. *They Saved the Crops: Labor, Landscape, and the Struggle over Industrial Farming in Bracero-Era California*. Athens: University of Georgia Press, 2012.

Moch, Leslie Page. *Moving Europeans: Migration in Western Europe Since 1650*, 2nd ed. Interdisciplinary Studies in History. Bloomington: Indiana University Press, 2003.

Moody, Kim. *US Labor in Trouble and Transition: The Failure of Reform from Above, the Promise of Revival from Below*. New York, NY: Verso, 2007.

Morris, Lydia. *Dangerous Class: The Underclass and Social Citizenship*. London: Routledge, 1994.

Nadel, Stanley. "Reds Versus Pinks: A Civil War in the International; Ladies Garment Workers Union." *New York History* 66, no. 1 (1985): 38–47.

Nelson, Bruce. *Workers on the Waterfront: Seamen, Longshoremen, and Unionism in the 1930s*. Urbana: University of Illinois Press, 1988.

Ness, Immanuel. *Immigrants, Unions, and the New U.S. Labor Market*. Philadelphia, PA: Temple University Press, 2005.

Ngai, Mae. *Impossible Subjects: Illegal Aliens and the Making of Modern America*. Princeton, NJ: Princeton University Press, 2004.

Noble, David. *Forces of Production: A Social History of Industrial Automation*. New York, NY: Knopf, 1984.

Nye, David E. *America's Assembly Line*. Cambridge, MA: MIT Press, 2013.

Ollman, Leah. *Camera as Weapon: Worker Photography Between the Wars*. San Diego, CA: Museum of Photographic Arts, 1991.

Orren, Karen. *Belated Feudalism: Labor, the Law, and Liberal Development in the United States*. New York, NY: Cambridge University Press, 1991.

Pagnamenta, Peter, and Richard Overy. *All Our Working Lives*. London: British Broadcasting Company, 1984.

Pedersen, Susan. *Family, Dependence and the Origins of the Welfare State: Britain and France, 1914–1945*. Cambridge: Cambridge University Press, 1993.

Perchard, Andrew. "'Broken Men' and 'Thatcher's Children': Memory and Legacy in Scotland's Coalfields." *International Labor and Working Class History* 84 (2013): 78–98.

Perea, Juan F. *Immigrants Out!: The New Nativism and the Anti-Immigrant Impulse in the United States*. New York: New York University Press, 1997.

Pink, Daniel H. *"Free Agent Nation."* sound recording. New York, NY: Time Warner AudioBooks, 2001.

Pink, Daniel H. *Free Agent Nation: The Future of Working for Yourself*, new ed. New York, NY: Warner Books, 2002.

Reich, Steven A. *A Working People: A History of African American Workers since Emancipation*. Lanham, MD: Rowman and Littlefield, 2013.

Ribalta, Jorge, ed. *The Worker-Photography Movement (1926–1939): Essays and Documents*. Madrid: Museo Nacional, Centro de Arte Reina Sofia, 2011.

Ribalta, Jorge, ed. *Not Yet: On the Reinvention of Documentary and the Critique of Modernism: Essays and Documents, 1972–1991*. Madrid: Museo Nacional, Centro de Arte Reina Sofia, 2015.

Riesman, David. *The Lonely Crowd: A Study of the Changing American Character*. New Haven, CT: Yale University Press, 1961.

Rogers, Rosemarie, ed. *Guests Come to Stay*. Boulder, CO: Westview Press, 1985.

Rogovin, Milton. *Triptychs: Buffalo's Lower West Side Revisited*. New York, NY: W. W. Norton, 1994.

Rogovin, Milton. *The Mining Photographs*. Los Angeles, CA: J. Paul Getty Museum, 2005.

Rogovin, Milton, and Michael Frisch. *Portraits in Steel*. Ithaca, NY: Cornell University Press, 1993.

Rosas, Ana Elizabeth. *Abrazando el Espíritu: Bracero Families Confront the US-Mexico Border*. Berkeley: University of California Press, 2014.

Rosen, Ellen Israel. *Making Sweatshops: The Globalization of the U.S. Apparel Industry*. Berkeley: University of California Press, 2002.

Rosenfeld, Jake. *What Unions No Longer Do*. Cambridge, MA: Harvard University Press, 2014.

Ross, Andrew. *No Sweat Fashion, Free Trade, and the Rights of Garment Workers*. New York, NY: Verso, 1997.

Rowbotham, Sheila. *A Century of Women: A History of Women in Britain and the United States*. New York, NY: Viking, 1997.

Sacks, Karen Brodkin. *Caring by the Hour: Women, Work, and Organizing at the Duke University Medical Center*. Urbana: University of Illinois Press, 1988.

Schor, Juliet. *The Overworked American: The Unexpected Decline of Leisure*. Reprint Edition, New York, NY: Basic Books, 1993.

Sekula, Allan. "Dismantling Modernism, Reinventing *Documentary* (Notes on the Politics of Representation)." *Massachusetts Review* 19, no. 4 (1978): 859–83.

Serlin, David. *Replaceable You: Engineering the Body in Postwar America*. Chicago, IL: University of Chicago Press, 2004.

Siegelbaum, Lewis H., and Daniel J. Walkowitz. *Workers of the Donbass Speak: Survival and Identity in the New Ukraine, 1889–1992*. Albany: State University of New York Press, 1995.

Slater, Joseph. *Public Workers: Government Employee Unions, the Law, and the State, 1900–1962*. Ithaca, NY: ILR Press, 2004.

Slaton, Amy E. *Race, Rigor and Selectivity: The History of an Occupational Color Line.* Cambridge, MA: Harvard University Press, 2010.

Sontag, Susan. *On Photography.* Harmondsworth: Penguin, 1977.

Soyer, Daniel. "Class Conscious Workers as Immigrant Entrepreneurs: The Ambiguity of Class among Eastern European Jewish Immigrants to the United States at the Turn of the Twentieth Century." *Labor History* 42, no. 1 (2001): 45–59.

Standing, Guy. *Work after Globalization: Building Occupational Citizenship.* Cheltenham: Edward Elgar, 2009.

Standing, Guy. *The Rise of the Precariat: The New Dangerous Class.* London: Bloomsbury Academic, 2011.

Steichen, Edward, ed. *Family of Man.* New York, NY: Museum of Modern Art, 1955.

Stein, Judith. *Pivotal Decade: How the United States Traded Factories for Finance in the Seventies.* New Haven, CT: Yale University Press, 2010.

Stone, Dan, ed. *The Oxford Handbook of Postwar European History.* Oxford: Oxford University Press, 2015.

Storrs, Landon R. Y. *Civilizing Capitalism: The National Consumers' League, Women's Activism, and Labor Standards in the New Deal Era.* Chapel Hill: University of North Carolina Press, 2000.

Strangleman, Tim. "Deindustrialisation and the Historical Sociological Imagination: Making Sense of Work and Industrial Change." *Sociology* 51, no. 2 (2017): 466–82.

Sugrue, Thomas. *The Origins of the Urban Crisis: Race and Inequality in Postwar Detroit.* Princeton, NJ: Princeton University Press, 1996.

Tatum, Charles M. *Lowriders in Chicano Culture: From Low, to Slow, to Show.* New York, NY: Greenwood Press, 2011.

Thompson, Heather Ann. *Whose Detroit? Politics, Labor, and Race in a Modern American.* Ithaca, NY: Cornell University Press, 2001.

Todd, Selina. *The People: The Rise and Fall of the Working Class.* London: John Murray, 2014.

Vargas, Zaragosa. *Proletarians of the North: A History of Mexican Industrial Workers in Detroit and the Midwest, 1917–1933.* Berkeley: University of California Press, 1993.

Vinel, Jean-Christian. *The Employee: A Political History.* Philadelphia: University of Pennsylvania Press, 2013.

Walkowitz, Daniel J. *Working with Class: Social Workers and the Politics of Middle-Class Identity.* Chapel Hill: University of North Carolina Press, 1999.

Webb, Sidney, and Beatrice Webb. *Industrial Democracy.* 1897 ed. Reprinted, New York, NY: Augustus M. Kelley, 1965.

Weber, John. *From South Texas to the Nation: The Exploitation of Mexican Labor in the Twentieth Century.* Chapel Hill: University of North Carolina Press, 2015.

Weiemair, Klaus, and Christine Mathies. *The Tourism and Leisure Industry: Shaping the Future.* New York, NY: Routledge, 2012.

Weil, David. *The Fissured Workplace: Why Work Became So Bad For So Many and What Can Be Done to Improve It.* Cambridge, MA: Harvard University Press, 2014.

Wolensky, Kenneth C., Nicole H. Wolensky, and Robert P. Wolensky. *Fighting for the Union Label: The Women's Garment Industry and the ILGWU in Pennsylvania.* University Park: Pennsylvania State University Press, 2002.

Zaretsky, Natasha. *No Direction Home: The American Family and the Fear of National Decline, 1968–1980.* Chapel Hill: North Carolina University Press, 2007.

Zieger, Robert H., Timothy J. Minchin, and Gilbert J. Gall. *American Workers, American Unions: The Twentieth and Early Twenty-First Centuries.* 4th ed. Baltimore, MD: Johns Hopkins University Press, 2014.

INDEX

accidents 13, 20, 104, 144–6
Aid to Families with Dependent Children (AFDC) 7, 134, 135
art and artists 40–57
    conceptual artists 40, 54, 56, 57
    Farocki, Harun 58–9
    portraiture 43, 47–53, 56
    Rivera, Diego 42–3
    Ukeles, Mierle Laderman 54, 57
assembly 90, 96, 100, 101, 105, 131
    assembly line 4, 14, 59, 77, 89, 93, 97, 132, 141, 144, 150–3
automation 10, 13, 15, 68, 93–4, 96, 101–4, 108, 121, 151–4
automobiles 130, 141–56, 162, 164–5

Bracero Program 30, 116–18, 125
Brecht, Bertolt 47, 50
Buffalo, New York 46, 48

childcare 2, 27, 36, 96, 105, 131, 171
child labor 18, 85
children's play 14, 46, 162, 165, 167, 171
cinema 39, 40, 57–9, 93, 159–61, 167–8
citizenship 109, 127, 138–40, 165
    economic 17, 21, 80
    and race 112, 114, 116, 125–6
class 1–3, 6–14, 21, 37, 49, 72–3, 107, 116, 136–8, 162–3, 168–70
    middle class 31, 32, 71, 157 (*see also* class)
    and race 120–2, 125, 126, 162, 165, 167 (*see also* class)
    working class 17–18, 20, 77, 82, 86, 128–9 (*see also* class)
coal industry 1, 10–13, 42, 49, 82–6, 103–4, 113, 130, 166
collective
    action 5, 137, 141, 142, 148, 149
    bargaining 21, 24–5, 28, 32, 115, 170
    identity 8, 17, 20, 40, 41, 71–2, 75, 100–1, 134, 146
colonialism 79, 96, 109, 123, 124. See also empire; post-colonial
containerization 65–9, 103

contingent worker 70–1, 73, 74, 140
Cowie, Jefferson 79, 105–6
crafts 65, 80, 89, 99, 132
    unionism 22, 137
    work culture 73, 81–2, 86, 142–4

deindustrialization 2, 78–82, 86, 90–2, 103, 111, 121, 126, 130, 133, 136–7, 155
    mining 9–13, 49–50, 59
deskilling 89, 94, 103
discrimination 9, 27, 105, 127–8, 132–3, 152
division of labor 94, 95, 144, 153
dockers 61, 65–70, 101–3
domestic labor 7, 18–19, 27, 32, 36, 54, 111, 114, 124, 131, 134, 166

electricity companies 4, 20, 35, 62, 87, 97
empire 30, 111–13, 123. See also colonialism; postcolonial
empty labor 145, 149
ethnicity. See race/ethnicity

Fair Labor Standards Act (1938) 22, 27, 64, 129, 158, 161
family 8, 11, 21, 40, 45, 57, 82, 87, 105
    and community 72, 77
    economy 2–3, 15, 17, 24, 114
    policy 109–10, 134
    welfare 2, 5, 26–7, 31
feminism 27, 54, 108, 132, 171
feminization 5, 31, 105, 114, 115
Ford, Henry 87, 89, 97
    Fordism 22, 82, 142–4, 153
    Motor Company 4, 14, 19, 25, 43, 131, 141, 147–8, 151, 156
freelancer 61, 70–5
full employment 33, 127–8, 130, 134, 136, 140, 161

gender 92, 97, 100, 104–5, 125, 131–3, 144, 157, 171. See also masculinity; feminization; sexuality; women
    family and 3, 21, 109, 116, 125

labor market 14, 17, 27, 37, 94, 95, 97, 110–11, 114–15, 127, 130, 140
space 77, 81, 87
work culture 2, 3, 5, 12, 108
Germany 3, 5, 10–11, 25, 79, 116, 143, 161, 170
art 41, 45, 48
guestworkers 119, 123, 125
Nazi 21, 61, 82, 113, 158
unemployment 128, 161
Google 14, 89, 171
Great Britain 104, 111, 144, 158
labor market factors 21, 129, 133, 161, 166, 170
labor and unions 25, 26, 33, 89, 131, 149, 166, 167
leisure 160, 167, 172
mining 10–13, 85
social class 128, 136–8, 169
welfare 3–5, 133, 134, 136, 139
Great Depression 3, 20, 37, 41, 43, 71, 110, 114–16, 142, 146
grievance procedures 24, 29, 31–2, 61–2, 103, 142, 148–9, 154
guestworkers 29–30, 109, 110, 116–20, 125

Hawthorne Experiments 4, 14, 97–8
health care 26, 27, 36, 107, 127, 134, 156, 171
labor market 31, 34, 166–7
hours of work 1, 4, 18, 20, 27, 29, 36–7, 62, 65, 74, 103, 155–8, 170
flexible 14, 36, 71

immigration. *See* migration
imperialism. *See* colonization; empire
inequality 14, 94, 105, 127–40
intermodalism 66, 102
Italy 3, 41, 79, 113, 119, 143, 161–2, 170
fascist 5, 21, 82, 112, 158

Japan 3, 82, 85, 153, 155, 158, 166
Japanese/Americans 2, 112

labor market 11, 18, 27, 30, 32, 34, 36, 107, 136, 170
gender/race 2, 3, 27, 29, 130, 133
leftists 46, 146
leisure 20, 45, 73, 80, 157–72. *See also* cinema; television; theatre
mass amusements 157, 161, 162
sites 137, 138, 158
sponsored leisure 4, 33, 157–9, 161, 165, 172
sports 161, 165, 169
Linkon, Sherry Lee 77, 80
living standards 18, 28, 121, 140, 159
longshoremen. *See* dockers
Lordstown 144, 152–4

masculinity 12, 70, 77, 84–6, 127, 144
mass production 21, 22, 96, 112, 142–4, 161
Mayo, Elton 88, 97–8
mechanization 94, 101–4, 108
Mexico 42, 120–2
Mexican Americans 21, 115, 117, 125, 132, 144, 162
Mexicans 21, 30, 109–10, 112, 114–18, 122, 125, 158
micropreneurs 72, 73
migration 3, 81, 109–26, 132
Mills, C. Wright 1, 80
moral economy 84, 92
motion pictures. *See* cinema
motorcycles 162–4

neoliberalism 2, 33, 104, 120–2, 125, 142, 148, 155, 170
New Deal 17–33, 115–16, 125, 133–4, 148

output 19, 93, 97–8, 142, 145, 153

photography 40, 45, 47, 52, 57, 59
Lange, Dorothea 43
Lonidier, Fred 55, 57
Rogovin, Milton 40, 46–53, 179
Sekula, Allan 55–8
Steichen, Edward 46
post-colonial 57, 110
precarious work 18, 28, 34–5, 37, 50, 61, 80, 90, 105
protocol 61–4

race/ethnicity 1, 4, 6, 8, 13, 29–30, 73, 81, 87, 89, 92–100, 104, 108–9, 112–15, 124–7, 130–9, 144. *See also* Mexicans; Japanese; Bracero Program
RCA 79, 105, 121
Reagan, Ronald 89, 103, 120–1, 134–5, 166, 167
Reaganism 33, 104
realism 40–9, 57
resistance
cultural 84, 141, 145

passive/covert 142, 146, 148, 149, 152, 154
worker 9, 22, 89, 90, 100, 121, 137, 156
right to work 64, 139, 155
Rivethead (Ben Hamper) 155–6
Russia 3, 13, 41–2, 45, 112. *See also* Soviet Union

seniority 24, 100, 103, 105
sexual harassment 18, 144, 154
sexuality 3, 8, 104, 108, 135
  reproductive 110, 114, 116
smoking 156–8
Social Security 7, 21, 23, 25, 80, 115, 134, 165. *See also* welfare
Soviet Union 13, 21, 45, 46, 79, 145. *See also* Russia
Spain 3, 5, 6, 13, 119
Springsteen, Bruce 77–8, 80–2, 90, 92
Strangleman, Tim 80, 82
sweatshop 29, 61, 64

Taft-Hartley 9, 29, 68, 148, 151
Taylor, Frederick Winslow 4, 89, 97, 98, 105, 108
  Taylorism 20, 62, 103, 142, 153
television 13, 72, 74, 105, 167–70
temp work 32, 34–7, 53, 71, 74, 109–10, 115
Thatcher, Margaret 89, 103, 136, 166
  government 10, 34, 167
  Thatcherism 33, 104
theatre 47, 158–62, 168
tourism and leisure industries 12, 164, 168, 172

undocumented immigrants 109, 110, 114, 118, 121, 122, 125
unions 2, 3, 4, 10, 24, 25, 27, 161, 165, 167. *See also* collective, bargaining; resistance; crafts

American 6–7, 9, 31, 64–8, 137, 144, 148
European 89, 129, 132, 134, 143
membership 22, 31
power (and attack on) 33–4, 35, 79, 103, 120–1, 144, 148, 155–6, 167
United States Department of Labor 27, 30, 36, 106, 117, 119

wars
  interwar 109, 113, 125, 134, 136
  postwar 28, 29, 92, 110, 116, 119, 130–1, 143–4, 157, 161–5
  World War I 1, 4, 8, 41, 97, 114, 116
  World War II 17, 23, 28, 45, 100–1, 127–8, 132, 148, 154
weapons of the weak 141–2, 146, 156
welfare 9, 18, 29, 31, 53, 72, 122, 130
  welfare capitalism 4, 20, 25, 26, 34, 88–9, 133, 153, 158, 171–2
  welfare policy 7, 109, 114, 123
  welfare state 3, 5, 23, 24, 26, 27, 32–4, 115, 117, 125, 127, 134–40, 161
women. *See also* feminization; gender; temp work
  citizenship 138–9
  discrimination and marginalization 2, 3, 6, 27, 97, 100–2, 104, 111, 130–2
  economic sectors 4–6, 12, 28, 30, 85, 166, 170
  migrants 114, 119, 124–5
  resistance 7, 17, 147, 152, 154, 155, 158–9
  welfare 9, 18–19, 26, 134, 163
  workforce 5, 24, 32, 38, 53–4, 72, 97, 104, 128, 156, 170–2
Workers Leaving the Lumière Factory in Lyons 39–40, 59

Youngstown (Ohio) 77, 80, 90